JESUS
REBURIED?

Claims that two tombs in Jerusalem are those of Jesus and his family (one a temporary resting-place for his body, the other a family tomb where his bones and those of members of his family were interred) have been widely publicized in the last few years. Most scholars have been entirely unconvinced but their arguments have not been easily accessible to the general reader. Now John Pryor has conducted much the most thorough investigation of the two tombs and the many different issues connected with their interpretation. His work is a model of careful presentation of evidence and sound historical judgment. He replaces sensationalism with sober assessment and his conclusions are highly convincing.
    Richard Bauckham
    Emeritus Professor of New Testament Studies, University of St Andrews, Scotland

An outstanding example [of] how to popularise sound scholarship. I am impressed [with] how you have mastered the vexed questions of the talpiot ossuaries. Your book is very readable for interested lay people, but also of interest to specialists. It argues a "conservative" case but with prudence and sober criticism.
    Rainer Riesner
    Professor of New Testament, Technische Universität, Dortmund, Germany.

"*Books that argue that ... the Jerusalem tombs... once contained the bodies of Jesus and his wife and other members of his family always attract attention. At such a time, what is needed is a careful appraisal of the evidence and some guidance on what conclusions may reasonably be drawn on the basis of it. I commend John Pryor's Jesus Reburied? as such a book.*"
    John Painter
    Professor of Theology, Charles Sturt University, Canberra, Australia

John Pryor combines sharp archaeological analysis, insightful New Testament interpretation, and theological acumen in this timely contribution to the ongoing debate about the discovery thirty years ago of first century Jewish tombs near Jerusalem and their significance. This is a must read for any scholar of the gospels and early Christianity, and for anyone interested in the always fascinating intersection of archaeology and Jesus research.
    Mark Harding
    Dean, Australian College of Theology

JESUS REBURIED?

THE MYSTERY OF THE JESUS FAMILY TOMB

JOHN W. PRYOR

WIPF & STOCK · Eugene, Oregon

Wipf and Stock Publishers
199 W 8th Ave, Suite 3
Eugene, OR 97401

Jesus Reburied?
The Mystery of the Jesus Family Tomb
By Pryor, John
Copyright©2013 Mosaic Press
ISBN 13: 978-1-62564-316-2
Publication date 7/29/2013
Previously published by Mosaic Press, 2013

For Yu yu

True Companion and Yokefellow

TABLE OF CONTENTS

Preface 1

Part A
Jewish Burial

Past Practice, Recent Discoveries and a Radical Interpretation

1. Burial Practice in First Century Jerusalem. 7
2. Two Burial Tombs in South Jerusalem 15
3. The Ossuaries in the Tombs 19
4. The James Ossuary – the Missing Tenth?. 39
5. Jesus and the Post-Easter Community – the Narrative Reconfigured . 51

Part B
Four Major Hurdles

Introduction – Historical and Textual Hurdles 56
6. Was Jesus Celibate?. 61
7. Mary Magdalene – Wife and Apostolic Leader?. 67
8. Joseph of Arimathea and the Burials of Jesus 95
9. Resurrection in Early Christian Thinking 115

Part C
Under the Microscope

The Talpiot Ossuaries and the Jesus Family Tomb Thesis

10. Three Talpiot B Ossuaries – Witnesses to Judaeo-Christian Faith? . .127
11. The 'Jesus Tomb' Ossuaries. .153
    Conclusion. 181
    Bibliography. 188
    Index of Passages Cited. 193
    Author index 198
    Subject Index 200

PREFACE

"This promises to be one of the greatest and most controversial archaeological finds in history." James Tabor, 2007.

In 1980 and 1981, during routine excavation and land clearance on a new housing site just south of Jerusalem, two ancient tomb complexes were unearthed – something not uncommon in that part of the world. Nor is it uncommon to find within such tombs evidence of their previous use – bone fragments and bone boxes (called ossuaries). What has been different about these two tombs are the claims that have been made for them.

Consider the following:

> … *it [is] probable that this was indeed the final resting place of Jesus of Nazareth.*[1]

This discovery

> *"provides the earliest archaeological evidence of faith in Jesus' resurrection from the dead, the first witness to a saying of Jesus that predates even the writing of our New Testament gospels, and the earliest example of Christian art."*[2]

Nor does it rest there, according to the judgement of James Tabor and Simcha Jacobovici. Their interpretation of the evidence leads them to further conclusions, among them being:

- The tomb complex housed the family of Jesus, and was given to them by the wealthy Joseph of Arimathea
- It is likely that in an ossuary marked with his name Jesus' skeletal remains were housed;
- Jesus was married to Mary Magdalene, whose ossuary was located in the complex;
- Jesus was the father of a person named Jude, also buried in the complex;
- An ossuary, bought in the illegal antiquities market, and labelled "James son of Joseph brother of Jesus", probably originated from the same tomb complex;
- Mary the mother of Jesus was also buried in the tomb complex.

Little wonder that Tabor is able to claim: "This promises to be one of the greatest and most controversial archaeological finds in history."[3] And one

---

[1] James Tabor, *The Jesus Dynasty* (Simon and Schuster, 2007 edition) 323.
[2] James Tabor and Simcha Jacobovici, *The Jesus Discovery* (Simon and Schuster, 2012) 1
[3] Tabor, *Jesus Dynasty* 319.

cannot but agree – but only so long as the conclusions can withstand close scrutiny. And therein lies the difficulty, for few others are persuaded, in spite of the superficial attractiveness of the evidence and the conclusions they draw from it.

James Tabor is an academic, Chair of the Department of Religious Studies at the University of North Carolina at Charlotte. His special interests relate to Judaism around the time of Jesus (known as Second Temple Judaism) and early Christianity. Simcha Jacobovici is a filmmaker with a particular interest in matters archaeological. Charles Pellegrino has also been associated with the Jesus Family Tomb project. His early research was in the field of palaeobiology, and he has now turned his attention to popular writing on subjects that involve archaeological interests. In a series of interviews, along with film and literary releases, these three have set a cat among the pigeons of the staid and cautious world of biblical archaeology.[4]

There has been no shortage of reactions and responses to the Jacobovici/ Pellegrino/ Tabor claims - via internet blogs, journal articles, booklets, even an international academic conference held in 2008.[5] This present study does not claim to break new ground. Indeed, it is unlikely that there is much more to be said on the claims. What I am wanting, however, is to provide both a summary of the arguments presented initially by Jacobovici and Pellegrino, and now more recently by Tabor and Jacobovici, and also to offer a balanced evaluation of their claims.

Part A sets the scene historically, and offers a summary of the contents of the tombs along with the interpretation of the tombs and their contents offered by Tabor and Jacobovici. Their interpretation, in effect, results in a radical rethinking of major elements of the life and beliefs of the earliest Christian community. **Part B** provides a detailed historical analysis of those areas of early Christian life and thought that are challenged by Tabor and Jacobovici:

---

[4] Everything that is claimed about the tombs is contained in the two most recent books, listed at notes 1 and 2 above. In what follows I have decided to concentrate on these two books for two reasons. Firstly, they are the most recent major works to come from the Jesus Family Tomb advocates. Secondly, behind them stands the academic judgement of James Tabor, and so one would expect that they represent the most careful assessments on the subject. Readers may also wish to read Simcha Jacobovici and Charles Pellegrino, *The Jesus Family Tomb* (HarperCollins, 2007), which is written in a more 'popular' style. Occasional reference will be made to this latter work. Readers may also wish to consult James Tabor's web site at jamestabor.com.

5 Papers from the conference, the Fourth Princeton Symposium on Judaism and Christian Origins, are due for publication by Eerdmans in late 2012/early 2013.

the celibacy of Jesus; the resurrection faith of the Christian community; the role of Mary Magdalene and James the brother of Jesus in the early church; and Joseph of Arimathea and the trial and burial of Jesus. Finally, in **Part C** we evaluate the claims made for the two tombs and their contents. Nine ossuaries in all, six in the first tomb and three in the second, have inscriptions on them, markings that Tabor and Jacobovici (and Pellegrino) claim revolutionise our understanding of Jesus and the earliest Christian community. We examine whether the inscriptions on the ossuaries will bear the weight of meaning given them.

A Final Word. I have written this book for the benefit of a wide group of people. I hope that it will be of help not just to those who are abreast of the controversies surrounding the Talpiot tombs, and those at home in matters relating to the historical Jesus, but also to those for whom all of this is something quite new and intriguing. In the case of the first two groups, Chapters 2 and 3 can safely be passed over, and possibly much of Chapter 4. For the benefit of all, I have attempted to keep the body of the book free from terms that are overly technical, though this has not always been possible. The footnotes are for those who wish to pursue matters further.

Part A

Jewish Burial

Past Practice, Recent Discoveries and a Radical Interpretation

Chapter One
BURIAL PRACTICE IN FIRST CENTURY JERUSALEM

In every human culture, the burial of the dead is observed with the utmost care and with developed ceremony. We instinctively recognise that the proper disposal of the body is important for the ongoing life of the society. Through its burial practice the family, and society as a whole, are able to honour those who have gone before and to express their confidence that death does not destroy the ongoing life. Through its burial rituals, a society not only expresses its beliefs about the state of the dead; it is also able to face the future with confidence.[1]

The debate over the burial of Jesus that has been raised by the claims of James Tabor and Simcha Jacobovici takes us to the heart of Jewish burial practice in the late Second Temple period (i.e. the first century AD). Before we turn to consider the discovery of the family tombs at Talpiot and their contents, it will be helpful for us to note what can be said in general of burial practices in Jerusalem in the time of Jesus.

1. Secondary Burial in Jewish Tradition

In Jewish tradition, as in other ancient cultures as far back as the Chalcolithic Age (ca 4000 BC), the secondary burial in family tombs of the bones of the deceased appears to have had an honoured place. In 2 Sam 21.12-14 we are told that King David showed respect for Saul and Jonathan when he '*took the bones of Saul and the bones of his son Jonathan ... and buried the bones of Saul and of his son Jonathan in the land of Benjamin, in the tomb of his father Kish*'. On many occasions in the Old Testament, we read of a person dying and being 'gathered to his people' (Gen 25.8, 17; Judges 2.10; 1 Kings 13.22; 2 Kings 9.28). Genesis 49.29-33 is especially informative, for it tells us that according to tradition, the Cave in the Field of Machpelah (according to tradition, in modern day Hebron) was the burial site for Sarah, Abraham and their early descendents. It was the family burial tomb, and it was there that Jacob requested to be 'gathered to my people'.

Passages such as the above, and the frequency of the verb 'to gather' in reference to burial, have suggested to scholars that the practice of collecting the bones of the deceased into family tombs, was quite ancient in Judaism. And behind it probably lay the belief that the dead and the living continue to have a kind of

---

[1] See the helpful comments in Byron McCane's introductory chapter, 'Death as a Fact of Life' in his *Roll Back the Stone – Death and Burial in the World of Jesus* (Trinity, 2003).

shadow-relationship, not completely removed from each other. Verses such as 2 Kings 13.21; Isa 8.19; 29.4 reflect the popular beliefs of the time.[2]

2. The Herodian Period Development

But in the 100 year period from about 30 BC until the end of the first Jewish Revolt in AD 70, in and around Jerusalem there was a significant development in relation to Jewish burial practice. And it is this development that is central to the recent claims relating to the death and burial/s of Jesus. In this period more than ever before or after,[3] many Jews in and around Jerusalem adopted the practice of isolating the bones of individual family members after the decay of the flesh and organs, and of collecting them in limestone boxes, called ossuaries. A family tomb, carved out of the limestone cliffs and rocks of the area, was used to house several generations of the dead of a family, and into these tombs were placed the ossuaries.

Figure 1. *Tomb Complex and Ossuaries: Dominus Flevit, Mt of Olives*

What percentage of the population adopted this practice? We cannot be certain. Magness suggests that 'only the wealthy members of Jewish society could afford rock-cut tombs' to serve as trans-generational family burial sites.

---

[2] See further, Craig Evans, *Jesus and the Ossuaries* (Baylor Uni Press, 2003) 26-28.

[3] It is not correct to say that ossuaries for secondary burial were employed only in this period of Jewish life. See Evans, *Jesus and the Ossuaries*, 28. Jodi Magness is cautious in her wording, affirming that ossuaries disappear from Jerusalem after AD 70, but acknowledging their continued use in Galilee and southern Judea until the third century. See Magness, 'Ossuaries and the Burials of Jesus and James,' in *Journal of Biblical Literature* 124/1 (2005) 129.

The poor would bury their dead in simple shaft graves, where the body would eventually rot and leave no archaeological record. McCane, however, suggests that burial in underground chambers was the norm rather than the exception, and he provides statistical evidence in support.[4] In relation to Jerusalem, in the modern period well over 1000 tomb complexes have been uncovered, and probably many more have disappeared. That statistic in itself should lead us to be cautious in suggesting that the affordability of family tomb complexes was confined to the wealthy few. Granted, such expenditure was beyond the reach of the abject poor, but many families would have taken it as a matter of honour to establish their own family complex.[5]

3. The Family Tomb Complex and its Ossuaries

Family tomb complexes of the time of Jesus had a typical design. Carved out of the local limestone rock, they would consist of a central chamber which could be entered by means of a narrow entryway. The chamber itself was rectangular, and usually large enough for several people to stand. Branching off from the central chamber, it would be normal for there to be up to nine niches. These niches are also called *loculi* (Latin) or *kokhim* (Hebrew). Finally, many burial chambers also had carved along one or two sides a ledge beneath an arch. The ledge is called an *arcosolium*.

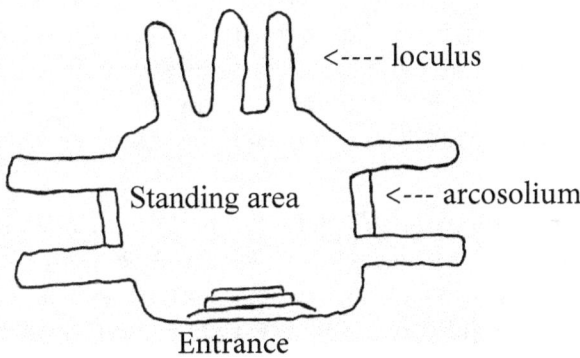

Figure 2. *Typical Jerusalem Tomb Complex*

Initially, the body of a deceased family member, anointed and wrapped, would either be placed on an *arcosolium* or slid into a niche. There it would remain undisturbed for about a year, allowing time for the flesh and organs to

---

[4] Magness, 'Ossuaries and the Burials of Jesus and James' 121, 123; McCane, *Roll Back the Stone*, 56-57 n 4.

[5] In many traditional societies today, there is great social pressure to spend lavishly at family weddings and funerals, often leading to long-standing debt.

decompose. After about a year, the bones would then be collected and placed in a small limestone box, or ossuary, which was then repositioned in one of the niches in the burial chamber. Ossuary dimensions vary considerably, but a typical ossuary would be about 600mm x 300mm x 250mm, large enough to hold all the bones of an adult, including the longest adult bone (the femur).

We mentioned earlier that more than 1000 tomb complexes have been unearthed in the Jerusalem area. Given the widespread practice of tomb robbery, we will never know how many ossuaries and bodies those tombs contained. Robbers not only take away the best objects, but they also frequently destroy those that are of lesser commercial value to them, smashing ossuaries, for example, into many pieces. But even so, over 2000 ossuaries have been listed in one catalogue or another.[6]

Three further details about ossuaries should be noted. Firstly, inscriptions.[7] It was not unusual for an ossuary to have inscribed on it the name of the person whose bones are inside. Of the 897 ossuaries catalogued by Rahmani, approximately 230 of them have some kind of inscription, written in either Hebrew, Aramaic or Greek. The inscription may be a single name; occasionally it may add the patronymic (x son of y), and, more rarely, it may give a nickname or even the birthplace of the deceased. The inscription could be found on any of the faces of the ossuary, on the lid, or even on the inside. And, as we shall see when we consider the Talpiot ossuaries, the inscription may be crudely or ornately written. Its purpose was obviously to serve not as a public display, but primarily as an identifier for the family in future years. As Rahmani says, they are often 'carelessly executed, clumsily spaced, and often contain spelling mistakes.'[8]

The second feature of the Herodian period ossuaries is that while most ossuaries appear to have held a single set of bones, this was not always the case. Many ossuaries held the remains of more than one person. Children and wives could be gathered in the ossuary of a family head, but some ossuaries were found to be packed with the bones of multiple people.

Finally, as we shall also note with those in the Talpiot tombs, ossuaries (and, indeed, burial chambers as a whole) could either be beautifully adorned or left remarkably plain. Typical adornments were rosettes on the front and rear faces of the box, as well as carved columns down the edges and around the

---

[6] The standard study of Jewish ossuaries is L Y Rahmani, *A Catalogue of Jewish Ossuaries in the Collections of the State of Israel* (Israel Antiquities Authority, 1994). Rahmani has listed 897 ossuaries.

[7] Very useful is Evans, *Jesus and the Ossuaries*, chapters 3 and 4.

[8] Rahmani, *Catalogue of Jewish Ossuaries*, 11-12.

sides. What is important to note is that such adornment, or its absence, does not appear to have been a strict indicator of a family's wealth. For example, a plain and unadorned tomb complex found in 1990 in the north Talpiot area of Jerusalem contained twelve ossuaries. One was ornately carved and had the inscription 'Joseph son of Caiaphas' and contained the bones of an elderly male, four children and a woman. It is generally agreed that this tomb complex has some association with the Caiaphas known from the gospels as High Priest at the time of Jesus (Matt 26.57; Jn 18.13), but the precise nature of the connection remains open for debate.[9] But in spite of the ornate style of the 'Caiaphas' ossuary, the tomb complex itself is not large and is quite roughly carved. McCane's summary is worth noting:

> Most Jewish burial caves in this region and period, however, are not luxurious at all, but roughly hewn, with irregular dimensions, unfinished surfaces, and an absence of decoration. It is not unusual, for example, for loculus niches to be so unevenly arranged – and cut into the wall at such odd angles – that one niche actually runs into another. A poorly constructed tomb might appear to be evidence of a family's lower social and economic status, but conclusions of this sort require careful review, since rich families may have had the means to build a splendid tomb but simply chose to use their wealth in other ways.[10]

4. The Ossuary Phenomenon

All of the above data lead to the obvious question: why? Why did ossuaries suddenly become so popular in late Herodian Jerusalem? Was it theologically driven, or was there some other, more mundane, explanation for the phenomenon?

One explanation that has been offered is the suggestion that the ossuary symbolised the heightened Jewish hope of bodily resurrection.[11] There are three problems with this proposal. Firstly, we simply lack any literary evidence that links *ossilegium* (the technical term for gathering bones) with resurrection hope. Secondly, why should the ossuary phenomenon be confined to Jerusalem, when other Jews, who did not make use of ossuaries, also believed in the resurrection hope? Indeed, the evidence from the Qumran cemetery clearly shows that the sectarians there were not even secondarily buried. Each body was buried in its own trench grave, facing north-south. More importantly,

---

[9] Richard Bauckham has presented a strong case for 'Caiaphas' being a kind of nickname for the wider family, so that the mere occurrence of the name 'Joseph son of Caiaphas' does not necessarily point us to the figure known from the gospels. See his 'The Caiaphas Family', *Journal for the Study of the Historical Jesus* 10 (2012) 3-31. For earlier comments, see Evans, *Jesus and the Ossuaries*, 104-112.

[10] McCane, *Roll Back the Stone*, 35.

[11] This interpretation is supported by Rahmani, *Catalogue of Jewish Ossuaries*, 53-55.

it has been claimed that the evidence of the Caiaphas family tomb indicates that Sadducean families, who did not hold to the doctrine of resurrection (see Acts 23.3-8), fully adopted the practice of gathering bones into ossuaries. On this point Rahmani is not convinced. He cites the Jewish historian Josephus (*Antiquities* 18.17: the Sadducees submitted 'to the formulas of the Pharisees') and also the confession of bodily resurrection expressed in the second of the 18 Benedictions, recited daily by all Jews.[12]

A second proposal draws attention to the happy co-incidence in timing between the enormous increase in ossuary usage and the extensive building projects initiated by Herod the Great. In particular, Herod's enlargement of the Temple Mount and the construction of the enlarged Sanctuary on the Mount, which continued well beyond his death (in 4 BC) until AD 64, required the employment of thousands of masons and other craftsmen. These craftsmen were also available to apply their skills for the private needs of the population.[13] Moreover, it is suggested, Jerusalem's building expansion also led to an increased population, and that in itself placed pressure on the need for more economical use of burial sites.[14] While there may be some merit in these suggested links, I believe we should be wary of suggesting that the availability of craftsmen and population pressures in themselves led to the 'ossuary phenomenon'. After all, apart from Jericho, where, admittedly, Herod also had a major building project, we do not find widespread ossuary usage outside of Jerusalem, not even in the immediate region of Herod's grand defensive fortress, the Herodion, outside of Bethlehem. And population pressure alone cannot explain why ossuary usage became so popular.

Another way forward is suggested by noting the following factors:

- This was a time when, under the influence of Herod himself, the aping of hellenistic ways reached considerable heights. While the impact of

---

[12] Rahmani, *Catalogue of Jewish Ossuaries*, 54. Rahmani also cites the second century AD Mishnah at *Sanhedrin* 10.1. But that text explicitly excludes from the world to come those who say there is no resurrection of the dead. This could well be an anti-Sadducean sentiment.

[13] This line of thinking is endorsed by Evans, *Jesus and the Ossuaries*, 29-30.

[14] Estimates of the first century population of Jerusalem vary considerably. J Jeremias provided an estimate of 55,000 to 95,000, based on the known inhabited area of the city. See Jeremias, *Jerusalem in the Time of Jesus* (SCM, 1969) 83 n 24. A more recent estimate suggests a growth from about 38,500 in AD 6 to 82,500 in AD 70. See H Shanks, '"Brother of Jesus" Inscription is Authentic,' *Biblical Archaeology Review* 38/4 (2012) 64.

hellenistic ways spread across the whole of Palestine, it was particularly strong in Jerusalem among the elite of the city.[15]

- Hellenistic economic and cultural influence led to a heightened sense of individuality.
- Jewish ossuaries display a remarkable resemblance both in shape and in some of the external decorations (rosettes and other geometric designs) to Graeco-Roman funerary boxes.
- Jews never adopted the hellenistic practice of cremation. In other words, the cultural influence of Hellenism, while extensive, could only go so far. The long-standing Jewish practice, honoured even by the Sadducean elite, of collecting the bones into a family tomb, remained the norm.

Did the conjunction of these elements lead to the popularity of individual secondary burial in ossuaries, rather than the hitherto practised collective secondary burial? As McCane suggests, 'The ossuary is best understood … as an artefact of the intersection between Judaism and Hellenism…', an intersection that was most marked in Jerusalem.[16] This sociological analysis is provocative, but it comes against two important observations. If heightened individualism is the explanation for the popularity of the ossuary, why are the majority of ossuaries left unmarked rather than having the names of the deceased inscribed on them? In fact, while approximately 25% of the ossuaries in Rahmani's catalogue are inscribed, it is acknowledged that even that percentage needs to be adjusted down to account for the large number of uninscribed ossuaries that would have been discarded by excavators or otherwise not collected.[17] Anonymity would seem to sit awkwardly with individuation. And why do so many ossuaries contain the bones of more than one person?[18] When an ossuary contains the bones of multiple persons, it is very unusual for more than one person to be identified on any inscription. So then, hellenistic influence and heightened individualism may have been contributing factors, but it doesn't appear that they alone can be the sole explanation.

In the final analysis, we need to remain open as to the reasons for the popularity of the ossuary in this period.

---

[15] The standard study is still Martin Hengel's seminal work, *Judaism and Hellenism* (SCM, 1974).

[16] McCane, *Roll Back the Stone*, 40. See his general discussion in pages 39-47.

[17] Rahmani, *Catalogue of Jewish Ossuaries*, 11.

[18] To his credit, McCane acknowledges this point in an extended footnote on p 59 n 27.

Chapter Two
TWO BURIAL TOMBS IN SOUTH JERUSALEM

As a result of the 1967 Six Day War, the Jewish State of Israel took control of the whole of the Jordanian territory west of the Jordan River, including Jerusalem. Hitherto, its presence in Jerusalem was limited to parts of today's West Jerusalem. Since 1967 the Jewish population of Jerusalem has increased enormously, and a veritable housing and construction boom has resulted – and continues to this day. But Jerusalem is an ancient city, and beneath its surface lie untold historical treasures waiting to tell their stories. It is not uncommon, therefore, for mechanical excavators to be forced to cease their digging, while the archaeologists and the Israel Antiquities Authority personnel get to work and examine what has just been uncovered.

1. The Talpiot Complexes

And such was the case in 1980 and 1981 when mechanical excavators, preparing the ground for the construction of new housing a couple of kilometres south of Jerusalem in the suburb known as East Talpiot, accidentally uncovered first one and then another tomb complex. Nothing uncommon, and certainly nothing newsworthy. But newsworthy is exactly what they have both become in the following years. We shall hereafter call these tomb complexes Talpiot A and Talpiot B.[1]

1.1 The First Complex: Talpiot A

Talpiot A was a modest-sized complex consisting of a low entrance with a stone carved façade that led into a rectangular open area, less than 3 metres square and about 2 metres from floor to ceiling. Leading off from each of three sides of the open area were two *loculi* – six in all. As well, two flat stone shelves, or *arcosolia*, were carved out of the rock face. As indicated in Chapter 1, these would have been used for laying out and preparing the body prior to its placement in a *loculus*. Alternatively, a shrouded body could be left lying on the *arcosolium* during the period of its decay.

---

[1] A third cave complex was also found nearby, but it was destroyed in the building process. What it contained will never be known.

Figure 3. *Entrance to the Talpiot A Tomb Complex*

At the time of discovery, ten ossuaries were identified and removed for cataloguing and storage by the Israel Antiquities Authority, the body legally responsible for the care and protection of all such ancient sites and their contents. What is puzzling is that one of the ten ossuaries, identified as "plain" in the original report, and given the catalogue number 80.509 by the IAA, has since disappeared, and become the subject of speculation by Tabor and Jacobovici, as we shall later indicate.

On the outside of six of the ten ossuaries inscriptions, in various degrees of clarity, have been detected. Their inscriptions have been read as follows:

Maramene Mara (a rare form of Mary; written in Greek)

Jehuda bar Jeshua (= Judah son of Jesus; written in Aramaic)

Matya (= Matthew; written in Hebrew/Aramaic)

Jeshua bar Yehosef (= Jesus son of Joseph; written in Aramaic)

Yose (a contraction of Joseph; written in Hebrew/Aramaic)

Marya (a rare latinised form of Mary; written in Hebrew/Aramaic)

At the time nothing was made of this discovery – after all, none of these names is notable, all of them being common among Jews of the time, as we shall later discuss. Then in 1995 a BBC Easter programme, entitled "The Body in Question", brought to public attention the discovery of Talpiot A and the inscriptions on the ossuaries. Public imagination was aroused by the presence of the name Jesus on a first century ossuary, and the obvious 'Easter question' was raised: have archaeologists uncovered the final burial tomb of Jesus of

Nazareth? More provocatively, since the official report in 1996 indicated that the ossuaries originally held bones,[2] were the bones of Jesus once housed in one of those boxes?

In the years that followed, Jacobovici (later assisted by Tabor) has pursued the speculation on the significance of Talpiot A and its contents, even in 2005 re-opening the tomb which had by now been sealed over with a concrete slab. What he discovered then was that in the intervening period since 1980, the tomb had been filled with old religious texts by Orthodox Jews and then re-sealed.[3] Reflecting on the original finds, he and Tabor have now presented what they believe to be the meaning and significance of the tomb and its contents.

1.2 The Second Complex: Talpiot B

About 50 metres from Talpiot A, another tomb complex was discovered in 1981. At the time of discovery it was entered and found to have nine *loculi* leading off from a central chamber. Seven ossuaries were noted as well as at least two skeletons and skeletal remains. But as a result of ultra-Orthodox Jewish protests,[4] a thorough examination could not be undertaken, nor were the ossuaries removed by the IAA for safekeeping. In 2010, however, Jacobovici and Tabor were able to obtain both official permission as well as the agreement of the ultra-Orthodox Jewish authorities to inspect Talpiot B by means of photographic probes into the tomb complex. Agreement with the religious authorities was reached on the understanding that none of the tomb's contents would be touched, disturbed or moved.

The photographic probe revealed three ossuaries of significance. Ossuary 3, which has an incomplete rosette on its face, also has some faint Greek letters inscribed above the rosette, which appear to be MARA. Tabor and Jacobovici have suggested that these letters, found also on the Mariamene ossuary in Talpiot A, are a pointer to a link between the two tombs. (*Discovery* 67)

But it was ossuaries 5 and 6 that have caused the greatest stir. Ossuary 5 was clearly seen to have a four line Greek inscription. The letters, along with the proposed translation, are as follows:

---

[2] Amos Kloner, "A Tomb with Inscribed Ossuaries in the East Talpiot," *Atiqot* 29 (1996) 15-22.

[3] This is known as a *geniza*, and such rooms were created in Judaism in order that scriptures and other religious texts that contain the divine name of Yahweh might be preserved and not destroyed.

[4] Ultra-Orthodox Jews are opposed to any disturbance of human remains. As a result, they do their utmost to prevent archaeological examination of tomb sites.

ΔIOC (= read as an adjective: Divine or Wondrous)

IAIO (= read as Greek lettering of the divine name Yahweh)

ΥΨΩ (= abbreviation of the Greek verb: lift/raise up)

ΑΓΒ (= unknown abbreviation; perhaps also 'lift up')

Ossuary 6, now partly hidden behind ossuary 5, but in 1981 located in the first *loculus* (perhaps the place of honour, suggest Tabor and Jacobovici), could only be photographed in part. On one end of the box was seen a bell-shaped object along with what later Christian art would describe as a cruciform engraving. At the other end was engraved an incomplete fish/vase similar to what was observed on the front panel. The front panel has an intricate, if asymmetrical, border. In my judgement, the crude and incomplete engraving on the right side, along with the poor quality of the front bordering, are important clues for the interpretation of the front panel, for they indicate something of the level of sophistication of the engraver/s. On the left section of the front panel is clearly seen a detailed vertical engraving – but what is it? Tabor and Jacobovici have asserted that it represents a fish, and that what is being spewed from the mouth of the fish is a representation of Jonah. Here, in their judgement, is the earliest known use of the Jonah symbolism to represent the Christian hope of resurrection from the dead.

Chapter Three
THE OSSUARIES IN THE TOMBS

Most (though not all) of the details listed in the last chapter are not in dispute. But such data, even more so than the historical documents of early Christianity, are not self-explanatory, as all historians agree. Tabor himself reminds us: 'neither our sources, nor our own attempts to make sense of them, are transparent windows'. (*Dynasty* 316) It is not the tombs and their ossuaries but what Jacobovici and Tabor have concluded from them that is controversial. Before proceeding to a detailed outline of their conclusions, a general overview will be helpful. The Tabor/Jacobovici thesis run as follows:

Talpiot A is the family tomb of Jesus and his immediate relatives resident in Jerusalem. After the crucifixion and resurrection of Jesus, most of his siblings, along with Mary his mother, relocated to Jerusalem, as indicated both from the New Testament (e.g. Acts 1.14; 15.13; Gal 1.19) as well as from traditions handed down by Eusebius, the 4th century church historian.[1] Joseph, Jesus' father, had died some years earlier in Galilee. The tomb was given to the family by a wealthy benefactor, and the suggestion is presented that Joseph of Arimathea was the benefactor in question. Thus, in this tomb were buried all of the Jerusalem-based family members of Jesus who died in the period between his crucifixion and the Jewish revolt of AD 66-70. Jesus himself also was buried there, and his bones eventually placed in the ossuary that bears his name. Resurrection faith for these earliest and closest disciples never meant the disappearance of his body! There was one person buried in the tomb who was not related by blood to Jesus, and that was the woman whose name is given on the ossuary as MARIAMENE MARA. This is none other than Mary Magdalene, the wife of Jesus, and the mother of the son of Jesus whose name on his ossuary is given as Yehuda (or Jude).

The Talpiot B tomb serves to confirm the interpretation of the Talpiot A complex. Deliberately constructed to be close to the tomb of the Lord Jesus, it is perhaps the family tomb of Joseph of Arimathea. For Tabor and Jacobovici, two ossuaries provide assurance that these contained the remains of early Judaeo-Christians. The engraving on ossuary 6 is confidently presented as that of a fish regurgitating a human – and thus it becomes the earliest Christian

---

[1] For example, Eusebius provides detailed tradition concerning the martyrdom of James, the Lord's brother in AD 62; and also the election of Jesus' cousin Symeon as James' successor as head of the Jerusalem church. See Eusebius, *History of the Church*, 2.23 and 3.11. Tabor presents the case for Symeon being Jesus' half brother, as we shall discuss.

attempt to use the motif of Jonah delivered from the belly of the fish as a type of the Christian hope of resurrection. The authors make much of the tradition lying behind Matthew 12.40 as being the inspiration for this artwork. The four line inscription on ossuary 5 likewise points to the hope of resurrection. Though no names emerge from Talpiot B, Tabor and Jacobovici are confident that it is the tomb of a well to do Judaeo-Christian family who deliberately chose its location alongside that of the 'resurrected' Jesus.

Now let us turn in detail to the ossuaries and the 'readings' of them that Tabor and Jacobovici offer.[2]

1. The Talpiot A Ossuary Inscriptions

Six of the ten ossuaries found in Talpiot A are recorded as having named inscriptions. Critical to the Tabor/Jacobovici thesis is their claim that every name can be associated with Jesus of Nazareth. The list, and their claimed associations with Jesus, are as follows:

1.1 "Jesus son of Joseph" (Aramaic: *jeshua bar jehoseph*) (*CJO* 704)[3]

This is a very simple and unadorned ossuary – that is, it has no scrolls or rosettes on the outside, and no elaborate bordering.

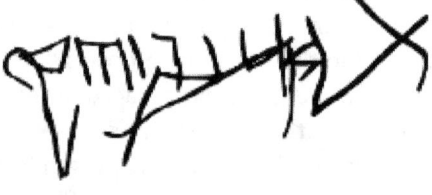

Figure 4. ישוע בר יהוסף

The writing on one end of the ossuary is in a cursive, informal style, scratched onto the surface as if with a nail or other sharp object. The word 'Joseph' is clearly visible, as is 'bar' (son of). Deciphering the first markings, however, has been more difficult and has proved contentious. Tabor himself acknowledges that it is 'nearly illegible' (*Dynasty* 23), though he accepts the eventual suggested translation of Levi Rahmani, who has been responsible for providing a catalogue of all ossuaries held by the Israeli Antiquities Authority up to 1994.

---

[2] What follows in the rest of this chapter are the various claims and interpretations offered by Tabor and Jacobovici. These can be found in *The Jesus Dynasty*, especially the Introduction, Chapter 14, and the Epilogue of the 2007 edition, and in *The Jesus Discovery*. Page references will be given only when necessary.

[3] For the ossuaries in Talpiot A, I have given their listing number in L Y Rahmani, *A Catalogue of Jewish Ossuaries*.

The difficulty is compounded by the fact that there are more scratches than are necessary to create the word 'jeshua'. These points are not insignificant, as we shall see in our analysis in Chapter 11. Though now empty, Jacobovici and Tabor were able to detect sufficient scraps of bone within the box to enable DNA sampling to be undertaken. The results of these tests will be considered later.

1.2 "Joseph" (Aramaic: yoseh) (CJO 705)

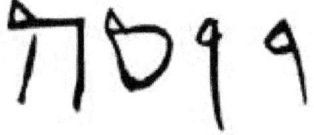

Figure 5. יוסה

Another plain and unadorned ossuary. The name is written quite clearly in formal script on the front face of the ossuary. The claimed link with Jesus is justified by reference to the brothers of Jesus named in Mark 6.3: James, Yōsēs, Judas and Simon. Matthew 13.55 follows Mark's text except that he changes Yōsēs to his full name Joseph, and reverses the order of Judas and Simon. In support of the claim that this *Yoseh* in the ossuary could be a brother of Jesus who died before AD 70, after which date such Jewish burial chambers appear to have been no longer permitted, the authors need to explain the absence of any ossuary naming Judas and Simon. In *Jesus Dynasty* Tabor argues that both these brothers lived well beyond AD 70, hence their absence from the family tomb. In respect of Jude, known to tradition as either the author of or the source behind the New Testament Epistle of Jude, Tabor writes of evidence from Eusebius, Epiphanius, and the 4th century document *Apostolic Constitutions*, which suggests that he was elected to succeed Symeon after about AD 106. This, of course, would have made Jude a very old man at the time of his appointment! As to Simon, matters are a little more complicated. Tabor claims that this brother is none other than the Symeon, son of Cleophas, whom Eusebius tells us was appointed successor to James after the latter's murder in AD 62, and who lived until the time of Trajan (Emperor from AD 98-117), and was martyred at the age of 120.[4] Against the claims of Eusebius, Tabor suggests that after the death of Joseph, Mary was given in marriage to Joseph's brother, Cleophas, so that the resultant children born to Mary and Cleophas, including Simon, were half-siblings to Jesus.[5] All of this still does

---

[4] See, for example, Eusebius, *HE* 3.11; 3.32.
[5] See *Jesus Dynasty*, 85-94, 163-165. Tabor, in fact, claims that three, and possibly four (Matthew), of the twelve apostles of Jesus were his blood brothers or half-

not explain why Jesus' brother, *Yoseh*/Joseph, probably died before AD 70. The reason for this claim is the conviction of Tabor that after the death of Jesus, James, the next eldest brother, established a dynastic succession, so that when he died in AD 62, the Jerusalem leadership should have passed to the next surviving brother. Since there is no mention of Joseph in the traditions passed to us by Eusebius, Tabor feels justified in his presumption that *Yoseh*/Joseph must have died before AD 62, when James was martyred.[6] We return to these claims of Tabor in Chapter 11.

Thus, of Jesus' four named brothers, only James and Joseph could possibly be buried in the Jesus family tomb, as only they died before AD 70.

There is one further detail that convinces Tabor and Jacobovici about this ossuary, and that is the name *Yoseh*. This, they claim, is a nickname for 'Joseph'. Though 'Joseph' accounts for 8.6% of Jewish male names in the first century period, the use of the nickname is much more rare, found on only seven ossuaries. And yet Mark's Gospel (corrected by Matthew) refers to this brother by this nickname. Since Mark represents the 'earliest New Testament gospel tradition' (*Discovery* 111), there 'appears to be a complete "fit" between text and artifact' (*Discovery* 112). The authors thus feel confident to challenge the suggestion of Rahmani, who proposed that the *Yoseh* on the tomb classified by him as *CJO* 705 is none other than the Joseph referred to on the 'Jesus son of Joseph' ossuary.

There are important issues to be considered here, and we shall return to this ossuary in Chapter 11.

1.3 "Mary" (Hebrew/Aramaic script: marya) (CJO 706)

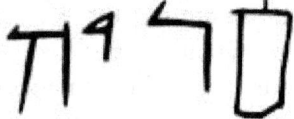

Figure 6. מריה

A plain and unadorned ossuary. The name Mary is found for nearly 22% of all Jewish women of the period. This inscription, however, represents what may be described as a latinised version of the name transcribed back into Hebrew text. In *The Jesus Family Tomb* Jacobovici and Pellegrino attempt to make much of this: the early church spoke of Jesus' mother as Maria, and here

---

brothers, namely, James, Jude and Simon. Except where it is important to the Jesus family tomb case, I do not intend to enter into dialogue on this claim.

[6] *Jesus Dynasty*, chaps 15, 17.

in a Jerusalem tomb is that same name, written in Hebrew script. And when you take into account that only eight instances of a Hebraic Marya are found 'out of thousands (*sic!*) of ossuaries', one is justified in presuming some kind of link between this ossuary and the Mary of early Christian tradition, that is, the mother of Jesus.[7] James Tabor also seems initially to have been attracted to this line of argument. In the second edition of *Jesus Dynasty* he wrote: 'The more common form of the name Mary in Hebrew or Aramaic is *Mariam*, but the relatively rare Aramaic name *Maria* fits Jesus' mother. That is the exact name she is given in the Greek New Testament and other early Christian texts.' (*Dynasty* 327) In the 2012 published *Jesus Discovery*, however, these claims disappear and the authors seem to acknowledge that nothing could be made of this ossuary were it not for the presence of the other inscribed ossuaries linked to the family of Jesus. (*Discovery* 107, 185) However, given their interpretation of the other five inscriptions, and given the fact that tradition (as reflected in Acts 1.14) tells us that Jesus' mother, Mary, took up residence in Jerusalem, the authors find no problem in suggesting that this Mary is none other than the mother of Jesus.

In the analysis of the Talpiot A ossuaries in Chapter 11, we will not pursue further the earlier claims made concerning the spelling of *Marya* on the ossuary. There is nothing special about it. As to the way Jesus' mother Mary is spelled in the New Testament, there is no 'exact same spelling' as Tabor claims. *Mariam* is the most frequent (12 occurrences, principally in Luke/Acts), but *maria* is also found (7 occurrences). Matthew and Luke use both forms. It is thus clear that nothing can be made of any similarity between the ossuary and the early Christian spelling of Mary.

1.4 "Matya/Mata" (Hebrew/Aramaic script: Matthew) (CJO 703)

Figure 7. מתיה

Written by different hands, 'matya' appears clearly and neatly inscribed on the outside of the ossuary, and 'mata' is found crudely scratched on the inside. Both are contractions of 'Matityahu'. Linking this name with Jesus' immediate family has proven more difficult for our authors, and hence more speculative.

---

[7] *Jesus Family Tomb* 16-17 and 202-203. The quote is from a footnote to p 202. The reference to 'thousands of ossuaries' is quite misleading. In Rahmani's Catalogue, only 233 are inscribed. That means that the 8 instances of *Marya* are quite unremarkable.

The first observation made is that in the lineage of Jesus' putative father, Joseph,[8] recorded by Luke in Lk 3.23-38, variants of the name Matthew are found six times, and two of these Matthews are sons of Levi. Having already established that three of his brothers were among the band of Twelve (namely, James, Jude and Simon), Tabor had initially suggested that Jesus would have been unlikely to have ignored his fourth brother, Joseph/*Yoseh*, and so concluded that Matthew/Levi the tax collector was none other than that fourth brother, now renamed after their deceased father. (*Dynasty* 164) This solution, however, would not fit the Jesus Family Tomb thesis, for *Yoseh* is already accounted for, and so between 2007 (*Dynasty*) and 2012 (*Discovery*) a different take on the Matya ossuary is given. Still drawing attention to the common occurrence of the name in 'Mary's' (see footnote 8) family tree, Tabor and Jacobovici are now satisfied to suggest that it is not impossible that such a name may have been given to someone in Jesus' immediate family, someone otherwise unknown to us. The name is common in Jesus' lineage yet is relatively rare in the records (found among fewer than 3% of males of the time).

1.5 "Yehuda bar Jeshua" (Aramaic: Jude son of Jesus) (CJO 702)

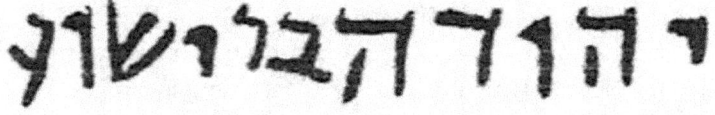

Figure 8. יהודה בר ישוע

The inscription is deeply incised on the front of its decorated ossuary. The symmetrical front face decoration consists of two deeply incised rosettes with a neat border encircling both the rosettes, and the edges of the box. A centre-line decoration separates the two rosettes. Rahmani concluded that the *Yeshua* of this ossuary, father to Jude, is the person referred to at the beginning of the ossuary catalogued by him as *CJO* 704, the so-called Jesus son of Joseph ossuary. *If* he is correct, and *if* this Jesus is Jesus of Nazareth, who then is the mother of his son, Jude? Enter Mary Magdalene!

---

[8] In both *The Jesus Dynasty* (p 53) and *The Jesus Discovery* (p 107), the authors mistakenly claim that the Lukan genealogy relates to Mary's lineal ancestors. It is quite clear that Luke is writing of Joseph's genealogy. See R Bauckham, *Jude and the Relatives of Jesus in the Early Church* (T&T Clark, 1990) 315-73. R E Brown, *The Birth of the Messiah* (Geoffrey Chapman, 1977) 89 n 65 provides us with the *very* few scholars who have sought to reconcile the Matthean and Lukan genealogies by claiming Luke's follows Mary's ancestry.

2. The 'Mary Magdalene' Ossuary (CJO 701)

The sixth ossuary with inscription in Talpiot A has proven to be the most contentious of them all. Indeed, it is probably no exaggeration to suggest that the whole Jesus family tomb thesis stands or falls on the interpretation if its inscription. Jacobovici and Pellegrino acknowledge in the following statement: 'From the beginning, we focused on this particular ossuary because it seemed to be the key to the whole story. Everything depended on this unique artifact.' (*Jesus Family Tomb* 204) Tabor has now joined them in concluding that this is the ossuary of Mary Magdalene, the wife of Jesus and the mother of the person in the 'Jude son of Jesus' ossuary. Their case is built upon a combination of factors, as we now will see.

2.1 The Ossuary Itself.

In excellent condition, the ossuary is carefully adorned with a pattern similar to, but more delicate than that of the *Jehuda bar Jeshua* ossuary, with its rosettes and borders. It is obvious that much care was given to the preparation of this resting place.

2.2 The Inscription.

Figure 9. *The Disputed 'Mary Magdalene' Inscription*

This is written on the back of the ossuary in Greek cursive. While the first seven letters can be easily read: MARIAME, the following letters have proven difficult to determine. Rahmani concluded that what follows, without a break, were three more letters, NOU. Then followed a slight break. Between this word and the next a vertical stroke appears, which Rahmani took to be the Greek letter *eta*, which he read as an abbreviation for the Greek *hē kai*. These two words stand for 'who is also', used on ossuaries to link two names. The final letters are in a more cursive style, and read as MARA. In the judgement of Rahmani, the result was a two word inscription: MARIAMENOU (also known as) MARA. The first word was taken to be a rare form of Mary, namely Mariamene in its Greek genitive singular form, 'of/belonging to Mary'. The second word was understood to be an expression of dignity, derived from the Aramaic word *mar* in its feminine form, and meaning 'lady'.[9] The

---

[9] When we comment on the MARA ossuary in Talpiot B (Chapter 10) we will have cause to correct this understanding of the Aramaic word *mara*. The Greek

full translation was thus given as 'belonging to Mariamene, [also known as] honourable lady'.

We need to return to this reading and interpretation of the inscription, for it has certainly not gone unchallenged, but Tabor and Jacobovici have indicated their acceptance of Rahmani's judgement. It is true that they reluctantly concede the possibility that MARA may refer to a second person, Martha, buried with her sister (why not daughter?), but are not persuaded to change their opinion: 'We are convinced otherwise, namely, that *Mara* is more likely a title of honor for Mariamene …'. (*Discovery* 157) And they conclude that the person to whom it refers was obviously someone held in high honour and respect. Who can this possibly be?

2.3 The DNA Analysis.

All except the so-called Jeshua and the Mariamene ossuaries had been thoroughly emptied and cleaned, and so DNA analysis of contents could not be undertaken to determine family relationship for most of the persons deposited. In the Jeshua and Mariamene ossuaries, however, 'more than enough' (*Discovery* 44) particles had remained to enable testing to be done. What the DNA results determined was that there was no *maternal* blood relationship between the two persons they represented. They could not share the same mother; they could not be brother and sister. Tabor and Jacobovici then made several (unstated) assumptions. Firstly, they presumed that the person in the Jesus ossuary was (i) male; (ii) the person referred to by its inscription, and (iii) the same person referred to as father of Jehuda. They then also presumed that the person in the Mariamene ossuary was the same as the name inscribed, and therefore female, and who could possibly be the honoured wife of Jeshua and mother of Jehuda. And so the search commenced for someone in the early Christian movement who was unrelated to Jesus by blood, but who was held in high honour, and who was given the name 'Mariamene'.

2.4 Mariamene in Early Christianity[10]

Though Mary Magdelene disappears from the scene immediately after the New Testament records of the death and burial of Jesus and the finding of the empty tomb, her name crops up in the subsequent early centuries of the

---

transliteration *mara* can represent both the masculine and the feminine of the Aramaic word for master/mistress. But for the purpose of the reading of this ossuary the correction *probably* (see Chapter 10) does not need to be made.

[10] Both the place of Mary Magdalene in early Christianity and the question of her marital status *vis à vis* Jesus are examined in depth in Part B. There will inevitably be some repetition of material presented here.

Christian movement. As well as some brief honorific mentions in the writings of those theologians and bishops of the church whom the orthodox revered (for example Irenaeus, Hippolytus, Origen), Mary Magdalene became the focus of attention for other groups and their writings deemed heretical by the mainstream church.[11] The earliest such writing is probably the (mid-second century?) *Gospel of Thomas*, where the Mary referred to in Sayings 21 and 114 is generally agreed to be a reference to Mary Magdalene. Here, as also in some later writings, she is the focus of a negative reaction from Peter: 'Simon Peter said to them, "Make Mary leave us, for females are not worthy of life"' (Saying 114). In other gnostic writings, however, Mary plays a positive role as visionary and bearer of revelation to the disciples of Jesus. For example, in the fourth century Greek text called *Acts of Philip*, Mary stands alongside Christ when the apostles are commissioned, holds the register of lands to be evangelised, and encourages her brother Philip when he is daunted by the charge to evangelise the Greeks. She even eventually travels to Jordan.[12] In the Coptic *Gospel of Mary*, Peter takes a more positive attitude to Mary, and says to her, "Sister, we know that the Saviour loved you more than the other women. Tell us the words of the Saviour that you remember, which you know and we do not, since we did not hear them." Mary then recounts her vision.[13]

This prominence (both negative and positive) of Mary Magdalene in early Christianity is important to Tabor and Jacobovici for two reasons. The first is that it supports their claim, as we will later consider, that Mary in fact played a major leadership role in the earliest Jerusalem based Jesus movement, a role that has been suppressed by the New Testament and their 'orthodox' descendents. In other words, given the profile that Mary received in such a

---

[11] A thorough treatment, from a feminist perspective, of the 'Mary Magdalene story' in early Christianity is presented by Jane Schaberg, *The Resurrection of Mary Magdalene* (Continuum, 2002). An abbreviated version of this book is *Mary Magdalene Understood* (Continuum, 2006). History, of course, is written by the winner, who will always describe itself as orthodox and its enemies as heretical. I use these terms as they have come down to us, reflecting the triumph of what became catholic Christianity over variant gnostic and other groupings.

[12] A Google search of *Acts of Philip* will supply the early 20th century translation of MR James. Typical of the frequent blending of persons with the same name, Mariamne in Acts of Philip has a sister named Martha. It is clear that Mary of Bethany and Mary Magdalene are considered one and the same person.

[13] Text taken from Bart Ehrman and Zlatko Pleše, *The Apocryphal Gospels* (OUP, 2011). The origin of this gospel is unknown and it was not referred to in the early church. Discovered in Cairo in the late 1800s, it was not published until 1955. Greek fragments of the work have also been found, bringing its date of origin back to the 3rd century.

number of early writings,[14] one is justified in wondering whether the silence (spoken of as a 'deafening silence' in *Discovery* 46) in the earlier records does not hide something that needs uncovering. The second point made is that even though Mariamene is rare, in later church writings it crops up twice in application to Mary Magdalene: in a quote by the 3rd century writer Hippolytus, and then in the fourth century Greek copy of the *Acts of Philip*. Could it be that this diminutive use of 'Mary', inscribed on an ossuary, lived on in the memory of early Christianity, only to surface several centuries later? Possibly, but there will need to be more to support such a claim, and for Tabor and Jacobovici it comes by way of a re-appraisal of the marital status of Jesus.

2.5 Mary, Wife of Jesus?

A careful re-reading of several texts provides confidence to Tabor and Jacobovici that Jesus may well have been married, and that his wife was Mary Magdalene. The following points are made:

Marriage was expected of all Jewish males in Jesus' time, and it would have been unusual if Jesus had not followed the custom. The links of John the Baptist and Jesus to the Essenes cannot take us far, for Tabor and Jacobovici dissent from the usual understanding of the Dead Sea Scrolls, Qumran, and the Essene movement in suggesting that celibacy was not an expectation. "The Scrolls are full of instructions about marriage, divorce, and avoiding fornication, or sex outside of marriage." (*Discovery* 144)

When writing to the church of Corinth in the mid-50s, Paul devoted considerable space to marriage, separation and divorce. He also presents a strong case for the unmarried to remain single. He admits he has no 'command of the Lord' to support his preference for celibacy, and so is left to give his own opinion (1 Cor 7.25). If Jesus had been unmarried, Paul would certainly have instructed that "all men should live like Jesus". (*Discovery* 145) At the very least, Paul's silence suggests that he presumed Jesus had been married.

But if everything supports the likelihood that Jesus would have been married, who was his consort? All the evidence points to Mary Magdalene. The earliest gospel, Mark, written in the 60s or 70s, tells us that women followers of Jesus witnessed his crucifixion and his hasty deposition and burial by Joseph of Arimathea, and these same women came to the tomb after the Sabbath in order to anoint and properly bury him. Matthew and Luke are dependent on Mark and essentially agree with his details. What is notable is that Mary Magdalene heads the list whenever women's names are mentioned. See Mk 15.40-41, 47; 16.1. The task of anointing the deceased involved intimate

---

[14] Schaberg, *Resurrection* 126, lists eight writings.

association with the naked body. Hence, a task for a wife, mother or sister. The suggestion is made that Mark and the other evangelists, writing decades after the event, know of a tradition that links Mary Magdalene with the burial of Jesus but have 'no idea who she was or why she was so prominent in the story ...'. (*Discovery* 133)

John's Gospel, written late in the first century, preserves an encounter between Jesus and Mary Magdalene outside the tomb (Jn 20.11-18). Drawing upon, but also extending, an interpretation proposed by Jane Schaberg,[15] Tabor and Jacobovici point to elements in the narrative that are sexually charged and suggest that the relationship between Jesus and Mary had been intimate: the single word addresses (Miriam; Rabboni), and the touching prohibition (which imply that prior to his death, Mary and Jesus had been physically intimate and had had a 'familial connection').

Finally, the early gnostic Christian document, the *Gospel of Philip*,[16] contains this slightly flawed section: "And the companion of the [...] Mary Magdalene. [...] loved her more than [all] the disciples [and used to] kiss her [often] on the [...]. The rest of [the disciples] said to him, 'Why do you love her more than all of us?' In spite of the breaks in the text, scholars generally acknowledge that 'mouth' or 'lips' should be understood after 'kiss her [often] on the'. This, along with the reference to Mary as Jesus' companion, which can mean partner or consort, also perhaps brings to the surface a truth about the relationship between Jesus and Mary suppressed by the dominant orthodox church.

There is one further clue to the real status of Mary, and it lies hidden in the word 'Magdalene'. She may well have come from come from Magdala, a town on the Sea of Galilee, midway between Capernaum and Tiberias. But more than that: just as others of Jesus' disciples had descriptive nicknames (Cephas became Peter [Matt 16.18]; James and John were named Boanerges [Mk 3.17]; and Simon was named the zealot [Lk 6.15]), so there is a hidden meaning in 'Magdalene'. The word comes from the Hebrew/Aramaic *migdal*, meaning tower – and so Mary may have received this name, not so much because of her town of origin, but because of her 'strong personality'. A further possibility is also canvassed: a later rabbinic tradition contains a story of two Miriams – one is a hairdresser (presumably Jesus' mother), the other is called the *megadla* –

---

[15] Schaberg rejects the attempt to turn Mary Magdalene into the wife of Jesus as 'just another attempt to complete the process of her "redemption" from a whore to a "normal" (married) woman'. See *Mary Magdalene Understood*, 62. Also *Resurrection of Mary Magdalene*, 102.

[16] We have it as a Coptic text, but it is a translation from Greek, possibly from the third century (Tabor and Jacobovici suggest second century).

the baby tender, the one who grows the child. Tabor and Jacobovici conclude: 'We are convinced that these are cryptic references to Mary the mother of Jesus and Mary Magdalene'. (*Discovery* 141)

Why has it taken so long to uncover the truth about the relationship between Jesus and Mary? At this point the logic becomes somewhat messy. Mary Magdalene is mentioned eleven times in the gospels (some of them duplicates or triplicates), and none presents her in a negative light. (*Discovery* 148) Indeed, Mary is presented as the first witness to the resurrected Jesus, and as the witness to the apostles. Nonetheless, early Christianity quickly suppressed the status of women – they were forbidden to speak in church (1 Cor 14.34-35), and the early credal list of witnesses to the resurrection makes no mention of women (1 Cor 15.5-8). In the process, suggest Tabor and Jacobovici, Mary's real leadership role was both suppressed and lost, and certainly her status as wife to Jesus and mother to their child disappeared from all records. Little wonder that when Mark writes his gospel, 'so many decades after the events', he knows of Mary Magdalene by name, but is totally unaware of her significance to Jesus.

But her true dignity was never lost, for when she died a suitable ossuary was set aside for her, beautifully adorned, and witnessing by its wording 'Lady Mariamene', that she held a place of high honour among those who knew the truth about her and Jesus.

3. The Ossuary Names and Statistical Analysis

None of the names inscribed on the ossuaries is unique, and most are among the most common names known from the time of Jesus. At the end of *Dynasty*, Tabor has given us the breakdown of the most common male and female names known from various epigraphic and literary sources in Palestine from 330 BC to AD 200.[17] Male names listed come to 1842, and females to 162.[18] The most frequently occurring names are as follows:

---

[17] The list is derived from Tal Ilan, *Lexicon of Jewish Names in Late Antiquity* (Mohr Siebeck, 2002). A more detailed listing, also derived from Tal Ilan, but giving slightly differing numbers, is presented in R Bauckham, *Jesus and the Eyewitnesses – the Gospels as Eyewitness Testimony* (Eerdmans, 2006) 85-89. Also in Bauckham, 'The Names on the Ossuaries' in C Quarles (ed), *Buried Hope or Risen Savior?* (B&H Publishing, 2008) 106-107.

[18] Bauckham provides similar individual numbers, but totals quite different from those given by Tabor. He lists 2625 males from 447 names, and 328 female occurrences from 74 names. If he is correct, the percentages will be significantly lower. For example, Mary/Mariam, for which he gives a total of 70 occurrences, will become 21%, which is closer to what is generally accepted. Likewise Joseph, which he lists as

Male Names	Frequency	Percentage
Simon	257	13.95
Joseph	231	12.54
Judah/Judas	179	9.71
Eleazar	177	9.60
John	128	6.94
Jesus/Jeshua	103	5.59
Hananiah	85	4.61
John	75	4.07
Matthew	63	3.42
Menahem	46	2.49
James	45	2.44

Female Names	Frequency	Percentage
Mary/Mariam	80	49.38
Salome	63	38.88
Shelamzion	25	15.43
Martha	20	12.34
Joanna	12	7.40
Shipra	12	7.40
Berenice	10	6.17
Sarah	9	5.55
Imma	7	4.32
Mara[19]	7	4.32

As indicated at footnotes 17 and 18, Bauckham has given slightly differing totals for individual names, and more significantly, very differing totals for males and females. The most noticeable contrast between the two relates to the name Mary. Tabor's chart lists her as occurring 50% of the time, while Bauckham's rates her at 21%. This is much closer to what is accepted among scholars, and Tabor himself has written: 'About 25 percent of women were names Mary ...'. (*Dynasty* 323) Even allowing for Bauckham's lower percentages, it is not surprising that when the Talpiot A ossuaries were brought to the Rockefeller Museum for cataloguing and storage, the names inscribed raised no eyebrows. Joseph, Mary, Jesus, Judas, Matthew - they are all among those most frequently occurring in the records of the time. Nor was the combination of names unique. For example, another ossuary inscribed

---

occurring 218 times, will become 8%.

[19] As we shall later mention, Mara may well be an abbreviation for Martha in many instances.

'Jesus son of Joseph' came to light in the Rockefeller Museum 1931, though its origin is unknown.

Convinced, however, that the *combination* of names associated with the family of Jesus and found in the one tomb is significant, Pellegrino, Tabor and Jacobovici have sought the assistance of statisticians. In *Dynasty*, Tabor refers to the question given to John Koopmans: what is the [statistical] likelihood of the following cluster of names and relationships occurring in a single family in first century Jerusalem: *Mary, a second Mary, Jesus son of Joseph, Jude son of Jesus, Joseph and Matthew*? On the presumption of a family size of six, the chances of this combination of names occurring in one family was given as 1/253,403 – equating to a population of 1,520,418, approximately thirty times the estimated population of Jerusalem in the period! Tabor concluded, 'Thus, statistically, it is nearly certain that this particular combination of names and relationships within one family is unique.... [so that] it is statistically all but impossible for more than one such family to have existed in first century A.D. Jerusalem.' (*Dynasty* 324-5) Initial statistical analysis had already been undertaken in 2005 by Pellegrino. He had calculated that 'the number of men likely to be called "Jesus, son of Joseph", to be found in a tomb with a latinised "Maria", and to be associated in that same tomb with a Greek-inscribed "Mariamne also known as Master" accounted for one out of about 365,928'. That equates to about four times the number of males living in Jerusalem in those generations.[20] Further statistical studies have been undertaken and are referred to in *Discovery*, most notably those by Prof Andrey Feuerverger.[21] It is acknowledged that the results will change significantly, depending on how some of the names are treated – we return to this consideration in our later analysis in Chapter 11. Tabor and Jacobovici are also willing to concede that statistics alone will not 'prove one way or the other that the Talpiot Jesus tomb is that of Jesus of Nazareth...'. (*Discovery* 118) Nonetheless, it is clear that for the authors, the statistical results are a powerful support to their thesis. That support becomes, in their judgement, overpowering and unassailable when they factor in the data from the 'James son of Joseph brother of Jesus' ossuary – to be considered in Chapter 4.

4. The Talpiot B Ossuary Inscriptions

For Tabor and Jocobovici, two further treasures complete the picture that leads to their conclusions about Jesus and earliest Jerusalem-based

---

[20] See Jacobovici and Pellegrino, *The Jesus Family Tomb*, 74-77.
[21] Feuerverger's contribution is also detailed in *The Jesus Family Tomb*, 111-115.

Christianity. The one is the second Talpiot tomb and its contents, the other is an unprovenanced[22] ossuary, the so-called James ossuary (see Chapter 4).

Without doubt, those involved in the photography of the Talpiot B tomb are to be congratulated on their technical skill and the results they were able to obtain from the probes. The results of the probes may seem to have been modest – a single word (MARA); a four line inscription; and a fish-shaped incision. But for Tabor and Jacobovici they are of profound significance, providing 'for the first time in history tangible *archaeological* evidence related to the resurrection faith of Jesus' first followers' (*Discovery* 182).

4.1 Ossuary 3 – MARA Inscription

'Etched faintly' into the front face of Ossuary 3 and just above an incomplete rosette were the Greek letters MARA. The presence of this word on an ossuary is rare: the authors mention four other occurrences. Ilan's list gives 5 other instances, though on one ossuary the same woman is named both Martha and Mara.[23] That one of those four other ossuaries is only a few metres away suggests that 'maybe the two tombs were related in content, not just in proximity'. (*Discovery* 67) The potential significance of this find for the Jesus thesis is never really spelled out.

4.2 Ossuary 5 – the Four Line Inscription

Figure 10. *Reproduction of Ossuary 5 in Talpiot B*

The four line inscription on Ossuary 5 is unusual for ossuaries of this period, but not unique. Most such inscriptions invoke a prohibition on the disturbing of the body within. Not until the 3rd century AD Jewish tombs at Beth She'arim in Galilee do we find unambiguous evidence of an inscription expressing hope for life beyond. The most notable Hebrew inscription reads: 'This is the grave

---

[22] That is, an artifact whose origins are unknown. Such artifacts normally surface having been illegally stolen from their site and then sold on the antiquities market.

[23] See Bauckham, *Jesus and the Eyewitnesses*, 89 n86. This point in fact becomes significant as we later ask what MARA was meant to signify.

of dear father Yehudah known as Gurk. May his resting place be with the righteous, his resurrection with the worthy'. A Greek inscription also from Beth She'arim reads: 'Good luck in your resurrection!'

The inscription on Ossuary 5 is written in Greek capitals as follows:

Line 1	ΔΙΟΣ
Line 2	ΙΑΙΟ
Line 3	ΥΨΩ
Line 4	ΑΓΒ

Figure 11. *The Four Line Inscription (letters enhanced for clear reading)*

All but the first letter of the second line are unambiguous. Whereas the second I in the line is written without the cross bars top and bottom (according to the practice of the day – rather like an English 'I'), the first I on the line has the cross bars. We return to this point in our examination of the interpretation.

Line 1 seems to represent a blending of Greek and Latin words for 'god' – thus instead of ΞΕΟΣ or DEUS we are left with ΔΙΟΣ. This word, used adjectivally, is found in Classical Greek poetry and means something like divine, wondrous, brilliant. This is how it is understood by Tabor and Jacobovici. Line 2 is read as a reference to the Hebrew god, Yahweh. In Hebrew, that name is written by four Hebrew letters, the Tetragrammaton: יהוה, which can be transliterated into Greek as either IAO or IAIO. The first two lines thus are taken as an address to Israel's god: divine or wondrous Yahweh/Jehovah. But what of the next two lines?

Line 3 appears to revert to Greek, and derives from the first two letters of the Greek verb *hupsoon*, along with an *omega* which is used in some of the verb's endings. The verb has a range of meanings, among which is the notion of raising up from death and of exalting to honour. The authors quote Jn 12.32, Acts 2.32-33; 5.31 and Phil 2.9 as examples of these 'theological' uses of the verb applied to the death and resurrection of Jesus.

With the interpretation of line 4 the authors are prepared to remain agnostic, since it is not a known Greek word. It could be an abbreviation of the name of the deceased; or it could possibly represent a Hebrew verb, *hagbah*, which also means to lift up. If that were so, lines 3 and 4 would be saying the same thing – in Greek and Hebrew. We are left, then, with a symmetrical four line inscription, alternating Greek/Hebrew/ Greek/Hebrew, the first two lines being the address to Yahweh, the second two expressing the prayer request.

The end result, *especially when taken alongside their reading of Ossuary 6*, is for Tabor and Jacobovici a clear indication of the Christian allegiance of the person in the ossuary. This is established on two counts. Firstly, the authors claim that the inscribing of the name of Israel's god, Yahweh, was considered heretical at the time. No traditional Jew would have done it. This ossuary is thus the property of someone who owes allegiance to that god, but who has broken free from some of the constraints of his/her upbringing. That leads to the second consideration: the third line reference to raising up is best taken either as an expression of faith in Yahweh who raised up Jesus from the dead, or as a calling upon Yahweh to raise up their Messiah, that is, to bring him back among them as he promised. Either way, it is a Christian and not a Jewish affirmation, based upon faith in the already resurrected Jesus, for no other first century Jewish ossuaries make explicit reference to resurrection hope.

4.3 Ossuary 6 – The Jonah Ossuary

But it is this ossuary which, in the judgement of the authors, is the capstone to the whole edifice of interpretation they have given, not only to the other ossuaries in Talpiot B, but also to those in Talpiot A. That the image depicted is that of Jonah and the fish is 'clear and unambiguous', (*Discovery* 184) a pointer to an early Christian family's faith in the resurrected Jesus – not the resurrected Jesus of the later Christian tradition, but the Jesus who was buried in his own family tomb just metres away. This and the four line inscription 'provide for the first time in history tangible *archaeological* evidence related to the resurrection faith of Jesus' first followers'. (*Discovery* 181) In our evaluation we shall see that this claim has little or no foundation.

Photos taken in 1981, when the tomb was first opened, reveal that this ossuary was full of bones and was located in the first niche to the right upon entrance into the chamber, the place of prominence. The ossuary itself is quite heavily scored with markings, but not markings that give the appearance of being professionally done by a skilled worker. Our authors interpret this as indicating that the owner intentionally bought an 'off the shelf' ossuary so that they could adorn it with their own distinctive message. At one end, an incomplete engraving is observed, as though the engraver planned badly and ran out of space. The intended object is the same as on the front panel. At the other end, the authors photographed 'some kind of doorway, with double crossed panels or bars'. The authors interpret this as symbolic of entering the gates of death, prior to being rescued from death's jaws by the means of the fish at the other end. This interpretation depends entirely for its credibility on the correctness of the image on the front panel.

Only half of the front panel was visible to the probe, but what it revealed is central to the thesis of Tabor and Jacobovici. Surrounded by typical borders is an object incised onto the ossuary on a vertical axis. The authors are confident that this object is intended to represent a fish, complete with detailed scales, fins and a tail. But not just any fish, for out of its mouth something is being spewed forth, and that provides the clue to its interpretation. So then, what Tabor and Jacobovici suggest is being projected is the biblical character Jonah, covered in weed (as in Jonah 2.5), and being spewed forth safely to land from the mouth of the great fish. In fact, in a later news release on April 12, 2012, Tabor announced that in the line markings at the base of the image, line markings that seem to represent the arms, body and legs of a human figure, Prof James Charlesworth had detected the four Hebrew letters that spell the name Jonah.[24] Here, in symbolic representation, is a clear expression of Christian faith in the hope of resurrection from the dead. The background to this interpretation is as follows:

- Reference to Jonah is found in the gospels, from a tradition taken over by Luke and Matthew. This tradition, independent of Mark, is known as the Q source. Scholars continue to debate whether this source was a written document, or simply a block of oral tradition to which Matthew and Luke had access. (Tabor and Jacobovici seem to side with those who think of it as an early gospel, written about AD 50.) (*Discovery* 74-75) In the Q tradition shared by Matthew and Luke, when asked to provide a sign, Jesus responds by saying, ' … no sign shall be given to [this generation]

---

[24] The announcement can be found at www.bibleinterp.com/PDFs/Jonah_2012.pdf. In a later conversation with Prof Ben Witherington, Charlesworth personally confirmed the earlier report's accuracy. However, he does not believe the tomb is that of Joseph of Arimathea, nor does he believe it is necessarily a Christian, as opposed to Jewish, site. See www.patheos.com/blogs/bibleandculture/ 2012/05/14/dr-jim-charlesworth-on-talpiot-tomb-b/.

but the sign of Jonah'. In Luke's account, Jesus goes on to say: 'For as Jonah became a sign to the men of Nineveh, so will the son of man be to this generation'. But in Matthew Jesus is even more explicit: 'For as Jonah was three days and three nights in the belly of the whale, so will the son of man be three days and three nights in the heart of the earth' (Matt 12.39-40/ Lk 11.29-30). Here, then, on an ossuary, is a figurative representation that shows evidence of reflecting the saying of Jesus known to us in Matthew's Gospel.

- In Christian iconography from the 3rd and 4th centuries, representations of elements of the Jonah story became the most common of all the images carved onto sarcophagi or painted on the walls of tombs and catacombs. Jonah and the fish becomes '*the quintessential early Christian biblical image*' – more frequently found than even the shepherd or cross images. The authors suggest that was due to the dominant influence of the Jonah tradition in the gospels, seen as the most powerful image of the hope of resurrection from the dead. The Jonah image on the Talpiot B ossuary predates the later Christian iconography by at least 150 years. The inscriber had no patterns to work from, simply the verbal tradition reflected in Q.

- In passing, the authors also draw attention to the fact that the person of Jonah is rarely referred to in Jewish writings of the period. They suggest that the reason for this is that when, in the 4th and 5th centuries, the rabbis were editing their earlier traditions, they had no interest in drawing attention to a figure whom the Christians had adopted as the primary iconographic expression of the resurrection of Jesus. Be that as it may, this ossuary is unique among the two thousand ossuaries catalogued for the period, and its uniqueness indicates that the fish representation was a deliberate attempt by the owners to convey a message. Though 'crude and homemade' it was intended to convey something 'deeply meaningful ... a specific message'. (*Discovery* 84)

- Having uncovered the fish/Jonah/resurrection symbolism on this ossuary, the authors now suggest that it is time to rethink the markings on several other ossuaries. Hitherto, these markings have been thought of simply as roughly scratched circles around a name; they now suggest that they also are early Christian fish drawings, with the tailpiece clearly in evidence. An ossuary fragment uncovered in the 1970s appears to have 'Jesus' inscribed, encircled by a rough fish; and the wording on the Mariamene Mara ossuary is also encircled by the fish symbol. It would appear that the impact of Jesus' Jonah saying took hold quite early, so that well before AD 70, the fish was adopted as a symbol of resurrection hope.

Chapter Four
THE JAMES OSSUARY – THE MISSING TENTH?

The authors have one more piece of the jigsaw to fit into place – the audacious claim that the famous James ossuary, brought to public attention in 2002, originally came from the Jesus Family Tomb (Talpiot A) and may well be the missing 10th ossuary. Already in his 2007 revised edition of *The Jesus Dynasty* Tabor signalled his belief that the James ossuary had originally belonged in the Talpiot A tomb. (*Dynasty* 320-322) Indeed, it would appear that by late 2005/early 2006 Jacobovici, Pellegrino and Tabor were actively seeking evidence, including DNA analysis, that might establish the case.[1]

1. The Story of the James Ossuary

In October 2002, Hershel Shanks, editor of *Biblical Archaeology Review*, unveiled to the public a plain ossuary that had inscribed on one of the front panels, in formal and neat Hebrew script, the simple words *ya'akov bar-josef akhui deyeshua*. Despite some initial doubts, this has been established as correct 1st century AD Aramaic for 'James son of Joseph brother of Jesus'. It transpired that the ossuary was the property of an Israeli collector, Oded Golan, who claimed to have had it in his possession for many years, and who acquired it from an antiquities dealer. Indeed, during his subsequent trial for forgery, Golan presented two photos of the ossuary in his parents' living room and which, if accurate,[2] support his claim that he had the ossuary in his possession in 1976, well before Talpiot A tomb was opened up.

Figure 12. *The James Ossuary*

---

[1] See pages 176-192 of *The Jesus Family Tomb*.
[2] Golan presented expert witness at the trial to support his claim that the photos are genuine and date from the mid-1970s.

The 'modern' story of the James ossuary is a fascinating one. It covers the acquisition of the ossuary by Oded Golan, its public 'unveiling' at an academic conference in Toronto in 2002, the subsequent scholarly furore over its authenticity, and finally charges of forgery levelled against Golan, leading to a prolonged trial in the Israeli courts. After many years, the trial judge delivered his verdict on 14th March, 2012. Golan was acquitted of the charge of forgery. In the words of the trial judge: 'the prosecution failed to prove beyond all reasonable doubt ... that the ossuary is a forgery.' He also added: 'This is not to say that the inscription is true and authentic and written 2000 years ago.'[3]

And so, after ten years of public debate, the scholarly community remains divided over the authenticity of the ossuary. A summary of the issues can be presented as follows:

2. What All Agree On

All agree that the ossuary itself is authentic. That is, while it cannot be precisely dated, it may well have come from the first century AD. It is simple and unadorned, except that the borders have the same edged pattern as the Herodian ashlars that are typical of the great building projects of Herod the Great, including the stones that to this day still form the foundation of the Temple Mount.

Also generally, though not universally,[4] agreed is the strong possibility that if the inscription is genuine it refers to James the brother of Jesus of Nazareth. Though not unique, it is unusual for an inscription to include reference to someone else in addition to the deceased's father or husband. The inscription suggests that the Jesus to whom James is related as sibling, was more well-known or important than either himself or his father.

---

[3] The best presentation of the early days of the 'James ossuary story' is Hershel Shanks and Ben Witherington III, *The Brother of Jesus – The Dramatic Story and meaning of the First Archaeological Link to Jesus and His Family* (HarperCollins, 2003). In 2004 John Painter published a revised edition of his *Just James – The Brother of Jesus in History and Tradition* (Uni South Carolina, 2004) to take account of the James ossuary debate. See Chapter 9 along with pages xvii-xxv and 345-355.

[4] Jodi Magness makes a strong case against the brother of Jesus of Nazareth being the person intended by the ossuary. Her judgement is based on two main considerations: (i) from the epistle that goes by his name, we know that James\ was an outspoken opponent and critic of the wealthy, and would not have approved of such a lavish burial; and (ii) the burial in Jerusalem of those from elsewhere normally refers to their place of origin – thus we might expect, 'James, son of Joseph from Galilee/Nazareth, brother of Jesus'. See Jodi Magness, 'Ossuaries and the Burials of Jesus and James', espec 149-154.

Statistically, while the three names are all well known among the list provided by Tal Ilan, and while Joseph and Jesus are particularly common, James comes fairly well down the list, as we saw in Chapter 3. Only 2.44% of males are named James. The statistical likelihood thus becomes quite high that this is a reference to the eventual leader of the Judaeo-Christian community in Jerusalem who was martyred in 62 AD. On the basis of an average family size of six, one statistician has concluded there is one chance in 34,160 families in contemporary Jerusalem that there would be a James who had a father named Joseph and a brother named Jesus.[5]

But the fact that the ossuary is unprovenanced places a high degree of uncertainty against the last two paragraphs. Did the ossuary originate from Jerusalem or Galilee or Jericho? We simply do not know (though see the later claims of Tabor and Jacobovici).

Finally, it *needs* to be logically agreed by all that even though the verdict of the Golan trial acquitted him of forgery, asserting that the prosecution was not able to establish its case beyond reasonable doubt, this judgement of the Israeli court does not prove either that Golan did not forge all or part of the inscription, or that it was not forged by someone else. It was not an academic judgement, but a legal one: the prosecution had not established its case against Golan. That still leaves the academic question quite unsettled.

יעקוב בר יוסף אחוי די ישוע
Reading right to left: Jacob son of Joseph brother of Jesus
Figure 13. *Inscription on the James Ossuary*

3. Where the Scholarly Community Divides

From the outset, the experts among the scholarly community have been divided. The issues revolve around the following three questions:

(i) Palaeography. Does the inscription reflect the orthographic style one would expect from first century AD Aramaic? To put it in modern terms: handwriting styles change over time and a handwritten text can

---

[5] *Dynasty*, 320. A different set of statistics is provided by Prof Camil Fuchs and referred to by H Shanks in '"Brother of Jesus" Inscription is Authentic' 33, 62, 64.

usually be placed to a certain era in the language in which it is written. Does the text on the James ossuary have the look of something written in the first century AD? Are there any indicators that might suggest it does not belong in that period?

(ii) Single Hand. Is it clear that all of the inscription was written by the same hand, at the same time?

(iii) Patina Residue. Both the ossuaries and the tomb complexes in the Jerusalem region were made of limestone. Over time, naturally formed mineral and organic changes take place on the surface of the limestone, affected by the presence of moisture, both on the surface and in the air, and by other factors. That residue on the stone surface is known as its patina and it can be scientifically analysed. To our knowledge, patina cannot be artificially created. In respect of the James ossuary, is there evidence of ancient patina in the grooves formed by the letters?[6]

A fourth question arose from the fact that the James inscription was deeply cut and clear to read, whereas on the other flat face of the ossuary a heavily weathered rosette was barely visible. Why would the inscription be so visible and the rosette so weathered? It was apparently because of this conflict, and not because of any fault in the palaeography, that the late Prof Frank Moore Cross of Harvard University judged the inscription a forgery. Prof André Lemaire has since demonstrated that such inconsistent weathering is not unknown and is no reason to suspect forgery.[7]

The initial defence of the genuineness of the inscription came from renowned palaeographer Prof André Lemaire of the Sorbonne, who concluded that the writing style points to a dating in the final decades before the destruction of the Temple.[8] In the face of the doubters, including a negative conclusion in a report commissioned by the Israel Antiquities Authority, Lemaire has continued to defend his original judgement: '... the James ossuary inscription does not raise any palaeographic, linguistic, or orthographic (spelling) problems, and there is no reason on these grounds to cast doubt on its authenticity.'[9] From the start,

---

[6] A more detailed and precise definition of patination, along with its uses and limitations for scientific analysis, is given by Steven Cox in his paper, 'A Forensic Science Analysis of "The Lost Tomb of Jesus" Documentary', pages 2-3, at www.uhl.ac/Lost-Tomb/ForensicAnalysisOfTLTJ.pdf.

[7] André Lemaire, 'Engraved in Memory – Diaspora Jews Find Eternal Rest in Jerusalem' *BAR* 32/3 (2006) 57.

[8] André Lemaire, 'A Burial Box of James the Brother of Jesus,' *BAR* 28/6 (2002).

[9] See André Lemaire, 'Israel Antiquities' Authority Report Deeply Flawed,' *BAR* 29/6 (2003), reprinted in *The Brother of Jesus*. The quote is on p 256 of *The Brother of Jesus*.

scholars of international repute lined up to defend Lemaire's original opinion or to contradict it. At his trial, Golan brought forward a host of opinions from authorities to support his claim that the inscription is authentic, and thus not forged by him.[10]

As already mentioned, in 2003 the Israel Antiquities Authority established a committee to examine the authenticity of the ossuary (along with another inscription in Golan's possession, not relevant to our concerns). The Committee divided into two groups. The Writing and Content Committee had the task of investigating whether the script and language used are compatible with the Aramaic of the period. The Materials and Patina Committee had the task of examining the patina and any other materials on the surface of the ossuary. Each expert on these committees worked independently and gave his/her own judgement, and then came together to provide a summary judgement. Sample findings from the Writings and Content Committee members are:

- 'The inscription appears new. The writer tried giving the letters an ancient appearance by using samples from contemporaneous inscriptions.'
- '... I am of the opinion that the inscription is a forgery.'
- 'The inscription does not exhibit a combination of configurational or substantial effects that would imply forgery. But I was convinced that the inscription is a forgery when presented with the findings of the Materials Committee.' (*sic*!)
- '... the inscription is not authentic, and was added at a much later date (possible [*sic*!] in two stages).'

As can be seen, the third excerpt, written by Prof. Ronny Reich, is in conflict with the other three.

Sample findings from the Materials Committee members are:

- 'All the various scratches on the ossuary are coated in the original patina and only the inscription and its immediate surroundings are coated with an artificial "patina"-like material of round crystalline granules. The inscription cuts through the original patina and appears to have been written by two different writers using different tools.'

---

[10] In April 2011 Golan produced a useful list of scholarly opinions to support his claims. See his article, 'The Authenticity of the James Ossuary and the Jehoash Tablet Inscriptions – Summary of Expert Trial Witnesses' at www.bibleinterp.com/articles/authjam358012.shtml. A useful summary and analysis of the 475 page trial verdict was produced by Dr Paul Flesher: 'The Ossuary of James the Brother of Jesus: From Trial to Truth?' at www.bibleinterp.com/articles/fle368021.shtml.

- 'The end of the inscription "brother of Jesus" appears authentic; in some places there seem to be remains of old patina, but in order to produce a uniform effect, this too was spread with the same granular substance.'

This last opinion also flies in the face of the judgement of others, namely that the last two Aramaic words ('brother of Jesus') were written by a later hand. It acknowledges that traces of authentic patina were found in two of the letters for 'Jesus'.

The Chairman of the IAA committee, Prof Yoval Goren, summarised the findings of the committee thus:

> The inscription was inscribed or cleaned in a modern period. Its coating is not a result of nature, and was probably accomplished by crumbling and dissolving chalk (or perhaps the powder falling from the engraving process) in hot water and spilling the suspension on the inscription and surrounding area in order to blur the freshly carved inscription.[11]

We are left, then, with a range of conflicting data and opinions, as follows:

- We have no evidential reason to doubt that Oded Golan had the ossuary in his possession in the 1970s, that is, before the Talpiot tombs were opened up.[12]
- Some experts claim that the whole inscription appears to be authentic, and written by the same hand; others are equally convinced that it was written by two separate hands, using different tools to engrave. The first part ('James son of Joseph') may be authentic. (In fact, Dr Joe Zias is reported to have told several people that he saw the ossuary in an antiquities shop before it came into the possession of Oded Golan, and that at that time it lacked the last two words 'brother of Jesus'.)[13] On the other hand, one expert on the IAA committee suggested the opposite, namely, that the second part of the inscription is original.
- Some experts claim that patina tests reveal that the words have broken into the ancient patina, thus suggesting a later dating for the inscription.

---

[11] A summary report is provided by Dr Uzi Dahari, 'The Committees Establishment and Selection of Members', available at www.bibleinterp.com/articles/Final_committees_report.shtml.

[12] The ossuary was confiscated by Israeli authorities when he was charged with forgery. I am unaware whether, subsequent to the trial verdict on March 2012, the ossuary has been returned to him.

[13] This is referred to by Hershel Shanks in his column in *BAR* May/June, 2012, p 22. It is repeated in Shanks' subsequent article, '"Brother of Jesus" Inscription is Authentic!' in *BAR* July/August, 2012, 26-33, 62, 64-65. Zias' claim is referred to on p 32.

Others claim that the evidence of patina residue in at least two of the letters for 'Jesus' is an indicators of its antiquity.[14]

- In relation to the last point, Prof Goren appears to have changed his opinion, and during the trial acknowledged that traces of ancient patina in two letters of 'Jesus' now lead him to be 'undecided. I am deliberating.'
- Evidence of modern detergents and modern mechanical actions on the surface do not invalidate the claims to antiquity, for they may simply be indicators of a cleaning process in the modern period – either by the antiquities dealer or by Golan.
- Questions have been raised about Prof Goren's failure to use the most reliable scientific equipment to examine the patina on the ossuary.[15]

Where does all of this conflicting evidence leave us? Frankly, it gives us no confidence one way or the other on the authenticity of the inscription. We do not know where it came from (though see below). We do not know whether or not the inscription was the work of a single hand. For example, it is possible that an ancient ossuary originally was inscribed 'James son of Joseph', and in ancient times a Jewish Christian found it and, recognising the names, decided to add 'brother of Jesus'. (I should add that this is an unlikely scenario, for no other reason than that a later Christian would be unlikely not to add some kind of honorific, such as 'brother of the Lord', rather than simply 'brother of Jesus'.) Equally, it may be a modern forgery using techniques of such a level of sophistication that they evade modern science. But then again, it may be genuine.[16]

4. The James Ossuary and the Jesus Tomb

Tabor and Jacobovici acknowledge that early in the investigations they were attracted to the possibility that the James ossuary may have come from Talpiot A. The IAA catalogue, as well as the listings in Rahmani, make reference to ten

---

[14] A useful response of specialists to the trial verdict and the question of the patination of the ossuary and its inscription is given in a detailed article by Amon Rosenfeld, Shimon Ilani, Howard Feldman, Yoel Kronfeld and Wolfgang Krumbein, 'Implications of the "Forgery Trial" Verdict on the Authenticity of the James Ossuary', at www.bibleinterp.com/articles/ros368030.shtml.

[15] Hershel Shanks, 'Fudging with Forgeries – A Closer Look at Professor Yuval Goren's "Scholarship"' in *BAR* 37/6 (2011) 53-58, 71. Ryan Byrne and Bernadette McNary-Zak (eds), *Resurrecting the Brother of Jesus – the James Ossuary Controversy and the Quest for Religious Relics* (Uni of North Carolina, 2009).

[16] A useful set of articles critical of the claim to authenticity is in R Byrne and B McNary-Zak, *Resurrecting the Brother of Jesus* (Uni of Nth Carolina Press, 2009).

ossuaries. But there are fatal difficulties in the James ossuary being the missing tenth ossuary:

- The dimensions of the James ossuary (56.5 x 25.7 x 29.5cm) are not the same as those recorded for the tenth (60 x 26 x 30).
- Rahmani records that 'The Department retained nine ossuaries ... recovered from a double chambered loculi and arcosolia tomb in 1980; a plain, broken specimen was also found'.[17] This suggests that the tenth ossuary was removed from the site but was not retained by the IAA because of its poor state. Many ossuaries are listed by Rahmani as 'broken and reconstructed' (as is the case with six of the Talpiot A ossuaries). This one was obviously in such a poor state, and was seen to have no special features, that reconstruction was not undertaken.
- Oded Golan claims to have been in possession of the James ossuary before Talpiot A was opened up in 1980.

There is thus no reason to consider that the missing tenth has been found! But at this point, Tabor and Jacobovici claim that scientific analysis tells another story. In 2006 analysis was undertaken of the patina on three ossuaries from Talpiot A, the James ossuary, and ossuaries from 13 other local burial tombs. The results showed that the three Talpiot ossuaries shared a common 'chemical signature', a signature that was different from each of the other 13 randomly selected ossuaries. And the James ossuary? Its patina shared almost the same chemical signature as the three from Talpiot A. It begins to look as though the James ossuary spent much of its history in the Talpiot A tomb.[18]

On this score, Tabor and Jacobovici opt for the suggestion that the James ossuary is a missing *eleventh* one from the Talpiot A tomb. But there are major difficulties with this suggestion:

- When the tomb was opened up in 1980, there were no signs of human intrusion in the recent past. Photos taken at the time indicate that all of the ossuaries were covered with local terra rossa soil to a depth of 600mm. It is true that no sealing stone at the entrance to the tomb was in place, but even so, there were no signs of recent tomb disturbance or grave robbery. Nothing in the report that was eventually written, nor anything in the statements of those who were involved at the time suggests that they noticed any evidence of soil disturbed in order to remove one item. This is critical, for it is true that the tomb, discovered on a Thursday, appears to

---

[17] L Y Rahmani, *Catalogue of Jewish Ossuaries*, 222.
[18] *Discovery* 174-179. Also see *The Jesus Family Tomb*, both at chapter 14, and also the laboratory printouts in the colour section.

have been left unguarded over the following Jewish Sabbath. It certainly was entered in that time, for skulls were removed by children and used as soccer balls! However, no mention was made by anyone that one ossuary appeared to have been removed.

- The James ossuary is heavily weathered, as though it has been exposed to the elements over some considerable time. This is not the case with the nine ossuaries recovered from Talpiot A. The authors suggest that the James ossuary occupied a position 'near the door, less covered with soil, and thus easy to carry off'. (*Discovery* 179) This suggestion ignores the expert opinion of Dr Wolfgang Krumbein, who in 2005 wrote:

    Based on a comparison of the ossuary surface to many other ossuaries, it appears that the cave in which the James ossuary was placed either collapsed centuries earlier, or alluvial deposits penetrated the chamber together with water and buried the ossuary, either completely or partially. Further, the root or climbing plant marks as well as the severe biopitting on the top and bottom parts of the ossuary indicate that the ossuary was exposed to direct sunlight and atmospheric weathering and other conditions that are not typical of a cave environment, for a period of at least 200 years.[19]

- The marks of weathering and of root climbing are clearly observable on photos of the James ossuary.
- One further consideration gives cause to pause, and that is the question: how securely does the scientific analysis establish that 'the James ossuary spent much of its history over the past two millennia in the Talpiot tomb environment'? (*Discovery* 179) In particular, how accurate is it to speak of a match between the Talpiot ossuaries and the James ossuary? In a detailed study, Steven Cox, a forensic scientist with expertise in the area of microanalysis of materials, has highlighted major errors of procedure on the part of those involved in the analysis of the ossuaries. As well, he points out that the James ossuary was contaminated by cleaning, 'more than once over a period of many years', thus making it impossible to eliminate the real possibility of sample contamination. Cox also detailed several examples of procedural errors relating to sample preparation. Finally, Cox contested the claim that 'every ossuary discovered in a particular tomb will have the same patina fingerprint'.[20] Cox responds:

---

[19] Prof Dr Dr Wolfgang Krumbein, 'Preliminary Report: External Opinion on Three Stone Items' cited by Steven Cox, 'A Forensic Science Analysis of "The Lost Tomb of Jesus" Documentary'. It is not possible to repeat the detailed critique that Cox provides. I would encourage readers to read Cox's paper (see fn 6).

[20] Claim made in the documentary film version of "The Lost Tomb of Jesus", produced by Jacobovici, and screened in March 2007 on the Discovery Channel.

'This is absolutely an unproven statement.... It is a speculation that has not been established with scientific protocol and methodologies. Within a cave or tomb different ecologies and environments can and do exist which would cause different patina formation.' Cox concludes that it may be possible to determine that 'the ossuaries could have originated from the same quarry from where they were hewn', but that 'the possibility that the "James Ossuary" and the "Jesus Ossuary" share a common origin from the same tomb is beyond reason, scientific fact, and proper scholarship.'[21]

5. Exit the James Ossuary

It is obvious, then, that in the quest for the truth about the Talpiot tombs, the so-called James ossuary cannot be taken into account. Firstly, contrary to the claims of Tabor and Jacobovici, there is simply no scientifically established evidence that it came from the Talpiot A tomb complex. In fact, as Prof Krumbein pointed out, the external condition and markings of the ossuary suggest that it did not come from the enclosed Talpiot A tomb – at least not in the last several hundred years. And it is difficult to imagine a circumstance in which an ossuary, looted from a tomb well back in the times of Ottoman rule in Palestine, had been preserved and found its way into the hands of an antiquities dealer in the late 20th century! Secondly, the integrity of the inscription on the ossuary remains under a cloud. While it is true that highly respected experts defend its authenticity, others disagree – the academic community is divided, and not on confessional lines.[22]

But there is one further point that will perhaps not have gone undetected by some, and it's this. It's just possible that the following scenario is correct: (i) the James ossuary and its inscription are authentic; (ii) the James referred to on the ossuary is the brother of Jesus of Nazareth; and (iii) the James ossuary was never *in situ* in the Talpiot A tomb. If all three of those were to turn out to be correct, and that, I acknowledge, is a big, though not impossible, ask, then the Tabor/Jacobovici thesis about the Jesus family tomb becomes unsustainable from the start, for a key member of the Jesus family was not buried in the so-called family tomb! Or, to turn the point on its head: if Tabor and Jacobovici are convinced of the authenticity of the James ossuary, it is critical to their Jesus Family Tomb thesis that they be able to demonstrate that it came from Talpiot A – or at least demonstrate that it is not impossible that it came from

---

[21] See Steven Cox article cited above.

[22] Hershel Shanks also continues to defend the authenticity of the ossuary, without committing himself on the question of whether the James in question is the one known from Christian history. He is also silent on the claims of Tabor and Jacobovici in relation to its origin in Talpiot A. See his '"Brother of Jesus" Inscription is Authentic' 26-33, 62, 64-65.

Talpiot A. To my mind, it is therefore very damaging to their case that their treatment of the James ossuary in Chapter 6 of *The Jesus Discovery* contains no mention of and response to Prof Krumbein's report (even though they mention him at endnote 34), nor to the critical scientific report by Steven Cox.

Academic integrity compels us to discard the James ossuary as we come to assess the claims made for the two Talpiot tombs. We will effectively make no further reference to it in the chapters that follow.[23]

Postscript – Dr Joe Zias Speaks Out

As this book was about to go to print, on 24 November 2012 an article by Dr Zias was posted on the Bible and Interpretation web site.[24] In it, Dr Zias responds to earlier charges by Hershel Shanks[25] that Zias is at best mistaken in his claim to have seen the James ossuary, minus the 'brother of Jesus' wording, in the shop of an antiquities dealer in the early 1990s, well after Oden Golan claims to have acquired it, and years after the Talpiot A ossuaries were removed for storage by the IAA. Among the matters that Zias now places on record are:

- He saw the James ossuary in the shop of Mahmoud Abushakra in December, 2003;
- He was accompanied by Dr Ludwig Kempe, whose diary entry confirms the date;
- Contrary to the suggestion of Hershel Shanks, he has not confused the James ossuary with a larger and heavier one in the same shop that was worded 'Joseph, son of Judah, son of Hadas';
- At least one other reputable scholar admits to having seen the James ossuary in Abushakra's shop;
- Abushakra appears to have been aware of the lucrative potential of the James ossuary, and spoke of it as his future 'pension fund';
- In spite of earlier denials, it is clear that Abushakra knew Zias, as the photo of the two, along with Dr Kempe, in the front of the shop validates.

This article puts Zias in direct conflict with the claims of Oded Golan, supported by Hershel Shanks. We, who can only observe from the sidelines, are in no position to make an authoritative judgement, though we may have our suspicions as to where truth lies. What can be said with certainty is that if Zias is correct then the following conclusions follow:

---

[23] Apart from brief discussion in Chapter 11.
[24] Joe Zias, 'James and the BAR Crowd – I Cons or just another Amazing Dis-Grace?' at www.bibleinterp.com/articles/zia368029.shtml.
[25] See references at note 13.

- The ossuary was purchased by Oded Golan after 1993;
- The 'son of Joseph' part of the inscription was not evident when Zias saw it in 1993 and some time between 1993 and 2002 those words were added;
- There is no reason to associate the ossuary with the tenth Talpiot A ossuary;
- Most importantly, James, the brother of Jesus, remains absent from the so-called Jesus Family Tomb. In fact, he was never there. As we indicated above, that absence of James from the family tomb becomes an insurmountable problem for the Tabor/Jacobovici thesis.

I suspect we have not seen the end to the Zias/Shanks dialogue and that both participants will be drawn into further 'conversation'. Others will also make their contributions from the sidelines. In particular, Tabor and Jacobovici will themselves need to provide a response.

Chapter Five
JESUS AND THE POST-EASTER COMMUNITY – THE NARRATIVE RECONFIGURED

From the discovery of the ossuaries in Talpiot A and B and the interpretation that Tabor and Jacobovici give to them, what emerges is a radically new narrative both of the fate of the crucified Jesus and of the early years of the Christian movement. It is a narrative, they claim, that hitherto has been lost to history, thanks to the successful efforts of the eventual male leadership of the church and their 'official' historians, the four evangelists and Paul. These leaders managed to ignore and suppress what did not suit their own agendas. Thanks to the discovery of the Talpiot tombs, however, the true story has now come to light. The recovered and reconfigured narrative, as presented by Tabor and Jacobovici, reads as follows:

1. Jesus' Death, Temporary Burial and Reburial

When Jesus finally died (around 3 pm on Thursday)[1], there was little time before the commencement of Sabbath at sundown. Consequently, he was hastily wrapped and placed in a nearby tomb as a temporary measure, thus preventing his body being thrown into an open mixed grave.[2] This arrangement was undertaken through the good offices of Joseph of Arimathea, who had more dignified plans for the burial of the Master. The usual understanding that Joseph of Arimathea placed the body in his own tomb complex rests upon a single verse from Matthew's Gospel (Matt 27.60), and is unsupported by the other gospels. When, after the conclusion of Sabbath, various women made their way to this temporary tomb early on Sunday morning, their

---

[1] Tabor claims that Jesus was crucified on Thursday, 14th April, AD 30, so that Jesus was in his tomb for three nights before the tomb was found to be empty on the Sunday morning. The next day, Friday, was a Sabbath as it was the day of Passover, according to Tabor. See *Jesus Dynasty*, 198-207. I do not intend to respond to these claims, as they are not material to the 'Jesus tomb' issue. For all his naïve reading of the biblical texts, Colin Humphreys has presented a strong case for the date of Jesus' death being Friday, 3rd April, AD 33. See his *The Mystery of the Last Supper* (CUP, 2011).

[2] Tabor suggests that Jesus was crucified on the Mount of Olives, not at the site generally recognised in early tradition, that is, where the Church of the Holy Sepulchre is located. See *Jesus Dynasty*, 226-7. Again, I do not intend to respond to this suggestion, except to note that at such a remove from the city, it would not be inconceivable for Joseph of Arimathea to own a burial chamber nearby. This, then, would weaken the case for suggesting the Talpiot A tomb had originally belonged to Joseph. More importantly, it would remove any justification for the claim that the body of Jesus needed to be moved from its temporary depository.

intention was to anoint the body properly and wrap it and remove it to the tomb provided by Joseph. At this point the thesis is unclear: on one occasion Tabor suggests that Jesus' mother, Mary, his sister, Salome, perhaps assisted by other women including Mary and Martha from Bethany, were responsible for removing the body, perhaps on Saturday evening once Sabbath had concluded. (*Dynasty* 235) Elsewhere, Joseph of Arimathea is suggested either to have done the deed (*Discovery* 36, 126) or to have intended to complete proper burial rites in another tomb after Passover. (*Discovery* 120) In any case, Jesus' wife Mary Magdalene, as reported in John 20, obviously unaware of the removal arrangements, comes early and first to the tomb, finds it opened and empty, and reports back to the disciples.[3] That tomb was indeed empty, for by that time the body had been removed from its temporary holding to its more permanent location in the Talpiot A tomb, where, in the course of time, the bones of Jesus were collected and gathered into their own ossuary.

2. Jerusalem and the Jesus Family

The evidence from the New Testament (Mk 6.3/Matt 13.55; Jn 7.3; Acts 1.14; 1 Cor 9.5) makes it clear that Jesus had several brothers, along with at least two unnamed sisters. Their blood relationship to Jesus has been the subject of conjecture both in the early church and in modern scholarship,[4] but Tabor dismisses other views and presents the case, and then goes on to presume, that Jesus was the eldest child in the family. Jesus' father, Joseph, died well before Jesus commenced his Galilean ministry, and Mary was re-married to Joseph's brother, Cleophas. The four brothers (James, Joseph, Judah and Simon) were all the children of Mary and Cleophas, and hence Jesus' half-brothers.[5]

In the immediate period after Jesus' death and resurrection, many of the members of Jesus' family left Galilee permanently and took up residence in Jerusalem. In Acts 1.14 both Jesus' mother, Mary, as well as his brothers are spoken of as regularly gathering with the Twelve for prayer in Jerusalem. Moreover, in spite of Luke's attempts to suppress the evidence relating to James' leadership status, it is clear from what Paul says in Galatians 1.19 and 2.9, and from extra-biblical sources (such as the *Gospel of Thomas* 12) that

---

[3] In the Epilogue to the 2nd edition of *Jesus Dynasty*, Tabor appears to ignore his earlier comments about Mary Magdalene's lone visit to the tomb. He now suggests that Mary Magdalene is wife to Jesus, and so, along with his other female family members, would have had responsibility for the washing and anointing of Jesus' body.

[4] An excellent consideration of the evidence from the early church is given in Richard Bauckham, *Jude and the Relatives of Jesus*, Chapter 1.

[5] The paternity of Jesus is not relevant to the Talpiot Tomb proposals, but in *Jesus Dynasty* Tabor argues the case that Joseph was not the father of Jesus, and that 'quite possibly a Roman soldier' named Pantera was the real father. See Chapter 3.

from the beginning, James, as next eldest son of Mary, assumes leadership of the new Jesus community. He is the heir to the dynasty. In Tabor's judgement, James is in fact the 'disciple whom Jesus loved' mentioned in John's Gospel, so that at the point of death Jesus handed over care of his mother to the eldest surviving brother (Jn 19.26-27). And what of Jesus' sisters? We are probably safe to assume that by this time they have reached the age of marriage and have settled with their husbands in Nazareth or its surrounds, and so played no further part in the Jerusalem-based movement.

But it was not only James from the family of Jesus who exercised a leadership role in the earliest community. Mary Magdalene also, as the honoured wife of Jesus, had an 'apostolic' role. By the time the four canonical gospels were written, knowledge of her had all but been suppressed by the male leadership of the church. The gospel writers knew almost nothing about her, except that she was present in Jerusalem at the time of Jesus' arrest, crucifixion and burial. But traces of her leadership role persisted even in the documents that formed part of the New Testament. She was the first to see the resurrected Jesus, and she was commissioned to announce the Easter message to the male disciples. This detail was suppressed in the early creed repeated by Paul in 1 Cor 15.3-8, where only appearances to males are recorded. Mary Magdalene was never completely forgotten, however, and the memory of her leadership lived on in some early circles, only to surface in certain later gnostic texts, notably the *Gospel of Mary* and the *Gospel of Philip*. Eventually, upon her death, she was given an honourable burial in the Jesus Family Tomb, and her ossuary bears witness to the status she bore, at least in the eyes of the close knit Jesus family. She was known as *Mara* – Lady Mary. Of her and Jesus' son, Judah, we know nothing.

3. Rethinking Resurrection Faith

Burial, re-burial in Talpiot A, and then eventual gathering into an ossuary - all of this requires Tabor and Jacobovici to re-examine the earliest Christian notion of resurrection. For there can be no doubt that the Jesus movement lived on after his death, and that at the core of its conviction was the belief that the God of Israel, Yahweh, had raised Jesus from the dead. But what did the earliest Jewish believers understand when they spoke of Jesus having been resurrected? The fundamental point that the authors wish to make is that their faith in Jesus' resurrection was not compromised by their awareness that his body was interred in the tomb provided by Joseph of Arimathea. In order to sustain this case, time and again they affirm the following:

- The Apostle Paul, who is the earliest written witness to Jesus' resurrection, knows nothing about empty tomb traditions that we later read of in the gospels. In the mid-50s, writing to the Corinthian church, he cites an early Christian creed: 'Christ died for our sins in accordance with the scriptures, he was buried, and he was raised on the third day in accordance with the scriptures ...' (1 Cor 15.3-5). This early creed says nothing about the tomb being empty.

- Paul's own experience of the risen Christ was visionary, and did not involve seeing a physical body. Moreover, when he lists his own visionary experience of the resurrected Christ with those of the other apostles and James (1 Cor 15.5-8), he seems to imply that their experiences were visionary like his. (*Dynasty* 232)

- Paul's own view of future resurrection for believers excludes the possibility of a 'flesh and blood' body. In 1 Cor 15 he does speak of a spiritual body, but that body has no literal continuity with the flesh and bones of the old.

- Mark, the earliest gospel written, knows of the discovery of the empty temporary tomb, but knows nothing of resurrection appearance stories such as are found later in Luke and John. His narrative concludes with the simple angelic command that the disciples should return to Galilee where they will again meet Jesus (see Mk 16.1-8).

- The resurrection appearance stories in Luke and John are legendary, created quite late in the first century. Their emphasis on the physicality of the resurrected body of Jesus (he becomes nothing more than a 'resuscitated physical corpse') (*Discovery* 209), reflect the felt need to defend the Christian message against pagan critics and their claims that the women were hysterical and delusional.

- Where and how, then, did the early Christians come to believe that Jesus was raised from the dead? The authors do not appear to consider speculation on this question as part of their brief. The closest we come to an answer to the question is in the suggestions from Tabor that: 'Perhaps it was in Galilee that the followers of Jesus found the renewal of their faith that the Kingdom of God was indeed at hand', and also that James, too, realised there was work yet to be done, and he 'turned things around'. (*Dynasty* 238, 240)

In short, Paul, with his belief in the non-physical nature of both Jesus' and believers' resurrections, 'is our best link to the Talpiot tombs'. (*Discovery* 196)

Part B

Four Major Hurdles

INTRODUCTION – HISTORICAL AND TEXTUAL HURDLES

What are we to make of the interpretations that Tabor and Jacobovici have offered? Do they make sense? Are they credible? These questions direct us not just to an examination of the archaeological evidence (covered in Part C), but also to the historical and literary evidence relating to Jesus and early Christianity. In Chapters 6-9 we will examine four key historical issues that the Tabor/Jacobovici thesis has thrown up. However, before we turn to these, some preliminary observations are in order.

1. Text and Spade – Collaborators not Rivals

It is now widely recognised that in order to understand the world of Jesus and earliest Christianity it is no longer sufficient to depend simply on one field of evidence. Gone are the days when scholars, cosily resident in their European or North American universities and with no knowledge of the physical environment of Jesus, could rely solely on documentary evidence to create a picture of Jesus and his ministry. Archaeological discoveries are now equal partners in the task of uncovering Jesus' world. 'Text and spade' work hand in hand.[1] But at this point temptations arise: it is very easy to use selective evidence from archaeology to bolster a fixed interpretation of the text; and it is equally easy to engage in a selective reading of the text to support a hypothesis derived solely from what the spade has uncovered! Intellectual and academic honesty must be prepared to listen to the voice of each partner in this delicate marriage!

Tabor, of course, as an experienced archaeologist and scholar of early Christianity, is not unaware of the 'text and spade principle', and indeed, he endorses it in the following quote: 'One of the things one tries to do in archaeology, when possible, is combine textual or literary evidence with the material archaeological evidence. One is always cautious that the text not be used to overinterpret the archaeological evidence or vice versa.' (*Discovery* 112) Nor can one disagree with this earlier statement: 'Sometimes new evidence causes one to see things that were there all the time but were unnoticed.' (*Discovery* 46) But what do you do when your reading of the literary evidence and your reading of the archaeological data are in fundamental conflict?

---

[1] Some useful studies on archaeological research and its relevance to studies on the historical Jesus are Jonathan Reed, *Archaeology and the Galilean Jesus* (Trinity Press, 2000); John Dominic Crossan and Jonathan Reed, *Excavating Jesus* (HarperCollins, 2001); James H Charlesworth (ed), *Jesus and Archaeology* (Eerdmans, 2006); Craig Evans, *Jesus and his World: the Archaeological Evidence* (SPCK, 2012).

There is no simple formula to solve this dilemma. The problem may lie with the literary evidence: it may be factually incorrect, due to error, ignorance or bias on the part of the author; or it may be that we have simply been reading the evidence wrongly. But it is equally possible, and frequently more likely, that the problem lies with our reading of the archaeological data. And the reason for that is obvious: most archaeological data is silent, it comes with no words, and it is our task to try to make sense of what lies before us. To give just one example: the archaeological recovery of the sophisticated Hellenised Jewish city of Sepphoris located only an hour's walk from Nazareth, is an important piece of jig-saw evidence as we seek to put together our picture of the social, economic and religious world of Jesus and his ministry in that environment. But as we walk over the site, what exactly is it telling us? Can we infer that Jesus had often visited Sepphoris, had perhaps been employed there, had learned basic 'market-place' Greek? Is Tabor justified in claiming: 'I don't think there is much doubt that Jesus walked the streets and marketplaces of … Sepphoris'? (*Dynasty* 108)[2] Possibly so, but what, then, are we to make of fact that the gospels are totally silent in respect of any contact Jesus may have had with the Hellenised Galilean cities of Sepphoris and Tiberias? May it not be that Jesus had no sympathy with urban life and avoided contact with these centres of Galilean power? His vision of the coming kingdom of God, which would soon bring blessing to the poor, the meek and those who trust God for their daily food and clothing, had no place for those living in the comfort of the cities of the wealthy.[3] The evidence of the spade is silent – it is our task to help it to speak.

When it comes to the Jesus tomb thesis, my concern is that Tabor, Jacobovici and their associates have become so captivated by their reading of the archaeological evidence that they are led to commit three fundamental errors. Firstly, their interpretation of the archaeological evidence leads them to an unsustainable re-reading of the literary evidence relating to Jesus and early Christianity. Secondly, in their attempts to re-read the literary evidence, they are led into worrying inconsistencies and commit methodological flaws as they re-interpret the texts. Thirdly, even the starting point of their whole enterprise, namely, the conclusions they have drawn from the archaeological data, can be shown to be without solid foundation.

---

[2] This way of interpreting the evidence was strongly defended by R Batey in 'Jesus and the Theatre,' *NTS* 30 (1984) 563-574; and *Jesus and the Forgotten City* (Baker, 1991).

[3] See my *The Enigmatic Jew*, 174-178

As we now proceed with our analysis of the Jesus tomb theory, I believe we will see that text and spade fundamentally provide little, if any, support for the conclusions that Tabor and Jacobovici draw from the Jesus Family Tomb.

2. The Prosopographic Test – Can We Get a True Picture?

There is one further test that we need to apply to the Jesus tomb claims, one that I will call the prosopographic test. The term prosopography derives from two Greek words, *prosōpon* (meaning 'face'), and *graphein* (meaning 'to write'). The term refers to the task of drawing upon literary, epigraphic (i.e. writing on stone, pottery and other archaeologically sourced material) and other data, especially data relating to people's names and family relationships, in the attempt to determine whether the various data are referring to the same person.

Sometimes the literary, epigraphic and archaeological data do converge to a remarkably convincing extent. A good example of a prosopographic 'fit' is the Nicanor ossuary inscription found on the Mount of Olives in 1902. The combined Greek and Hebrew wording on the ossuary read: 'Ossuary of [4] Nicanor of Alexandria, who built the doors – Nicanor the Alexandrian'. Rabbinic tradition in both the Mishnah and the Talmud refer to one set of Temple gates given by Nicanor, who brought them from Alexandria. This convergence of archaeological, epigraphic and literary evidence has led the scholarly community to the conclusion that these sources refer to one and the same person.

Sometimes the prosopographic fit is not quite as close, but remarkable nonetheless. In Mk 15.21 we read, 'And they dragooned one Simon a Cyrenean, the father of Alexander and Rufus, as he came from the country, to carry his cross beam.' Notably, both Matthew and Luke, who draw upon Mark here, omit the reference to Simon's sons. In 1941 E L Sukenic uncovered in the Kidron Valley a number of ossuaries, one of which had various inscriptions on its front, back and lid. The Greek on the sides was not always grammatically correct, but was clearly intended to read, 'Alexander, son of Simon'. The Greek and Hebrew on the lid included the Hebrew word QRNYT. Does this refer to Cyrenaea in North Africa, as most scholars suggest, or is it a reference to a village in Judea? While the names Alexander and Simon are known elsewhere in Palestinian inscriptions, their presence with a probable reference to Cyrene tips the balance in favour of this ossuary being a link to the Alexander mentioned in Mk 15.21. Not all agree,[5] but it was enough to convince the late

---

[4] Another possible reading of the first seven Greek letters (ΟΣΤΑΤΩΝ) is 'bones of the [sons] of …'. See Craig Evans, *Jesus and the Ossuaries*, 91-94.

[5] For example, D Lührmann, *Das Markusevangelium* (HNT 3; Herder, 1987) 259.

Martin Hengel[6] and most of the academic community of the strong likelihood that one and the same Simon and Alexander are being referred to by Mark and the ossuary inscription.

Finally, we should note that at times what appears at first blush to be a prosopographic fit cannot be sustained. In 1931 E L Sukenik brought to public attention an ossuary he had found in 1926 in the basement of what is now the Rockefeller Museum in Jerusalem. On its decorated side could be read the words 'Yeshu' and then 'Yeshua son of Yehoseph' (= 'Jesus son of Joseph'). That Yeshu is a contracted form of Yeshua is confirmed by later rabbinic use of this contraction when making reference to Jesus.[7] Though the ossuary's inscription leads us to think of Jesus of Nazareth, the link could never be established. The ossuary's origin is unknown, and the two names, Joseph and Jesus, are among the most common in the register of Jewish names for the time. The ossuary adds nothing to our knowledge of Jesus of Nazareth.

When we come to the ossuaries in Talpiot A and Talpiot B, we will want to apply the same rigour for prosopographic fitting when we consider the suggestions put forward by Tabor and Jacobovici for the identification of the names on the ossuaries, and indeed, (in the case of Talpiot B) of the names no-where mentioned in the tomb.[8]

****

We turn now to consider each of these three concerns. In Chapters 6-9 we will examine the literary evidence relating to four key issues that are thrown up by the Tabor/Jacobovici thesis. On the way, we will observe and comment upon the methodological approach adopted by Tabor and Jacobovici in their handling of the literary evidence, both biblical and extra-biblical. What the evidence will reveal is that far from requiring a rewriting of the story of Jesus and early Christianity, the literary and historical data actually serve as major hurdles, hurdles which the Jesus tomb thesis struggles in vain to clear. In Part C we will then give consideration to the archaeological evidence thrown up by the Talpiot tombs.

---

[6] M Hengel, *The 'Hellenization' of Judaea in the First Century after Christ* (SCM, 1989) 67 n.39.
[7] For example, *b. Sanhedrin* 43a reads: 'On the eve of Passover Yeshu was hanged ....'
[8] A useful article introducing the importance of prosopography as it applies to the Talpiot ossuary claims is presented by Prof Christopher Rollston at http://www.jstor.org/stable/25067663.

Chapter Six
WAS JESUS CELIBATE?

In the Epilogue to *The Jesus Dynasty* Tabor acknowledges that up until the Talpiot A ossuaries came to his attention, he was always sceptical of any suggestions that Jesus might have married, especially of those speculative claims that associated him intimately with Mary Magdalene. In fact, in the Preface to the book's first edition, he is rather scathing of these Dan Brown type 'popularized notions' that are 'long on speculation and short on evidence'. (*Dynasty* 4) What changes his mind, however, are his takes on two of the ossuaries, 'Jude son of Jesus' and 'Mariamene Mara'. We deal with those in Part C, but first we must ask, how correct is it for Tabor now to claim: 'There is no reason to suppose Jesus would have necessarily chosen a celibate life'? (*Dynasty* 328) Indeed, by the time we get to *The Jesus Discovery* that rather tentative thrust at the received tradition becomes a fully blown presentation of the argument for Jesus having been married. (*Discovery* 142-147)

The gospels, of course, no-where explicitly state that Jesus was unmarried. Nonetheless, I believe that the traditional historical judgement that Jesus was in fact unmarried and celibate remains strong. Consider the following:

- Jesus' early adult life involved a close association with John the Baptist, a recognised celibate and ascetic preacher.[1] And why did he not marry? Because John had given up everything, including his priestly heritage and all the privileges that would have come with it. He had abandoned the comfort of village life in Judea and gone into the Judean wilderness by the Jordan River in obedience to what he considered to be a divine calling. He was convinced that Israel's God was about to break into history, that time was short, and that he must prepare Israel through the preaching of repentance and baptism. His sense of calling and ministry, and his belief in the urgency of the times, gave no place for married life. Instead, he was surrounded by a body of male disciples who lived with him in a communal existence (Jn 3.25; Matt 11.2; Lk 11.1). When Jesus commences his Galilean ministry, he also comes preaching with the same measure of urgency that John had brought to the Judean populace: repent, for the Kingdom of God has drawn near (Matt 3.2; 4.17/Mk 1.15).[2] He

---

[1] John's celibacy is fully acknowledged by Tabor, who wrote: 'There is no indication that John married or pursued a trade'. (*Dynasty* 133).

[2] Only Matthew, dependent on Mark, has applied Jesus' kingdom message also to John. He has done this to highlight the continuity between the forerunner (John) and the Messiah. Though this parallel wording in the summary of John's message and

has learned well from John during the months, or possibly years, spent with him in the south, preaching repentance and baptism (see Jn 3.26; 4.1-3). In fact, the urgency of the moment is now increased not lessened, for the signs of the Kingdom are present in his healing powers (Lk 11.20). This close relationship between the two prophets of the coming Kingdom of God carries with it a presumption (but, I grant, not a firm proof) that as one was unmarried, so was the other. Both were gripped by the same sense of urgency, and marriage would only have been a hindrance to their calling. In fact, we may go further to say that in the current debate over whether Jesus was an eschatological prophet as opposed to one who was a social reformer,[3] a sage,[4] or Cynic-style philosopher,[5] the more we accept the eschatological prophet option, the stronger will appear the case for Jesus' life being a celibate one.[6] Eschatological prophets have no time for marriage and family life (see also comments below on Matt 19.12). I would be prepared to say that if, after his time in Judea with John the Baptist and his subsequent return to Galilee, Jesus entered a marriage alliance, it must mean that he had fundamentally altered his theology from when he was in Judea with John. And to that proposal I believe the evidence stands opposed.[7]

- While it is true that the gospels are silent on so many historical details we would love to know about, here and there we can detect tantalising clues that assist. On two occasions Jesus' family is mentioned, and both references can really only be understood to mean that these are his only blood connections and there is no wife to add to the picture. In Mk 3.21 and 31-34 it is his mother, brothers and sisters who are concerned for his well-being and (presumably) the reputation he is bringing upon the

---

that of Jesus is the literary contrivance of Matthew, the urgency in John's preaching, evident in Matt 3.1-12 and Lk 3.1-9, 15-17, provides the justification.

[3] As in the writings of R A Horsley. See his *Jesus and the Spiral of Violence* (Harper and Row, 1987); *Bandits, Prophets and Messiahs* (Harper and Row, 1988); and *Galilee – History, Politics, People* (Trinity, 1999).

[4] As proposed by the scholars of the Jesus Seminar, See R Funk, R Hoover, et al, *The Five Gospels* (Polebridge, 1993).

[5] As proposed by John Dominic Crossan, *The Historical Jesus* (CollinsDove, 1991); and Burton Mack, *A Myth of Innocence: Mark and Christian Origins* (Fortress, 1988).

[6] This is the view of Jesus that I have presented in my *The Enigmatic Jew*. Also in support is the writing of Dale Allison. See his *Jesus of Nazareth, Millenarian Prophet* (AugsburgFortress, 1998), and *Constructing Jesus – Memory, Imagination, and History* (SPCK, 2010) 31-220.

[7] On the relation of Jesus to John the Baptist see my *The Enigmatic Jew – in quest of the historical Jesus* (Createspace, 2011) chaps 3, 4.

family. No wife is mentioned at this stage of his ministry. Then when he returns to Nazareth (Mk 6.1-6), no wife is mentioned as having been left residing there during his absence. Both incidents take place early in his ministry, so we are left to take the natural reading of them to conclude that at this stage in his life, Jesus has not yet married. He could conceivably marry after these incidents (and I presume the Mary Magdalene hypothesis would require such a scenario), but even so two observations can be made:

Firstly, the only way a wife can be brought into the picture is to claim that she has been erased from the list of family members, either by the evangelist or by the tradition he received. Of course this is possible, but where is the evidence? It simply doesn't exist. We will later be critical of the *The Jesus Discovery* and its use of the 'suppression of evidence' hypothesis in its attempted 'rehabilitation' of Mary Magdalene.

Secondly, at the time of the commencement of his Galilean ministry, Jesus will have been at least 30 years of age, possibly 35 or even more.[8] Even by the age of 30, Jesus had passed well beyond the years of marriage for a young man in his times (as Tabor and Jacobovici acknowledge in *Discovery* 143). Why? The questions about his paternity would have meant that many maidens would not have been available to him, but even so, a suitable *mamzer* girl could have been found.[9] In the light of his known association with John the Baptist, the natural reading of the evidence leads to the conclusion that Jesus has chosen the celibate life. There is thus no need to claim that the traditions about Jesus' family reflected in Mark 3 and 6 are other than essentially historical.

These two observations, then, lead to the most natural conclusion that at this stage in his life, well beyond the age by which a Jewish male would be expected to have married, Jesus has no wife because he has deliberately chosen the path of celibacy as part of his calling to preach the coming of the Kingdom of God. The burden of proof strongly rests with those who would seek to demonstrate otherwise.

- It is surprising that Tabor and Jacobovici do not comment on the saying of Jesus in Matthew 19.12: 'For there are eunuchs who have been so from

---

[8] If we presume that he was born in about 5 BC and was crucified in AD 33 (as convincingly proposed by Colin Humphreys in *The Mystery of the Last Supper*), and if, as I have suggested in my *The Enigmatic Jew*, Jesus' Galilean ministry lasted less than 12 months, then he was in his late 30s at the time.

[9] For consideration of Jesus' *mamzer* status, as a child whose paternity is uncertain, see *The Enigmatic Jew*, 49-59.

birth, and there are eunuchs made so by man, and there are those who have made themselves eunuchs for the sake of the kingdom of heaven.' We'll never know whether this saying goes back to Jesus or is a Matthean creation. The Jesus Seminar, for example gave it a pink colouring, indicating that for the majority of that group of scholars the saying goes back to Jesus, in some form or another. Others concur. The conservative scholar Robert Gundry, on the other hand, made the case that verses 10-12 were an elaboration by the evangelist on the divorce saying of Jesus.[10] Whatever interpretation we place on its meaning for Matthew (the three references given in footnote 10 offer differing interpretations of its meaning), and whether we see the verse as going back to Jesus, or as a Matthean extension of the Jesus tradition, one thing is for certain: the verse would not have seen the light of the Matthean day if Matthew and the churches he wrote to had had any knowledge that Jesus had been married, had not in fact been a 'eunuch for the sake of the kingdom of heaven'. For the final part of the saying is its punch-line, and it presents the single state as the highest ideal of dedication. Matthew could never have allowed that to come from the lips of Jesus if he had known that Jesus himself (and John the Baptist) had not been the exemplar/s of it.[11] We might also add that this verse is relevant to our later discussion (se Chapter 11) of the Talpiot A ossuary inscribed 'Jude son of Jesus': Matthew and his churches obviously had no knowledge of any child fathered by Jesus. Eunuchs leave no descendents!

- We need not enter into the debate on the extent to which the Essenes encouraged or practised celibacy. What can be said is that Tabor and Jacobovici are too cavalier when they make statements like, the Dead Sea Scrolls 'never hint at celibacy; quite the opposite is true', and 'it is mistakenly assumed that the Essenes practised celibacy'. (*Discovery* 144) It can certainly be acknowledged that the Essene movement that flourished in the villages of Judea appears to have had members who were married.[12]

---

[10] See Robert Funk, Roy Hoover and the Jesus Seminar, *The Five Gospels* (Polebridge, 1993) 220-221; WD Davies and Dale Allison, *Matthew* (ICC vol 3; T&T Clark, 1997) 21-26; Robert Gundry, *Matthew: A Commentary on his Literary and Theological Art* (Eerdmans, 1982) 381-383.

[11] Davies and Allison make the provocative suggestion that 'it seems probable enough that Mt 19.12 was originally an apologetical counter, a response to the jeer that Jesus was a eunuch' (p 25). And perhaps the plural 'eunuchs' embraces John the Baptist as well as Jesus, and any of the disciples who have either not married or who, for the sake of the coming kingdom, have abandoned their wives to live the celibate life as part of Jesus' inner group (see Lk 18.29 in contrast to Matt 19.29/Mk 10.29).

[12] On the Judean village-based Essene movement and Jesus' contacts with it, see my *The Enigmatic Jew*, Chap 5.

But a document like *The Community Rule* (1QS) can only be understood as establishing rules for the life of a monastic-like community. And the evidence from the Qumran cemetery, where nearly all of the bodies are adult male, supports this understanding.[13] That celibacy was honoured and practised among the Essenes cannot be dismissed as 'an invention'. Far to be preferred is the cautious judgement of Prof John Collins, 'In my judgement, the balance of evidence favors the view that the *yahad* [the community referred to in 1QS] was celibate....'[14] Thus, while it is true that celibacy was 'not considered an ideal or valued lifestyle among Jews in the Greco-Roman period' (*Discovery* 143), neither was it unknown.

- As mentioned in Chapter 3, Tabor and Jacobovici claim that the Apostle Paul provides support for the married status of Jesus. It is suggested that though Paul knows a saying of Jesus prohibiting divorce (1 Cor 7.10), when it comes to offering advice on celibacy, he is unable to offer anything from the traditions about Jesus, and must simply give his own advice (1 Cor 7.25). Thus 'Paul's silence strongly implies that he did not think that Jesus was unmarried'. (*Discovery* 145-6) But can this argument from silence bear the weight Tabor and Jacobovici want to place on it? If Paul knew, or presumed, that Jesus had been married, could he have presented the case for celibacy so forcefully? It seems hardly likely. We might also note 1 Cor 9.5: '*Do we not have the right to be accompanied by a believing wife, as do the other apostles and the brothers of the Lord and Cephas?*' If Paul had known that Jesus was married, and especially if he had been married to Mary Magdalene, since she is known to have accompanied Jesus on occasion (Lk 8.3), it would have greatly strengthened his case to bring forward his trump card, and add, 'and as did the Lord'!

- In the first half of Chapter 7 we direct our attention to Mary Magdalene. Tabor and Jacobovici detect evidence in John 20 and in the burial and resurrection accounts of a close physical/familial relationship between Mary and Jesus, a relationship that has been all but suppressed by the gospel writers. They also see evidence for Jesus' marriage to Mary Magdalene both in later gnostic traditions and in the Jewish Talmud. Our examination of these claims will turn up nothing of historical substance.

---

[13] Debates on the cemetery at Qumran have been extensive. An excellent survey and analysis is given by Joe Zias, 'The Cemeteries of Qumran and Celibacy: Confusion Laid to Rest,' in *Dead Sea Discoveries* 7.2 (2000) 220-253. See also Rachel Hachlili, 'The Qumran Cemetery Reassessed' in *The Oxford Handbook of the Dead Sea Scrolls* (Lim and Collins [eds]; OUP, 2010) 46-78.

[14] J J Collins, *Beyond the Qumran Community – The Sectarian Movement of the Dead Sea Scrolls* (Eerdmans, 2010) 150-151.

In the light of the above, it can be confidently affirmed that Jesus did not marry and that he considered his celibate state as part of his calling as prophet of the coming Kingdom of God.

Chapter Seven
MARY MAGDALENE – WIFE AND APOSTOLIC LEADER?

In the Jesus Family Tomb thesis, three characters take centre stage: Jesus, Joseph of Arimathea and Mary Magdalene. Important as the first two are, it can be argued that it is Mary who is pivotal to the whole case. Hers is the ossuary that has the intriguing inscription, and whose bone fragments have no DNA link with the fragments in the Jesus ossuary, and she is proposed as the mother of the Jude, son of Jesus, whose ossuary was also located in Talpiot A.

In the four canonical gospels, Mary Magdalene is referred to eleven times, twelve if you count her mention in the later long ending of Mark at Mk 16.9.[1] Who was she, what was her social status and background, why was she attracted to the Jesus movement, what was her role in Jesus' final hours on the cross and at his burial, and what became of her in the post-Easter period? Not only has Mary been the focus of much speculation in the history of Christianity (often understood, wrongly, as the paradigm of the repentant whore), but in recent years considerable scholarly attention has been devoted to her. Especially from a feminist perspective, there have been many articles and books written seeking to uncover the 'real' Mary Magdalene.[2]

As already indicated, Tabor and Jacobovici make much of Mary Magdalene, but their case can be boiled down to two central arguments: she was married to Jesus (hence her presence in the Jesus Family Tomb), and in the early years of the Christian movement in Jerusalem she had a prominent leadership role, a fact that was suppressed by the patriarchal leadership and which is all but hidden in the documents of the New Testament. We now need to examine the literary evidence for these two claims. In presenting their case, Tabor and Jacobovici are heavily dependent on the writings of Jane Schaberg, and so we will make frequent reference to her work.

---

[1] Matt 27.56, 61; 28.1; Mk 15.40, 47; 16.1; Lk 8.2; 24.10; Jn 19.25; 20.1, 18.
[2] Perhaps the most thorough study is that of the late Jane Schaberg, *Resurrection of Mary Magdalene*. A popular version of this appeared as *Mary Magdelene Understood*. Written from a feminist perspective, Schaberg's 2002 work is scholarly yet very readable. It suffers from the lack of a bibliography, which makes the tracing of footnoted references very difficult and time consuming.

1. Is There Literary Evidence of a Marriage Between Jesus and Mary Magdalene?

Taking the case well beyond that of Schaberg,[3] the Jesus tomb claim for Mary's marriage to Jesus is based on four literary considerations.

a) *John 20.1-2, 11-18 – Mary at the Tomb*. Is it possible that behind the words of intimate exchange between Mary and the risen Jesus (Miriam – Rabbouni), and behind the 'do not cling to me' prohibition at v17, lie evidence of a previous level of intimacy between these two people, indications of a 'familial connection' (*Discovery* 134), which the Risen One declares must not be resumed? We need to return to this incident when we consider Mary's status in the early Jesus movement, but for the moment the following observations can be made.

- Long ago, the great Johannine scholar C H Dodd noted the singularity of this incident and commented: '... the dialogue between Jesus and Mary has no analogue, and it shows a psychological subtlety which is quite exceptional in these stories'. Some years earlier he had written: 'Yet I cannot for long rid myself of the feeling (it can be no more than a feeling) that this *pericopé* has something indefinably first-hand about it.'[4]

- But even if Dodd's inner 'feeling' is correct, that doesn't solve our problem, for he readily acknowledges that 'if a traditional unit underlies this *pericopé*, it has been fairly completely remoulded'.[5] The incident recorded in Matt 28.9-10, where Jesus meets the women, including Mary Magdalene, coming from the tomb, obviously comes from the same tradition. There they touch him and do him reverence; and as in John 19.17, Jesus gives the women a message to convey to 'my brothers', a term in the gospels that is unique to these two incidents.[6] Tabor writes that Matthew's account is but a 'garbled version of the story' (*Discovery* 135) found in John, but he provides no real justification for such a sweeping claim. All that we can with confidence assert is that

---

[3] 'The making of Mary Magdalene into Jesus' wife or lover seems to me a patriarchal attempt to complete the process of her "redemption" from a whore into the form of a "normal" woman, reabsorbed into society' – Schaberg, *Resurrection of Mary Magdalene*, 102.

[4] CH Dodd, *Historical Tradition in the Fourth Gospel* (CUP, 1963) 146. The second quote, written in 1955, is reproduced on p 148 of *HTFG*.

[5] Dodd, *HTFG*, 146.

[6] In fact, Schaberg, *Resurrection of Mary Magdalene*, 295-297, lists 18 points of contact between Matt 28.9-10 and Jn 20.1, 11-18, which she claims 'indicate a common pre-Matthean, pre-Johannine tradition.'

behind Matthew and John lies a tradition of an appearance, either to one woman (Mary) or to several.

- What lies behind the account in John has been the subject of much debate and there is no scholarly consensus. It is worth noting that John 20 has two incidents where individuals meet with the risen Lord (Mary and Thomas), while elsewhere more than one person is involved. Thus, in Matthew several women go to the tomb and then are met by the risen Jesus (28.8-10); and on the mountain more than one disciple is said to doubt (28.17). Is it possible, as Lindars suggested, that John is responsible for expanding an original tradition either by introducing an individual, or by reducing several persons to one in order to make the point clearer? After all, John does like to present his story of Jesus in terms of individuals and their contact with him.[7] If that were the case, rather than personal memory (as Dodd considered) it would be John the evangelist who was responsible for the wording of the Jesus-Mary encounter.

- But let us, for the sake of the argument, accept that an original first hand account (as in John) was later modified (by Matthew or his source) to include other women and to involve an act of touching and veneration. What did the exchange signify? Can we draw from it the inference of familial intimacy that Tabor and others[8] wish to draw? Well, certainly not as far as John the evangelist is concerned. Tabor makes much of Mary's response, *rabbouni*, suggesting that it was a 'diminutive term of endearment' more intimate in expression than a mere *rabbi*. That interpretation, however, is incorrect and appears to derive from a suggestion of W F Albright that the term is a caritative variant of *rabbi*, implying 'my dear (or little) rabbi'.[9] In fact, however, it is used elsewhere in the New Testament at Mk 10.51 (by blind Bartimaeus) who at this stage had no relationship with Jesus; and John for his part simply gives it the translation 'teacher', denying any connotation of endearment in the word. As Lindars indicated: 'It is one of a variety of lengthened forms of *rabbi*, indicating greater respect and deference than the simple

---

[7] B Lindars, *The Gospel of John*, (Marshall Morgan and Scott, 1972) 595. See also CFD Moule, 'The Individualism of the Fourth Gospel,' *Novum Testamentum* vol 5 (1962) 171-190.

[8] For example Bp Spong in his *Resurrection – Myth or Reality?* (HarperCollins, 1994) 90-92.

[9] W F Albright, 'Recent Discoveries in Palestine and the Gospel of St John' in Davies and Daube (eds), *The Background of the New Testament and its Eschatology* (CUP, 1964) 158.

form.... John is quite correct in supposing that a woman would use this form, whereas male disciples use the simple *rabbi*.[10]

- As to the instruction 'do not cling to me' (v 17), can we see here an indication of earlier physical intimacy? Are we able to deduce that as originally spoken by Jesus, what was meant was: 'Do not touch me as you were wont to in our former relationship'? After all: 'For a woman to touch a man in this culture further implies a familial connection'. (*Discovery* 134) We do not know what the original Aramaic tradition said, nor do we know whether the assumptions of familial connection were present in the pre-Johannine tradition. All we can confidently say is that John has not taken it this way, and neither has the tradition reflected in Matt 28.9 seen anything incongruous in the women grasping the feet of Jesus. In other words, neither evangelist sees any need to suppress reference to physical contact between Jesus and non-familial women. For John, the ascended Jesus can be touched (v 27); Mary's intended act of devotion, however, does not come from the full assurance of faith in the Resurrected One, and so needs to be temporarily held back.[11]

b) *Leader in the Burial Rites*. In all of the biblical traditions except Jn 19.25, Mary Magdalene heads the list of women either present at the crucifixion and burial sites or coming on Easter morning to the tomb. Now, in traditional funerals of the time, anointing and preparation for burial was 'an intimate task for a wife, mother, or sister', and this suggests to Tabor and Jacobovici that even though Mark, (and Matthew and Luke, both dependent on Mark) know nothing about Mary Magdalene, they are witnesses to the lost tradition of Mary's relationship with Jesus (*Discovery* 133). The general truth of the authors' claim is probably correct, and in normal situations preparation for burial was the task of the women in a family. But in the case of Jesus the following serve to cancel the conclusion drawn.

---

[10] Lindars, *Gospel of John*, 606. Agreeing with Lindars are G Beasley-Murray, *John* (Word, 1987) 375; and R E Brown, *The Gospel According to John* (Anchor Bible; Doubleday, 1966) 2.991-992. Other major commentaries (Schnackenburg, Barrett, Haenchen, Carson) do not discuss the issue. R Bultmann, *The Gospel of John* (Blackwell, 1971) 686 n 6, persuaded by Albright, suggests that John's rendering of *rabbouni* as 'teacher' has failed to capture the caritative sense.

[11] The verse does present problems for understanding, not least the sense of the 'for/because' – is John suggesting that once he has ascended it will then be possible to touch Jesus? See the major commentaries, especially C K Barrett, *The Gospel According to St John* (SPCK, 1978) 565-6.

- No women were involved in the burial of Jesus, but only Joseph of Arimathea (and Nicodemus). We will discuss the reason for this when we consider Joseph and his role in the burial of Jesus. But at this point we must note that no tradition brings women into the action of anointing, wrapping and burying Jesus. The family of Jesus was definitely not involved in his anointing and burial.
- The traditions listing the names of the women who view the crucifixion or the burial, or who come to the tomb on Easter morning, are quite varied.[12] It is true that Mary Magdalene's name is found in each list, but what Tabor and Jacobovici fail to note is that apart from the list in John's Gospel, *none* of the women listed by the evangelists is a family member. In the case of Mark, alongside Mary Magdalene he lists another Mary, the mother of James the younger/less and Joses,[13] and Salome. Though a case has been made for this Mary to be the mother of Jesus,[14] I believe we can be confident that this was not Mark's intention. For a start, Mark would hardly have referred to her by the names of two other of her children.[15] Moreover, considering James' future importance in the life of the early church, it is unlikely that he would have been known as

---

[12] **At the crucifixion site**: Matt 27.56 has MM, Mary the mother of James and Joseph, and the mother of the sons of Zebedee; Mk 15.40 has MM, Mary the mother of James and Joses, and Salome; Lk 23.49 simply refers to women who had followed Jesus from Galilee. John 19.25 has Jesus' mother, Mary wife of Clopas, and MM.

At the tomb site: Matt 27.61 has MM and the other Mary; Mk 15.47 has MM and Mary the mother of Joses; Lk 23.55 again gives no names. John has no mention of women present.

Easter morning to the tomb: Matt 28.1 has MM and the other Mary; Mk 16.1 has MM, Mary mother of James, and Salome; Lk 24.10 lists MM, Joanna, Mary mother of James, and other women with them. Jn 20.1 has MM alone (but note v 2).

[13] Mark's Greek phrase may also be translated 'Mary the wife of James and mother of Joses', or even (to create another woman) 'Mary the wife of James; also the mother of Joses'. Neither of these options is to be preferred. See R H Gundry, *Mark* (Eerdmans, 1993) 976-77.

[14] E.g. by Gundry, *Mark* 977. Gundry's suggestion that with the centurion having just confessed Jesus as the Son of God, Mark did not wish to diminish this affirmation by referring to Mary as Jesus' mother, is not convincing. Bauckham, who rejects the suggestion, also lists claims in the early church to link this Mary and her children to the family of Jesus. See *Jude and the Relatives of Jesus*, 20, 22-23, 38, 42. Tabor also comes out in defence of this proposal (*Jesus Dynasty*, 77-80).

[15] Presuming, of course, that she was their mother and that they were not the children of Joseph by a previous marriage. See my *The Enigmatic Jew*, 42-45 for a defence of the latter option. Also Bauckham, *Jude and the Relatives of Jesus*, chap 1.

James *the Less*.[16] Finally, is it likely that Jesus' mother would be listed *second* behind Mary Magdalene? Jn 19.25 surely represents the correct order: mother first, then other family members, then others.

- As to Salome, whom Tabor and Jacobovici claim is 'possibly Jesus' sister' (*Discovery* 132), I suggest we can be confident that she is not a member of Jesus' family. For a start, John's account of the crucifixion scene lists the only two female family members present before mentioning Mary Magdalene (Jn 19.25) and with no reference to Salome. As well, while it is true that early Christian tradition gives the names of Jesus' two sisters as Mary and Salome, in those traditions his sister Salome is never linked to the gospel accounts as one who is present in Jerusalem at the time of the crucifixion. Finally, whereas Mark clearly distinguishes the two disciples of Jesus named Mary (15.40, 47; 16.1), he evidently knows of only one Salome, and yet in no way links her familiarly with Jesus. As Bauckham concludes: 'So it seems that Salome the disciple of Jesus was known by name to Mark's readers, but her namesake the sister of Jesus was not.'[17]

- What of the other two non-family members? Matthew replaces Mark's Salome with the (unnamed) mother of the sons of Zebedee. The reason for this is unclear. Perhaps the best answer is the suggestion that while Salome was unknown in the churches to which Matthew's gospel was written, Matthew did know that the mother of the sons of Zebedee had travelled with Jesus (Matt 20.20), and so he felt justified in including her name. He does not, however, feel justified in naming her as one of those who went to the empty tomb. The other non-familial member is named by Luke as Joanna (Lk 24.10), a person previously mentioned by him (8.3) as being the high born wife of Herod Antipas' steward. She certainly was no blood relative of Jesus.

- We are justified, therefore, in concluding, with Bauckham, that '*no relatives of Jesus appear among the women disciples named by the Synoptic evangelists*' *as being either present at the crucifixion scene or as coming to the empty tomb*.[18]

- And that, of course, puts a different light altogether on the question of the women's presence at the tomb on Easter day. Let us accept three propositions: (i) that it was normally the role of family-related women

---

[16] Bauckham presents a convincing case against any attempts to justify the epithet 'the less' to James the brother of Jesus. See *Jude and the Relatives of Jesus*, 14.

[17] On these last points see Bauckham, *Jude and the relatives of Jesus*, 37-44.

[18] Bauckham, *Jude and the Relatives of Jesus*, 15.

to anoint a body for burial; (ii) that the tradition mentions no family members of Jesus as coming to the tomb; and (iii) that the women came to the tomb bearing aromatic spices (both Mark and Luke refer to *arōmata*).[19] That leaves certain obvious questions: (i) Why did none of the family members go to the tomb? (ii) In the aftermath of Jesus' death were the family members in contact with the other Galilean disciples (men and women)? (iii) Did the other women go to the tomb with or without the knowledge and consent of the family? (iv) What did they think they were going to do at the tomb?

- In the attempt to answer these questions, the biblical traditions provide us with little assistance. Nonetheless, we know that funeral practices changed only slowly over time, so that evidence from both earlier and later times can be utilised to explain customs in Jesus' time.[20] I would also add that we Westerners need to remind ourselves that in the cultural world of Jesus (and as in many non-Western cultures still today), the role and importance of the family could never be ignored. In the next chapter dealing with Joseph of Arimathea we will provide reasons why the family members of Jesus were legally prevented from undertaking the normal mourning rituals, including anointing and preparation of the body prior to burial. That being the case, the evidence of the gospels suggests the following answers to our questions:

(i) The female family members of Jesus were legally prevented from involvement in the burial of Jesus;

(ii) The other women would not have dared to intrude into the private affairs of the family of Jesus without their knowledge and consent. Such an action would have been culturally unacceptable;

(iii) It is a justifiable presumption that the Galilean disciples, male and female, family and non-family, would have been in some form of contact with each other in the period after Jesus' burial. The traditions speak of the women rushing back to the disciples with news of the empty tomb – so they knew where to find them! It is simply not conceivable that the women would have planned their visit to the tomb without the knowledge and consent, not only of Jesus' family members, but also of the wider body of disciples.

---

[19] Matthew and John make no reference to the bearing of spices or an intention to anoint the body. In Matthew, the presence of the guard makes access to the tomb impossible, and in John, Jesus has already been richly and royally anointed. See my *Jesus Resurrected?* 129-130.

[20] This point is well demonstrated by Byron R McCane, *Roll Back the Stone – Death and Burial in the World of Jesus* (Trinity, 2003).

- (iv) Thus, the women went to the tomb to perform acts of devotion on the body of Jesus not just on their own behalf, but also *on behalf of the family*. This is an important point: *Mary Magdalene and the other women went to the tomb not because they were family members, but because they were not.*
- (v) What exactly they intended to do (unwrap and anoint the body? anoint any exposed parts? anoint the wrapped body?) we will never know and is immaterial. It is quite possible that they themselves did not have a clear idea of what might be possible. They certainly did not know what was to be done about removal of the stone. We are, as I have elsewhere written, in the area of the logic of the heart.[21]

Thus, Mary Magdalene's presence at the head of the list of women at the death and burial scene (with the exception of Jn 19.25), and at the tomb, in fact establishes the very opposite to what Tabor and Jacobovici claim. She is not a family member, but is the most well known and perhaps the most 'senior' of those female disciples who accompanied Jesus to Jerusalem. And they are the ones who, on behalf of the family, visit the tomb on Easter morning. As a final note: John's Gospel, for all its oddity in focussing solely on Mary Magdalene, supports this interpretation of the situation. The evangelist knows of family members present at the crucifixion scene (19.25), but provides no hint of their presence at the empty tomb.[22]

c) *Mary Magdalene in the Gospel of Philip.* As we shall note later in this chapter, Mary Magdalene assumes a prominent role in some of the literature of early Christianity, especially much gnostic literature. Two passages from the Gospel of Philip stand out. This gospel, known to us only in Coptic but acknowledged as probably originally written in Greek in the late 3rd century[23], writes thus:

> *There were three who always walked with the Lord: Mary his mother and her sister and Magdalene, the one who was called his companion. His (sic!) sister and his mother and his companion were each a Mary. (59.6-10)*

---

[21] See my *Jesus Resurrected? Sifting the Historical Evidence* (Createspace, 2011) 130.

[22] There would be no justification for suggesting that the 'we' in Jn 20.2 includes Jesus' mother and aunt (from 19.25) rather than the women known from other traditions.

[23] Tabor and Jacobovici (*Jesus Discovery* 155) give the impression that the Gospel of Philip derives from the 2nd century: some (without defining who) have suggested it was written by the 2nd century gnostic mystic Valentinus. Translation used here and for other Nag Hammadi texts is from James M Robinson (ed), *The Nag Hammadi Library* (Brill/Harper and Row, 1988).

> *And the companion of the (...) Mary Magdalene. (... loved) her more than (all) the disciples and (used to) kiss her (often) on her (...). The rest of (the disciples ...). They said to him, 'Why do you love her more than all of us?' The Saviour answered and said to them, 'Why do I not love you more than her? When a blind man and one who sees are both together in darkness, they are no different from one another. When the light comes, he who sees will see the light, and he who is blind will remain in darkness.' (63.32-64.9)*

The passages have been the subject of much interest among scholars.[24] In all of early Christian literature, only in these two passages is anyone ever called Jesus' companion, a term that certainly can convey the sense of a consort, and hence of a marital and sexual relationship. But is this what is intended, and if so, is it a pointer in the life of Jesus of Nazareth – does it reflect 'real history' as Tabor and Jacobovici suggest? (*Discovery* 156) And even if (with many scholars) we supply the missing word in the second quote to read 'kiss her often on her lips/mouth', what exactly is meant by this? The following can be said:

- The *Gospel of Philip* has many references to matters matrimonial: man and wife, the bridal chamber, sexual intercourse, motherhood, parenthood, conception (e.g. 64.30-65.28) . But we get the distinct impression that this marriage and sexual imagery is symbolic of something spiritual, relating to the union of believers with the divine realm: '... Christ came to repair the separation which was from the beginning and again unite the two [i.e. man and woman].... Indeed those who have united in the bridal chamber will no longer be separated.' (70.14-21) The jury is still out on what all this means. Is sexual/marriage language used as a metaphor for another realm of existence, or are the physical and the 'sacred' bonded, so that the one becomes a sign of the other? It is tempting to suggest that the sheer frequency of sexual language is proof that it is meant to be taken with some degree of literalness and not as mere metaphor. There is ambiguity, and perhaps it is deliberate.

- What, then, of Mary Magdalene? Are we meant to understand her as the spouse/consort of Jesus, or is the emphasis on her spiritual perception, as the one who is not blind but sees? Certainly the latter, but not necessarily to the exclusion of the former. Again, we need to be open to the possibility of deliberate ambiguity.

- But neither should we read too much, for example, into the kissing reference even if the missing word is 'lips' or 'mouth'. Just before the reference to the three Marys we read these slightly confusing, yet

---

[24] See the useful discussion and footnotes in Schaberg, *Resurrection of Mary Magdalene*, 151-155.

important, lines about the source of spiritual enlightenment and nourishment:

It is from being promised to the heavenly place that man receives nourishment. (...) him from the mouth. (And had) the word gone out from that place it would be nourished from the mouth and it would become perfect. For it is by a kiss that the perfect conceive and give birth. For this reason we also kiss one another. We receive conception from the grace which is in one another. (58.30-59.5)

- In the light of this last quote, the complaint of the disciples at 63.32ff is not primarily about their sexual jealousy, nor is the kiss a metaphor for sexual intercourse. Rather, 'Mary is seen as one who accepted and understood (Jesus') teaching and was therefore loved by him; she is a wise pupil kissed by her teacher'[25] Thus, in the kiss, Jesus reveals more to Mary than to the disciples; they too would like to be kissed and enlightened by Jesus. But they are spiritually blind, and not in a position to receive the light that he gives. This way of reading the meaning of the kiss is supported by a similar statement in the *Second Apocalypse of James*, another of the documents discovered in 1945 at Nag Hammadi in Egypt. At 56.14-15 James says of the risen Lord: 'And he kissed my mouth. He took hold of me saying, "My beloved! Behold I shall reveal to you those things that neither the heavens nor the archons have known."'

- So then, in the *Gospel of Philip* is Mary Magdalene to be seen as the spouse of Jesus? That is too historical, modern and prosaic a question. The Jesus of this gospel is the heavenly Master, and Mary is probably the ideal disciple. Yes, she possibly is the spouse of the Master, but that is also because she is more spiritually enlightened than anyone else. The physical and the spiritual are tantalisingly blended here. We cannot jump from this text to the conclusion that this writer thought that Jesus of Nazareth had been married to Mary. His/her mind is working on a different level. But let us return to our primary concern: is the presentation of Mary Magdalene in the *Gospel of Philip* a pointer to traditions that survived only in heterodox Christianity,[26] traditions that remembered her as the consort of Jesus? In the light of the fact (i) that

---

[25] Schaberg, *Resurrection of Mary Magdalene*, 154.

[26] I recognise that terms like orthodox, heterodox, and heretical are perhaps anachronistic for the early Christian centuries when the battles are still being fought among the early Christians as to who will be able to claim the title of bearer of the truth.

no other early Christian writings come close to echoing this thought; and (ii) that none of the orthodox fathers (Tertullian, Irenaeus etc) defend the celibacy of Jesus or seek to dispute such a claim about Mary Magdalene's marital status, that case has no merit. Mary's marriage to Jesus was obviously not on anyone else's radar screen. The *Gospel of Philip* opens up the intriguing question of Mary's relationship to Jesus as understood by this early Christian (Valentinian?)[27] group, but it provides no ammunition for those who wish to propose a marriage between the historical Jesus and Mary.

d) *Magdalene – Nickname for the Baby Tender?* There is one last clue that convinces[28] Tabor and Jacobovici that evidence about Mary Magdalene and Jesus exists outside the Talpiot ossuaries. It lies hidden in the word 'Magdalene'. While they acknowledge that the term seems to relate to Mary's town of origin, Migdal, just south of Tiberias on the Sea of Galilee, they also press two other claimants. One draws from the meaning of *migdal* as tower in Hebrew and Aramaic. Perhaps Jesus gave her this nickname as she became the leader of the women who supported Jesus in his Galilean ministry. Not only did she come from Migdal, but she was herself a tower of strength to Jesus. I find this an attractive possibility, in the light of the other nicknames that were given to disciples: Simon became Cephas/Petros (Mk 3.16); James and John became Boanerges (Mk 3.17). But it is the third option where the imagination of Tabor and Jacobovici seems to take flight. Later rabbinic tradition written down in the Talmud (5th-6th century AD) tells of two Marys. One is a hairdresser, understood elsewhere to be Jesus' mother seduced by a gentile named Pandeira. The other is called *megadla*, meaning one who grows the child. The authors conclude: 'We are convinced that these are cryptic references to Mary mother of Jesus and Mary Magdalene.'[29] Perhaps so, but how far does this take us?

Jewish attacks on the credibility of Christian claims can be traced back to the second century.[30] For evidence of these we are indebted to the 2nd century Christian apologist Justin's *Dialogue with Trypho*, and also to the 3rd century scholar Origen's account in *Contra Celsum* of an attack on Christianity by the earlier pagan Celsus and an unnamed Jew. In none of

---

[27] It is generally understood that the *Gospel of Philip* derives from adherents of Valentinian gnostic Christianity.

[28] 'We are convinced' is a frequent claim by Tabor and Jacobovici, a phrase rarely found in academic writings.

[29] *Jesus Discovery* 141. The Talmudic references are *b. Chagiga* 4b and *b. Shabbat* 104b.

[30] Or perhaps even earlier (see Matt 28.15). See my *Jesus Resurrected?* 69-71.

these accounts of Jewish confrontation with Christianity is any slur cast on Jesus' morality. Celsus certainly appears to know about Mary Magdalene. On two occasions he writes of Jesus being seen alive again by an 'hysterical female'.[31] Indeed, there is one earlier place where Celsus, appearing to know the tradition behind Lk 8.1-3, says that 'Jesus went about with his disciples, and obtained his livelihood in a disgraceful and importunate manner'.[32] There is no need to read into this any hint of an accusation that Jesus was living off immoral earnings.[33] Origen certainly doesn't understand the accusation that way and defends Jesus only by referring to the normal custom of philosophers receiving support from their followers. What all this tells us is that Celsus, and early Jewish tradition, knew a fair deal about Jesus, but there is silence all around on the matter of his marital status. And certainly silence on his ever having fathered a child.

The Talmudic reference to *megadla* may or may not be an allusion to Mary Magdalene, but even if it is, it arose not because of any ancient traditions about Jesus and Mary Magdalene. And did any early slanders against Christianity ever seriously suggest that Jesus' mother Mary was a hairdresser? None are known. Tabor appears to have misunderstood the meaning of the phrase *megadla neshaya* as it is applied to Mary in the Talmud: it is a slur on one who allows her hair to grow long, an indication of her loose morals – thus taking up the Jewish theme that Jesus' birth was the result of an illicit affair on Mary's part.[34] Jews and Christians lived together in the villages and towns of Palestine for some centuries after the time of Jesus. Some of the essential details of Jesus' life and doings would have been known among non-Christian Jews. It would not have taken much for someone to have invented a slur against Jesus by giving a linguistic twist to the name of one of his women followers. Attacking the morals of a religious leader is a sure way of attacking the movement as a whole. But to suggest that behind these Talmudic sayings may lie something of historical substance is to go way beyond the evidence.[35]

---

[31] Origen, *Contra Celsum*, 2.55; 2.70.

[32] *Contra Celsum* 1.65.

[33] Against Schaberg, *Resurrection of Mary Magdalene*, 84 and n 86.

[34] See Peter Schäfer, *Jesus in the Talmud* (Princeton Uni Press, 2007) 15-21.

[35] Tabor and Jacobovici have been cautious in not claiming too much from the Talmudic literature, but the very fact of their devoting two pages to discussion of alternate meanings to 'Magdalene' will lead the general reader to suppose that behind the rabbinic traditions lies historical substance. Otherwise, why include this material in a chapter whose central thesis is the marital relationship of Mary with Jesus?

2. Is There Literary Evidence for Mary Magdalene Having Held a Prominent Leadership Role in the Early Christian Movement?

This question is not really germane to the Talpiot A tomb claims but it crops up in subtle ways in the recent writings that Tabor has put his name to. And one can see the point of the suggestion: if Mary Magdalene is the honoured Mara of the Mariamene Mara ossuary, and if she is the mother of Jesus' child, and if James the brother of Jesus is also buried in the same tomb complex, and if James was the leader of the Jerusalem based Christian community – then it stands to reason that James himself acknowledged Mary's high standing in the early church. Otherwise she would not have been buried in the Jesus Family Tomb along with him. But Tabor takes the argument even further: the New Testament authors (especially Luke) have deliberately suppressed the leadership role of Mary Magdalene, but certain traces remain, and these, along with the loud chorus in early gnostic writings of later centuries, enable us to see that Mary Magdalene was a leader of a segment of early Jerusalem based Christianity. No wonder she was given such a dignified title on her ossuary! And the theological focus of that community, as revealed in the Epistle of James and the supposed document Q, was widely different from that which was developed by Paul and which came to dominate the emerging catholic church.

Responding to these suggestions would take us far from our primary concerns, but we can make certain observations.

a) *James and Mary Magdalene.* We commence with James. The evidence from a careful reading of both Acts and Paul (at Gal 1.18-2.14, 1 Cor 15.5-7) suggests that the brother of Jesus exercised a leadership role from the beginning of the early community. And this is supported by early church tradition and writings as reflected in Eusebius. There is room for debate on several questions. Was James' position dominant from the start, or did it emerge so only after the persecution that broke out in about AD 42 under Herod Agrippa I, and when Peter and other apostles left Jerusalem and commenced wider evangelism? What really was the attitude of James to the law free gospel that Paul preached? What were the differences between James, Peter and Paul? And so on.[36]

What is abundantly clear is that after the New Testament era James became the focus of attention in a range of early Christian literature. From the

---

[36] I have deliberately kept this note on James brief. The most thorough study of James is John Painter, *Just James – the Brother of Jesus in History and Tradition*. See also R Bauckham, 'James and the Jerusalem Church' in Bauckham (ed), *The Book of Acts in its Palestinian Setting* (Eerdmans, 1995).

possibly early 2nd century *Gospel of Thomas* (at Saying 12), many tractates that, to a greater or lesser degree, reflect different theological perspectives from those of emerging Christian orthodoxy, give a leadership role to James. This appears to be in contrast especially to Peter, the representative of orthodoxy. As Painter says:

> *The Nag Hammadi tractates affirm both the leadership priority of James and his superiority as a recipient and transmitter of esoteric tradition. Here there is no evidence of any dependence of James on the apostles for his authority or for the esoteric revelation.*[37]

And what can be said of the gnostic Nag Hammadi texts can apply also to the other literature of early Christianity.

Returning to the first generation after Jesus, there is no need to ascribe ulterior motives to Luke in Acts, such that he 'deliberately suppressed' the truth about the leadership of James and the family of Jesus in those early days, and that he 'managed to recast' the evidence. Nor do we need to read Luke's silence on the death of James in AD 62 as evidence of his attempt to remove James from Christian memory. These sweeping judgements of Tabor[38] do not do justice to the fact that at critical moments Luke acknowledges James as leader of the Jerusalem church (Acts 12.17; 15.13; 21.18). Yes, Acts does seek to minimise or smooth over the obvious tensions and theological differences among the earliest Judaeo-Christians, but we can agree with Painter that Acts is no more pursuing an anti-James agenda than an anti-Paul agenda. What he does do is fit the data concerning James into his broader theological presentation.[39]

Now, if the leadership role of James is recognised in the New Testament (Acts and Paul), in the early traditions quoted by Eusebius,[40] and in later 'heterodox' writings, and if (as Tabor and Jacobovici suggest) Mary Magdalene was an honoured leader in the Jesus family centred in Jerusalem, then we are surely entitled to ask: what does the material in the James tradition have to say about Mary Magdalene? And the answer, as we shall now see, is surprising.

In the New Testament, Mary Magdalene vanishes from sight after the accounts of the empty tomb and Jesus' resurrection. Both Luke and Paul affirm the leadership of James, but it is a leadership that appears not to

---

[37] Painter, *Just James*, 178.
[38] Found in *Jesus Dynasty*, 249-258, preceded by the claim on p 248: 'Luke more than any of the other gospels marginalizes the family of Jesus.'
[39] So Painter, *Just James*, 97.
[40] See Eusebius, *Ecclesiatical History*, 2.1.3; 2.1.4; 2.23.4.

be shared with any save, for a time, the senior male apostles Peter and John (Gal 2.9). James may be supported by a body of elders (Acts 21.18), but Luke makes no attempt to hide the senior, decision-making role that James enjoys. When it comes to decisions that have the potential to affect the lives of the conservative Jewish believers in Jerusalem, nothing takes place without the consent and authoritative backing of James. No wonder, after his release from Herod Agrippa's prison, Peter gives instructions that James should be notified (Acts 12.17). One gets the impression that at this juncture Peter is acknowledging the seniority of James. Even earlier than Acts and Paul, the primitive Christian creed that surfaces in 1 Cor 15.3-7[41] provides evidence of the seniority of James, a seniority that he obviously cared not to share with anyone else. Only he and Cephas are explicitly named.

Eusebius, writing in the 4th century, has much to say about the leadership of the Jerusalem church in the early days, and he is in part dependent on Hegesippus, a 2nd century Judaeo-Christian. As previously mentioned, he writes of the leadership of James, but he knows much more. He writes of James' death and of the appointment of Simeon, Jesus' cousin, to succeed James. He provides the names of a body of elders (probably erroneously named bishops),[42] and he knows of the beginnings of heretical teachings in the church.[43] In none of this does he make any mention of women leaders, including Mary Magdalene. Had he or Hegesippus had any knowledge of an ongoing role for Mary Magdalene we can be confident he would have mentioned it, probably negatively, as by the second century episcopal government was well and truly entrenched, which secured male church leadership until recent times.

In the literature of early Christianity the James tradition was employed in a variety of ways. His piety and his suffering for his faith were widely recognised across all traditions. The Judaeo-Christian tradition also knew his role as a defender of Jewish traditions; gnostic traditions stress his personal relationship with Jesus and his reception of special revelations; while the emergent catholic orthodoxy placed emphasis on his role as first bishop of Jerusalem and his subservience to the authority of the apostles.[44]

The first notable document is the *Gospel of Thomas*. This collection of

---

[41] It does not matter whether this early creed concluded at verse 5 (as I believe) or at verse 7. Paul early on learned of and taught a resurrection tradition that included James but none other of the family circle of Jesus. See my *Jesus Resurrected?* 9-26.

[42] See Bauckham, *Jude and the Relatives of Jesus*, 70-79.

[43] See Bauckham, *Jude and the Relatives of Jesus*, 45-106.

[44] Painter, *Just James*, 181.

sayings of Jesus, probably early to mid-second century in dating, appears to have come from a church tradition that gave allegiance to James at the expense of Peter. In Saying 12, the disciples ask Jesus who will be their leader after his departure, to which they receive the response: 'Wherever you are, you are to go to James the righteous, for whose sake heaven and earth came into being'.[45] At Saying 13, Peter and Matthew give inadequate answers to Jesus' question, 'who am I like?'. Only Thomas gets it right. Then, in the final Saying (114), we have the first of several instances in the gnostic tradition where Peter says a disparaging word about either Mary Magdalene or women in general: 'Let Mary leave us for women are not worthy of life.' Jesus' puzzling response is not exactly a ringing endorsement of women as worthy disciples: 'I myself shall lead her in order to make her male, so that she too may become a living spirit resembling you males. For every woman who will make herself male will enter the kingdom of heaven.' We must return to this saying later in the chapter, but for our present purposes, what is notable is that Mary Magdalene has no association with James, nor is she remembered other than as a woman follower of Jesus.

In the other literature of early Christianity where James is either a central character or receives a mention,[46] only in the *First Apocalypse of James*, one of the Coptic Nag Hammadi texts, is reference also made to Mary Magdalene. The original Greek text probably dates from about AD 200. Though badly damaged in parts, what we have presents revelations given by 'the Lord' to James the Just, who addresses Jesus as 'Rabbi'. These revelations include the 'passwords' that James needs to ascend to heaven past the rulers of the world. Towards the end of the document, we read: 'Cast away from yourself all lawlessness. And beware lest they envy you. When you speak these words of this [perception], encourage these [four]: Salome and Mariam [and Martha and Arsinoe...]' (40.20-29) . What exactly lies behind this instruction is difficult to say,[47] but it is quite clear

---

[45] Tabor's claim for this saying is too sweeping when he writes, 'The *Gospel of Thomas* provides us with our earliest and most clearly stated evidence that James succeeded Jesus as leader of the movement....' (*Jesus Dynasty*, 256). The saying may be a claim to that effect, but not evidence of its historical veracity.

[46] The following texts, many as only fragments or quotes in other authors, are known to us: The *Gospel of Thomas*; The *Gospel of the Hebrews* (quote only); The *Protoevangelium of James*; the *Pseudo-Clementine Homilies and Recognitions*; The *First Apocalypse of James*; The *Second Apocalypse of James*.

[47] This translation has been challenged by A Marjanen who reads it as: 'When you speak these words of this [perception/knowledge] be persuaded by this [testimony of] Salome and Mary etc'. See reference in Schaberg, *Resurrection of Mary Magdalene*, 131f. Even if correct, the women are put forward as examples of suffering in the face

that Mariam (whom we can presume to be Mary Magdalene, though possibly she is conflated with Mary, sister to Martha)[48] holds no distinctive position of dignity alongside James. She and the other women appear to be among the '[seven] women who have been your disciples. And behold all women bless you (i.e. Jesus)' (39.15-20)

Thus, while James was held in great honour among certain segments of early Christianity, what has survived from the literature of those segments makes it quite clear that Mary Magdalene held no corresponding position of special dignity. There is nothing in the literature of early Christianity that gives Mary Magdalene a standing of authority and dignity alongside her presumed (on the Tabor/Jacobovici thesis) brother-in-law James. If any literary support is to be found to support the claims arising from the Talpiot A ossuaries, we will need to search elsewhere.

b) *John 20, Mary Magdalene and the Elijah/Elisha Motif.* In our discussion of the question of Mary as wife to Jesus we gave some consideration to the Jesus/Mary Magdalene encounter in John 20. But there is something else about this narrative that convinces Tabor and Jacobovici that in John 20 are fragments of a tradition that looked upon Mary Magdalene as successor to Jesus. For this they are indebted to Jane Schaberg[49] who has boldly suggested that behind John 20 are to be seen the remnants of 'an imaginative reuse of 2 Kings 2.1-18' where Elisha witnesses Elijah's ascent and is himself empowered by the Spirit to be Elijah's successor. As Schaberg says: '... Mary Magdalene's claim to have seen the risen Jesus ascending carries with it the implicit claim to have inherited a double portion of the spirit that was in him.'[50] Schaberg is aware of the difficulties in her thesis. A succession narrative will normally name what it is that is passed on; it will include acts that symbolise the succession; and there will be some kind of confirmation that succession has taken place. In the Elijah/Elisha narrative these can all be seen in the references to the double portion of spirit, the mantle, and Elisha's striking of the water with the mantle. None of these is present in John's narrative of Jesus and Mary at the tomb. As well, Schaberg agrees that Acts 1-2 does present us with a succession narrative after the pattern of Elijah/Elisha: Jesus is taken from the disciples, the Holy Spirit

---

of persecution, not of their leadership.

[48] S J Shoemaker, 'Rethinking the "Gnostic Mary": Mary of Nazareth and Mary of Magdala in Early Christian Literature,' in a paper delivered at the 2000 annual conference of the SBL has argued that in some of the early gnostic materials there was a fusing of Marys into a kind of 'universal Mary'.

[49] In *Resurrection of Mary Magdalene*, 304-355.

[50] Schaberg, *Resurrection of Mary Magdalene*, 304-305.

comes upon them, and others are witnesses to the event. But for Schaberg the Acts 1-2 pattern is typical of Luke, who deals with the threat of female power by taking over a rival tradition, overwhelming it and blotting it out![51] Finally, Schaberg admits that in the gospels, the various traditions have all but erased the Elijah/Elisha motif: in Matthew 28 by including other women in the resurrection appearance; in John 20, where Peter, the Beloved Disciple, and male disciples as a whole surround and overwhelm Mary's story.

There are serious problems with Schaberg's Elijah/Elisha thesis:

- Contrary to Schaberg's several claims (e.g. on pages 305 and 325), Mary does not, in fact, witness the ascension of Jesus. In 20.17, where Jesus tells Mary he has not yet ascended, and where he commissions her with the news of his impending ascension, it simply is not possible to posit that Mary is a witness to the event. And yet this 'marker' as Schaberg calls it (p 304), is the major clue that points her in the direction of the Elijah/Elisha narrative.
- Schaberg takes great pains to demonstrate that in Jewish tradition, Elijah's ascent in a chariot did not mean he did not die. There may be room for debate on this point. However, what is undeniable is that Elijah did not die and get buried. Yet in John 20 Mary is talking to one who most certainly did die and was buried in the nearby tomb. No such scene is found in the Elijah/Elisha tradition.
- Elisha's vision of the ascending Elijah takes place at the moment of Elijah's removal from earthly existence. But this is not Mary's experience. She has already witnessed Jesus' death 36 hours earlier.
- Possible allusions to the Elijah/Elisha stories abound in John's Gospel, as Schaberg acknowledges: changing of water into wine; healing of the nobleman's son; feeding of the multitude; healing of the man born blind; and perhaps Jesus' prayer at the raising of Lazarus.[52] What Schaberg fails to mention is that several of the parallels are between Elisha and Jesus (raising of the Shunammite woman's son [2 Kings 4]; feeding the multitude [2 Kings 4.42-44]; healing of the gentile Naaman [2 Kings 5]).
- This supposed tradition of the empowering of Mary Magdalene whereby she becomes Jesus' successor finds no echoes in any of the literature of

---

[51] Schaberg, *Resurrection of Mary Magdalene*, 318, and note 105.
[52] Schaberg, *Resurrection of Mary Magdalene*, 339f. The links with Elijah were earlier presented by J Louis Martyn, 'We Have Found Elijah', in his *The Gospel of John in Christian History* (Paulist, 1979) 16-28.

early Christianity – so successfully has it been suppressed. Schaberg herself admits that it only comes to the surface in the community in which the gnostic *Gospel of Mary* was produced. We shall soon look at this document along with others that give a place to Mary. What we can say here is that there is nothing in these writings that have any points of contact with the kind of Elijah/Elisha succession motif that Schaberg detects in John 20.

- In seeking a location for the Magdalene Christianity that lies behind John 20, Schaberg, without any evidence, posits the possibility of the Upper Galilee region of Palestine.[53] But this creates a problem, for the further away from the main centres of the new faith such a tradition was nurtured, the more difficult it becomes to explain how John the evangelist would have got hold of it, and why he would have trusted it and bothered with it. If, on the other hand, the tradition existed in the major church circles from which John derived his material, the greater becomes the difficulty in explaining how it survived at all.

The fact that Schaberg needs to acknowledge that only 'shards' of this Magdalene tradition can be detected in John 20 leads us to suggest, with respect, that what she can see in the text is somewhat like the case of the emperor's new clothes! I have to admit that my response to what Schaberg has provided us with in Chapter 7 of her book, 'Mary Magdalene as Successor to Jesus", is, as she herself feared may be the response of many, 'sheer fantasy' (p 347).[54]

c) *Mary Magdalene and Peter – Competitors as First Witness to the Resurrection.* There is one final claim relating to Mary that Schaberg, with Tabor in agreement (*Discovery* 135-138), presents as evidence of an authority status for her, an authority that was suppressed by the patriarchal apostles. The argument runs as follows: there appears to be a clear contrast between those New Testament writings where Peter is presented as the first witness of the resurrection, and those where that privilege is given to Mary Magdalene. Now, there is a clear link between a claim to being recipient of a resurrection appearance and a claim to community leadership. So it follows that in 1 Cor 15.5 and Lk 24.34 the leadership credentials of Peter are being put forward at the expense of Mary. By contrast, Matt 28.9-10, Jn 20.14-17 and the later Markan appendix at Mk 16.9 preserve traditions

---

[53] Schaberg, *Resurrection of Mary Magdalene*, 347.

[54] This is typical of Jane Schaberg's ability to clothe her scholarship with a light touch, and even mild humour. Her recent untimely death from cancer has left a vacuum not only in feminist scholarship, but in New Testament scholarship in general.

where the honour of being first resurrection witness is given to Mary.[55] From all of this, Schaberg concludes that 'the widespread tradition [in later post New Testament writings] of Peter's hostility to Mary' finds its source in 'a certain unspoken rivalry between Peter and Mary Magdalene in – or better, behind – the Christian Testament.'[56] In fact, Schaberg favours the possibility that Luke and Paul actually knew of the tradition of a first appearance to Mary and deliberately replaced it with a Petrine first appearance – and 'thus rivalry is reflected in the Pauline and/or Lukan materials.'[57]

Again, this is a thesis that will not bear close scrutiny.

- Firstly, the neat division between the Petrine group (Luke and Paul) and the Mary group (Matthew, John and the Markan Appendix) will not hold. Matthew's Gospel strongly supports the leadership of Peter. He adds to the Petrine passages found in his source, Mark (e.g. at 16.17-19). As well, it can be argued that his emphasis on commitment to the Law (5.17-20) even in the mission to the nations (28.19-20 – 'teaching them to observe …') reflects the known theological emphasis of Peter. As Painter well demonstrates, 'Matthew is an expression of the Petrine tradition …'.[58]

- As to Luke's presumed bias against Mary Magdalene, this charge also needs to be rejected. The first prosecution evidence directs the reader to Luke's account of the sinner woman who intrudes into the Pharisee's house to anoint Jesus' feet. Luke follows this with the mention of women, including Mary Magdalene, who minister to Jesus in his Galilean travels. This pair of traditions, Lk 7.36-50 + Lk 8.1-3, along with the fact that Luke has omitted the later incident of the anointing of Jesus in Bethany, is taken as a clear indication that Luke wishes to disparage Mary Magdalene ('Luke's strategy' is what Tabor and Jacobovici call it). But this is a judgement without objective foundation, a reading into the text that presumes to know the mind of Luke. One is left to suspect that Luke is being blamed for the later sins of the church fathers who did turn Mary Magdalene into the repentant sinner woman in the Pharisee's house, and then compounded the error by blending her with Mary of Bethany. A case of the sins of the children being visited upon

---

[55] What follows is a very brief summary of Schaberg, *Resurrection of Mary Magdalene*, 200-299.
[56] Schaberg, *Resurrection of Mary Magdalene*, 200.
[57] Schaberg, *Resurrection of Mary Magdalene*, 201.
[58] Painter, *Just James*, 89. Pages 88-102 are relevant.

the father! In the same way, Luke's omission of Mary's name, or the name of any other woman, at the crucifixion and burial sites (23.49, 55) should not be negatively interpreted, for their names are brought forward, Mary Magdalene at the head, in the account of the visit to the empty tomb (24.10). But this does not satisfy Tabor and Jacobovici. Noting the absence of any mention in Luke of a resurrection appearance to Mary/women, we are told that 'Luke cannot write her out of the story completely so he minimizes her role'. (*Discovery* 151) But why could he not 'write her out of the story'? If he had an agenda against Mary, and if he omitted her and the women's names at the crucifixion scene, why would he not also remove her name at the empty tomb scene? Nor have we any grounds for presuming that Luke knew of any tradition of an appearance to Mary – nothing in Luke 24 provides us with any clue to that effect. More to the point, Lk 24.10 suggests the very opposite to what is claimed against Luke – by naming Mary Magdalene and the women just before the narrative moves to the next stage, it looks as though Luke actually wants the memory of the women's names to be preserved. Nor is there any justification for seeing in Lk 24.11 (the women's report taken as 'an idle tale') evidence of 'hostility of male disciples … toward Mary'.[59] On the contrary, in view of the fact that the reader knows the women's report to be correct, it is 'the eleven and all the rest' (24.9 – which surely included *female* family members) who are seen in a bad light.[60] And if the textually problematic 24.12 is accepted as original,[61] Peter ends up confirming the women's report. If, as we are led to believe, Luke felt such freedom to manipulate the traditions, and if he favours Peter at the expense of a known tradition of an appearance to Mary Magdalene, is it not surprising that he leaves us with no comparable account of a resurrection appearance to Peter, simply the enigmatic affirmation 'The Lord has risen indeed, and has appeared to Simon' (24.34)? Of course, 24.12 and 24.34 serve Luke's purpose to highlight the senior status of Peter at this critical juncture, but we have no grounds for claiming that he has done it at the deliberate expense of anyone, especially Mary Magdalene. If Luke is out to uphold the status of Peter and to put a lid on Mary Magdalene's pretensions, he has certainly done it with a very light brush! We must conclude

---

[59] Schaberg, *Resurrection of Mary Magdalene*, 200.

[60] Tabor and Jacobovici (*Jesus Discovery*, 138) miss this point altogether, claiming that Luke himself characterises the women's report as an idle tale. An equally serious error on their part: the women did not claim to have 'seen Jesus'.

[61] This is one of several problematic texts in Luke 24. See my *Jesus Resurrected?* 73-74.

that Luke's Gospel provides us with no evidence of a clash of authority claims between Peter and Mary.

- The credal statement that Paul repeats to the Corinthian church, 1 Cor 15.3-7, does pose real questions for us, as we note in Chapter 9. One problem that puzzles is the absence of any mention of an appearance to Mary Magdalene/women.[62] Though Schaberg is uncomfortable with the suggestion from R E Brown, I suspect that it is close to the truth:

    The tradition that Jesus appeared first to Mary Magdalene has a good chance of being historical .... The priority given to Peter in Paul and in Luke is a priority among those who became official witnesses to the resurrection. The secondary place given to the tradition of an appearance to a woman probably reflects the fact that women did not serve at first as official preachers of the church – a fact that would make the creation of an appearance to a woman unlikely.[63]

    After all, it is not just Mary Magdalene who fails to rate a mention in that early creed of 1 Cor 15 – so too does Cleopas and his companion.

- Finally John's Gospel. This is certainly, by Schaberg's definition, a 'Magdalene text', for of all the early Christian texts it is the only one in which the honour of being the first recipient of an appearance is accorded to Mary. But it is certainly no less a Petrine text. Here is not the place to enter the debate of the relationship of Peter and the Beloved Disciple in this gospel.[64] Nor can we enter the debate as to whether John 21 was integral to the original gospel or a later addition – the majority of scholars insist the gospel originally ended at 20.31, but a sizeable number continue to argue that 21.24-25 was the original ending.[65] What can be recognised is that Peter is a major figure for the evangelist, no

---

[62] See also my *Jesus Resurrected?* 12-14.

[63] R E Brown, *Community of the Beloved Disciple* (Geoffrey Chapman, 1979) 189 n 335. In my *Jesus Resurrected?* (pp138-39) I questioned whether Jesus' first appearance was to women. In this chapter we have also expressed doubt that it was Mary Magdalene alone or in the company of other women who saw the resurrected Jesus. Schaberg expresses her discomfort on p 201.

[64] The literature is considerable. Still valuable is K Quast, *Peter and the Beloved Disciple – Figures for a Community in Crisis* (JSOT Press, 1989).

[65] See Bauckham, *Jesus and the Eyewitnesses*, 358-411 (espec. p 363 n 12) for (i) a modern defence of the integrity of John 21 as original to the gospel; and (ii) a useful consideration of the evangelist's claims for Peter and the Beloved Disciple. Also R A Culpepper, 'John 21:24-25: The Johannine *Sphragis*' in P N Anderson, F Just and T Thatcher (eds), *John, Jesus, and History, Volume 2 – Aspects of Historicity in the Fourth Gospel* (Society of Biblical Literature, 2009).

less honoured than the Beloved Disciple. In the opening chapter, Simon is given the name (Cephas) by which he is to be known in his leadership role in the early church (1.42; cf 1 Cor 15.5; 1.12); he is spokesman for the faithful disciples (6.66-71); he, with the Beloved Disciple, confirms Mary's message about the empty tomb (20.1-10). Then in John 21 Peter is revealed as chief pastor of the church, by grace restored from failure, and destined to give his life. John's Gospel is a Petrine text through and through – and yet one which in no way diminishes the importance and faith of Mary Magdalene.

One is left to conclude that if, in the early days of the Christian community, there was a conflict of authority and power between Peter and Mary Magdalene, there is no evidence of it in the New Testament. Yes, Luke, Mark and Paul appear to know of no resurrection appearance to her, but that cannot be read as an attempt to suppress her memory or her standing. And the two gospels that, by Schaberg's definition, show evidence of earlier Magdalene claims, namely, Matthew and John, are strong defenders of Petrine primacy. If we are to find evidence for Mary's status as a successor to Jesus and of a Petrine/Mary division, we need to look elsewhere.

d) *Mary Magdalene, Peter and Post-New Testament Writings.* One of the most intriguing features of early Christian writings outside the New Testament is the prominence that some of them give to Mary Magdalene. And in some of these Peter appears as the apostle who seeks to denigrate her. Is it possible that these writings provide the evidence we are looking for: proof of Mary's original status as successor to Jesus, and proof of Peter's (and that of the male leadership in general) opposition to her?[66] Do they, in fact 'present an alternative "lost" portrait of Mary Magdalene and her role as Jesus' female apostle extraordinaire – quite literally *the* apostle of the apostles and the successor of Jesus'? (*Discovery* 153)

There are about 12 early Christian, mostly gnostic, documents known to us that mention Mary Magdalene.[67] Those of particular interest to us are the *Gospel of Thomas*, the *Gospel of Philip*, *Pistis Sophia*, the *Acts of Philip*, and the *Gospel of Mary*. Schaberg lists nine aspects to the profile of Mary as found in the gnostic literature:

> *(1) Mary is prominent among the followers of Jesus; (2) she exists as a character, as a memory, in a textual world of androcentric language and patriarchal ideology; (3) she speaks boldly; (4) she plays a leadership role vis-à-vis the male disciples; (5) she is a visionary; (6) she is praised for her superior understanding; (7) she*

---

[66] See *Jesus Discovery*, 152-156; Schaberg, *Resurrection of Mary Magdalene*, 121-203.
[67] See the list in Schaberg, *Resurrection of Mary Magdalene*, 122 (Nag Hammadi texts), 125 (other texts).

> *is identified as the intimate companion of Jesus; (8) she is opposed by or in open conflict with one or more of the male disciples; (9) she is defended.*[68]

In Schaberg's judgement, each of these aspects appears in at least four of the texts. In the Gospel of Mary, each of the nine profile elements can be detected.

With much of Schaberg's analysis we can agree. We have already seen how in the *Gospel of Philip* Mary is the special recipient of revelation from the risen Jesus; she has more insight that the other (male) disciples. In the *Gospel of Mary* also, Mary Magdalene is noted as one whom Jesus loved more than other women. This time, it is Peter himself who acknowledges Mary's special privilege, and asks her: 'Tell us the words of the Saviour that you remember, which you know and we do not, since we did not hear them.' (*G. Mary* 10) This looks like a request to learn teaching of Jesus while he was on earth, teaching not given to the male disciples. But in what immediately follows, it becomes clear that visionary, post-resurrection insight is what Mary will pass on: 'Mary replied, "What is hidden from you I will tell you.... I saw the Lord in a vision ....' On many occasions, then, Mary fulfils the role of one who passes on special post-resurrection gnostic information to the disciples.

But noteworthy as this is, can it be said to indicate a leadership role for her? What is interesting is that in just about all of the gnostic texts that give some prominence to Mary, there remains a distance between her and the male disciples. It is as if *their* prominence is presumed, *their* foundational leadership is taken for granted, and what is surprising is that another, namely Mary, has insights that they lack. Never at any stage does she become one of them. The logical conclusion to be drawn from this is that whatever led such groups to ascribe such a role to Mary Magdalene (see below), what lay behind it was no lingering tradition that ascribed to Mary an acknowledged equality with the male disciples, no leadership role hitherto suppressed and now come to the surface.

Nor is what I have just written challenged by the picture of Mary in the (possibly 6th century) *Acts of Philip*.[69] True, in this document Mariamne,[70] sister of Philip, is commissioned to accompany Philip in the evangelising

---

[68] Schaberg, *Resurrection of Mary Magdalene*, 129.

[69] Text is taken from M R James, *The Apocryphal New Testament*(Oxford; Clarendon, 1924).

[70] We cannot close off the possibility that here is an example of the blending of Marys, for at her first mention Martha, sister of Mary of Bethany, is spoken of in the same breath (8.94) . See n 55.

of the Greeks – dressed as a man (8.94)! On their travels, Philip journeys through 'Lydia and Asia', accompanied by 'Bartholomew, one of the Seventy, his sister Mariamne, and their disciples' (15.107). In the final sections of the document, Philip's glorious martyrdom is described, after which Mariamne is destined to travel to Jordan (15.148) where her 'body shall be laid up in the river Jordan' (15.137). Here we certainly glimpse a Mary who exercises a ministry alongside her brother Philip and Bartholomew. But even so, on the one occasion where we see her in action, Mary's ministry is to a woman, the wife of Nicanor the proconsul (15.114-115). Prior to that, Mariamne 'sat and listened to Philip discoursing' (15.109). This last reference, along with the earlier charge given by the Saviour to change from 'thy woman's aspect', indicates that even here there is retained a difference between the role of Philip and of Mary. I am thus not so certain that we should read her future travel to Jordan as a mission charge. It would appear that she travels to Jordan to fulfil her 'destiny' (15.142) ; it is there she shall die and be buried.

Thus, the fourth of Schaberg's profile aspects needs to be challenged. Mary's leadership role vis-à-vis the apostles is essentially restricted to her conveying of revelatory information to them, a point recognised by Schaberg herself.[71]

Peter's contacts with Mary Magdalene are to be found in three documents. Most prolific are the Peter/Mary/Jesus communications in a (possibly) late 3rd century Coptic text known as *Pistis Sophia*. In this document, which describes post-resurrection teachings of Jesus on the origin of sin and evil, the value of repentance and the nature of post-death existence, Mary Magdalene poses the overwhelming majority of questions to Jesus. Three times Peter is spoken of as opposed to Mary, primarily because 'this woman ... takes the opportunity from us, and does not allow any one of us to speak' (I.36-37; II.72; IV.146). What is clear is that the issue at stake for Peter, speaking on behalf of the male disciples, is not Mary's presumed authority, but that she, a woman, is spiritually more advanced than they are. 'He is envious, contentious, misogynistic' as Schaberg acknowledges.[72]

We have already noted the spiritual insight ascribed to Mary in the Nag Hammadi *Gospel of Mary*, and Peter's acknowledgement of her (*G Mary* 10). But this is not Peter's last word. Later, both Peter and Andrew dispute

---

[71] Schaberg, *Resurrection of Mary Magdalene*, 144.

[72] Schaberg's excellent survey of *Pistis Sophia* (pp 161-165) is dependent on a study by A Marjanen, *The Woman Jesus Loved: Mary Magdalene in the Nag Hammadi Library and Related Documents* (dissertation Uni of Helsinki, 1995; published by Brill, 1996), unavailable to me.

Mary's special place. Peter asks, 'Should we turn about, too, and listen to her? Did he choose her above us?' The text follows: 'Then Mary wept and said to Peter, "My brother Peter, what are you thinking? Do you think that I have thought up these things alone in my heart ....?" Levi responded and replied to Peter, "Peter, you are always angry.... If the Saviour made her worthy, who are you then, for your part, to cast her aside?..." When Levi said these things, they began to go out and to teach and proclaim.' (*G Mary* 17-19). What we note from this text is that (i) there is no antipathy on the part of Mary towards Peter or the other male disciples; (ii) it is the male disciples who are called to evangelise the world (*G Mary* 9, 19); and (iii) Mary is acknowledged as having superior spiritual insight by reason of her close relation to the Saviour.

Finally, we return to the earliest Peter/Mary conflict, in the final logion in the *Gospel of Thomas* (114), which has already had our brief attention. Whereas in *Pistis Sophia* and the *Gospel of Mary* Peter's problem appears to be his envy of Mary's superior spiritual insights, in the *Gospel of Thomas* his problem is more fundamental: she is a woman. Peter says to the male disciples, 'Mary should leave us, for females are not worthy of the life.' We need not again concern ourselves with Jesus' gnostic response.[73] As to the debate over whether *Thomas* represents traditions of Jesus sayings independent of and earlier than the canonical gospels – that continues unabated. Fortunately, we don't need to enter the lists in that academic battle. For the record, I incline to the view recently cogently argued by Mark Goodacre, that *Thomas* was familiar with the synoptic gospels and that, rather than being a mid- to late first century document, it is a mid-second century work with defined gnostic tendencies.[74] But even accepting *Thomas*' familiarity with the synoptics does not exclude the possibility that here and there echoes of traditions unknown to the canonicals found their way into *Thomas*.[75] And that may well be the case with our Saying 114. Though we could never establish the point, I would not be surprised if this logion is a gnostic reshaping of a memory that takes us back to the ministry of Jesus. After all, if Jesus' originally all-male band of disciples, drawn from John the Baptist's ministry, soon attracted the support of

---

[73] See the discussion in Schaberg, *Resurrection of Mary Magdalene*, 156-160.

[74] See Mark Goodacre, *Thomas and the Gospels. The Case for Thomas' Familiarity with the Synoptics* (Eerdmans, 2012).

[75] J Jeremias' *The Unknown Sayings of Jesus* (SPCK, 1964) is still a useful study of possible sayings of Jesus outside the New Testament. See also Bertil Gärtner, *The Theology of the Gospel of Thomas* (Collins, 1961) 49-52; R McL Wilson, *Studies in the Gospel of Thomas* (Mowbray, 1960) 41-42.

certain women (Lk 8.1-3), then we ought not to be surprised if it drew some initial resentment on the part of the males. Nor would any of the evangelists have had any interest in preserving such a memory in their gospels. The closest we get to such a memory is in Jn 4.27.

We have covered the limits of the Mary/Peter contacts in the early gnostic literature. What is abundantly clear is that whatever the background to them in the gnostic world of the early centuries, nothing of a lingering portrait of Mary as an authoritative female apostle can be detected. She does not threaten the male leadership, she enlightens and encourages it. The reason for this later prominence of Mary is an open, puzzling and unresolved question. Does it go back to John 20 and the revelation given her in the garden? Does Jesus' love for Mary in the gnostic gospels have its roots in Jn 11.5 where Jesus is said to love Mary, Martha and Lazarus? I suspect that the answer is yes to *both* of these questions, and that the Mary of later gnostic writings is indeed a blending of these two Marys. A fascinating question, but it need not concern us now. What we can be confident of is that *no early Christian writings provide any support for the notion that a memory of Mary Magdalene as an apostolic leader was initially suppressed and then resurfaced in these documents*. The gnostic Mary Magdalene does not threaten the male leadership, nor is she out to dethrone Peter; she enlightens and encourages, but she leaves them to their roles as leaders and apostolic preachers.

Conclusion

Mary Magdalene has been the focus of much scholarly interest in recent times, and not just from the feminist guild of New Testament scholarship. We would love to know more about this female disciple of Jesus who figures so prominently in the canonical gospels, only to disappear completely thereafter until she re-emerges as a figure of spiritual privilege and insight in early gnostic writings. Did she return to Galilee after the resurrection or stay on in Jerusalem? Did she play any active support role in the life of the church, or did she quietly retire with her memories, awaiting the return of the Son of Man? We will never know. But let us not forget that she is not the only known disciple of Jesus of whom we know nothing after their brief appearances in the gospels – what of Mary and Martha of Bethany, Salome, Bartimaeus, Nicodemus, Joseph of Arimathea, Simon of Cyrene? What we can affirm with confidence is that the broad literary evidence, both canonical and post-New Testament, offers no support for any suggestions that Mary Magdalene was married to Jesus or that she exercised (or was meant to exercise) any apostolic/leadership role in the post-Easter Christian community. Nor does the evidence support any claim that her memory was deliberately suppressed. On the contrary, I believe that we can assert with confidence that the literary evidence suggests the very opposite: Jesus was never married, and Mary Magdalene never exercised any position of leadership in the earliest community. As to her memory, far from being suppressed and essentially unknown to the evangelists, it was firmly treasured as being integral to the story of Jesus' final days in Jerusalem.

Postscript – the Jesus' Wife Papyrus Fragment

In late September 2012 news reports worldwide drew attention to an academic paper presented by Prof Karen King that made reference to a recently published papyrus fragment in Coptic, dated from the fourth century, in which Jesus refers to 'my wife'. Comments on the find have been numerous, and speculation is likely to continue for some time. Already some responses have seen in the fragment supporting evidence for the Jesus Family Tomb thesis with its claims for a marriage between Jesus and Mary Magdalene. But as many scholars have pointed out, the fragment really takes us no further along the path of uncovering evidence of the marriage of Jesus. Rather, it is typical of the language of parts of the gnostic tradition that developed from the late second century, a language already noted in our analysis. More to the point, however, is the question of the authenticity of the fragment. There is a growing body of opinion that is firmly of the opinion that it is a modern hoax.[76] So long as that cloud hangs over the fragment, it cannot be taken into consideration in the study of early gnostic thought.

---

[76] See *BiblePlaces.com* blogs for September 18 and 21, 2012 for a detailed list of articles and responses. Francis Taylor is among a growing number of scholars who have expressed the belief that the text is a modern forgery heavily dependent on the *Gospel of Thomas*. See his well argued response, 'Inventing Jesus' Wife' at www.bibleinterp.com/articles/wat368023.shtml. See also the website of Mark Goodacre for similar conclusions.

Chapter Eight
JOSEPH OF ARIMATHEA AND THE BURIALS OF JESUS

In the Tabor/Jacobovici thesis Joseph of Arimathea has a central role to play. Though his name is never found on any of the ossuaries in the two Talpiot tombs, for various reasons he is drawn into the reconstruction presented in *The Jesus Discovery*. And even prior to the publication of *The Jesus Discovery* Tabor's views on the question had been published in *The Jesus Dynasty*, and also defended in an SBL forum paper, 'Two Burials of Jesus of Nazareth and the Talpiot Jeshua Tomb'.[1] Before examining the literary evidence relating to the burial of Jesus, let us review the main points of the Tabor thesis relating to Joseph of Arimathea.[2]

1. Joseph of Arimathea and the Burials of Jesus

- Joseph is a follower of Jesus, but also a person of 'influence and means', a member of the Jerusalem Sanhedrin who arrest Jesus and hand him over to Pontius Pilate. (124)
- Just as disciples of John the Baptist collected his dead body for burial, so Joseph (and Nicodemus) decided to act in respect of Jesus, to comply with Jewish law and custom, which required a body to be buried before sunset, and especially before an oncoming Sabbath. (35-36)
- Joseph's request to Pilate for the body of Jesus was a bold act whereby he demonstrated his sympathy with Jesus and his movement. (90)
- Mark's gospel suggests that Joseph's action and choice of a nearby tomb was hasty, in light of the coming Sabbath, and he intended to complete the proper burial rites after the Sabbath. (120)
- John's gospel also presumes that the tomb was temporary and not permanent. (134)
- The initial burial site was not owned by Joseph, who would hardly have selected such a public area for his family burial cave. (119-120) Matthew alone tells us that the tomb belonged to Joseph (Matt 27.60), and this change to his source Mark is due to the influence of Isa 53.9 – the Suffering Servant makes his tomb with the rich.
- Mark's gospel implies that Joseph intended to complete the due burial rites once Passover was concluded. He 'had both the means and the

---

[1] *Jesus Dynasty*, 223-237; and http://sbl-site.org/Article.aspx?ArticleID=651.
[2] Unless indicated, all page references are to *Jesus Discovery*.

formal responsibility (italics mine) to honor Jesus and his family in this way.' (120)
- Apparently unbeknown to Joseph, the women also intended to return to the (temporary) tomb after Sabbath to complete the Jewish rites of burial. (36)
- Presumably some time on Saturday evening, at the conclusion of the Sabbath, Joseph removed the body of Jesus and placed it in the tomb complex on his family estate, which he had planned to dedicate to the family of Jesus. (36)
- As well, we can presume that Joseph informed none of the family or disciples of Jesus concerning his action, since the empty tomb narratives highlight the surprise of these persons when they discover or are told of the empty tomb. (126)
- The term 'Arimathea' refers not to a Judean village but derives from the Hebrew word for height. The noun in the dual form 'Ramathaim' therefore means twin heights. Even today two prominent heights can be seen as one looks south from Jerusalem towards Talpiot. (126-7) Luke refers to Arimathea as a 'city of the Jews' (Lk 23.51), but Luke's knowledge of the geography of Palestine is deficient. (229 n38)
- Joseph later selects another nearby site to serve as the burial cave for his own family.

2. The Questions that Remain

Readers will note that there is a sudden presumptive jump in the sequence of events, a jump for which there is no literary or archaeological evidence. The records all tell us that it was Joseph who received permission from Pontius Pilate to depose Jesus' body from the cross and bury it. But that is as far as our knowledge of Joseph extends. Neither the early Christian records nor any of the evidence from the Talpiot tombs provides us with any evidence that the tomb complexes found at Talpiot have any association with Joseph of Arimathea. No ossuary mentions the name of Joseph. The only substantive justification that Tabor can provide is his interpretation of the background to 'Arimathea'. We will need to return to this in due course.

There is one other presumption that many readers will not be aware of. Tabor presumes that Joseph of Arimathea was an historical figure. Among a small band of scholars and others, the account of the burial by the fictional character Joseph has been read as a figment of early Christian imagination. The story, along with the accounts of the discovery of the empty tomb, was invented to cover over the early Christians' embarrassment for their failure to retrieve the body of Jesus from the cross and their ignorance of where Jesus was buried.³ I do not intend to respond to this charge which requires a totally speculative reading of the gospels. Along with the overwhelming majority of scholars, Tabor is surely correct to presume the historicity of Joseph of Arimathea.⁴

But other questions remain, and these we must examine to see what light can be shed on them by Roman, early Christian and Jewish literature. We depend upon the gospels, evidence from Roman authors concerning crucifixions, and Jewish writings, including Josephus, the Mishnah and later rabbinic texts. We will proceed by posing and seeking a response to the following questions:

(i) What was Joseph's attitude to Jesus at the time of his, Jesus', death?

(ii) Why did Joseph, rather than Jesus' family, assume responsibility for Jesus' burial?

(iii) Is there any evidence to suggest that Joseph looked upon his Friday action as 'a temporary measure'?

(iv) What was the attitude of Roman authorities to those they crucified? What latitude did they give in relation to the burial of crucified people?

(v) What do Jewish writings reveal of Jewish attitudes and practice in relation to the burial of criminals condemned by their own authorities and the Romans?

(vi) Joseph's action must have been notified eventually to the disciples. But the whole biblical account rests upon the puzzle of the first empty tomb. Why the absolute silence on the second one?

3. At the Time of Jesus' Death, What Can be Said About Joseph?

The biblical testimony needs careful scrutiny. The Gospels of John and Peter and the synoptic gospels are quite different in their accounts of Joseph. We commence with Mark, which I take to be the earliest gospel.⁵ Mark 15.43

---

[3] See, for example, J D Crossan, *The Historical Jesus*, 391-94; idem, *Who Killed Jesus?* (HarperCollins, 1995) 160-77; JS Spong, *Resurrection: Myth or Reality?* (HarperSanFrancisco, 1994) 221-229. The majority of the members of the Jesus Seminar also voted that Joseph of Arimathea was a Markan invention. See R W Funk et al, *The Acts of Jesus* (Polebridge, 1998) 442.

[4] An excellent response to the kinds of arguments presented by Crossan is given by Dale Allison, *Resurrecting Jesus: The Earliest Christian Tradition and its Interpreters* (T&T Clark, 2005) 352-363.

[5] In my *Jesus Resurrected?* 46-55, I provided a critique of the thesis of Crossan that embedded within the Gospel of Peter is the earliest Christian gospel, which became the source of all others.

translates, '*Joseph from Arimathea, a respected member of the Council, a man who was himself awaiting the coming of the kingdom of God, dared approach Pilate and ask for the body of Jesus.*' This is a remarkably restrained narrative. There is nothing here that links Joseph to Jesus, either directly as a follower or indirectly as a secret admirer. Since we are not told he is a priest, we are probably entitled to assume that he is a man of some wealth and standing in the community, and was consulted from time to time by the High Priest and thus regarded as a member of the Council or Sanhedrin.[6] All Mark feels able to say of him is that, at this stage of his life, though wealthy and powerful, he is also (*kai autos*) piously awaiting God's kingdom, probably an indication of his Pharisaic sympathies. In this regard, he resembles the characters that we meet early in Luke's Gospel, Simeon (Lk 2.25) and Anna (Lk 2.36-37).

Luke's account (Lk 23.50-52) is dependent on Mark, as will be seen from the underlined words and phrases which correspond exactly with Mark: '*And behold a man named Joseph, a <u>member of the Council</u>, a good and righteous man – he himself did not agree with their decision nor with their deed – who came <u>from Arimathea</u>, a city of the Jews, and <u>who was awaiting the kingdom of God</u>, himself <u>came to Pilate and asked for the body of Jesus</u>.*' Luke's alterations to Mark are typical of his style and language,[7] and there is no reason to think he is dependent on another *written* source. He also says nothing to back up any claim that at this stage Joseph was a known Jesus sympathiser or adherent. But he does add one detail not given by Mark – his non-agreement with the council decision and action. Luke does not tell us whether Joseph was present at the meeting of the Council and was 'outvoted', whether he was present and kept his peace, or whether he was absent. What it does look like is that Luke is attempting to hold the balance: he knows only what Mark has told us about Joseph at this point in his life; but he also is aware that this man was absolved by the later Jerusalem Christian community of any complicity in the <u>arrest and trial of Jesus</u>. And that obviously because he had joined up with them. In

---

[6] It is important to recognise that the Council in Jesus' day appears not to have been a fixed body and number such that all members could be expected to be called to its meetings. This assumption, so often repeated among scholars, confuses later rabbinic references to the Beth Din or Sanhedrin, a formal body of 70 or 71 members, with the body referred to in the gospels and Josephus as the *sunedrion, gerousia, presbyterion*, and *boulē*. This latter body seems to have functioned more as a consultative list which the High Priest could consult as he desired. By the 2nd century AD this body had become a formal Sanhedrin. See my *The Enigmatic Jew*, 288-9. A detailed note on the Jerusalem Council is found in Joan Taylor, *The Immerser: John the Baptist within Second Temple Judaism* (Eerdmans, 1997) 172-185.

[7] For example, 'good' and 'righteous' are frequently found in Luke (and Matthew); and Luke's favourite term for even a village/hamlet like Nazareth is 'city'.

fact, that is why his name was known and remembered – even by Mark. We can agree with Bauckham, referring to many of those named in the gospels: '… all these people joined the early Christian movement and were well known at least in the circles in which these traditions were first transmitted.'[8]

Matthew takes us further. Notice how much of Mark he has removed, while adding his own comments. Matt 27.57-58 reads: '*When evening had come, there came a rich man from Arimathea, by the name of Joseph; and he was a disciple of Jesus. He himself came to Pilate and asked for the body of Jesus*.'[9] There's not much of Mark's text here. Matthew's Joseph is no longer just a good man, well respected and awaiting God's kingdom – he has become a card-carrying disciple of Jesus! And his membership of the Jerusalem Council has also been covered over, so that he can in no way be suspected of having had any role in the recent events.

In emphasis, John 19.38 is close to Matthew, though it is unlikely that there is any literary dependence.[10] It reads: '*After these things, Joseph from Arimathea, being a disciple of Jesus, but secretly out of fear of the Jews, asked Pilate that he might take the body of Jesus. So he came and took his body*.' Again, no mention of Pilate's Council membership, nothing about his righteous character and piety. He has no connection with the Jewish authorities responsible for Jesus' death. He is simply a private individual who takes upon himself an appeal to Pilate. Like Matthew's Joseph, he is a disciple of Jesus,[11] but he has kept his allegiance to himself. His wealth is displayed in the following verses when the volume of the embalming ointments is given.

Joseph's role in the non-canonical *Gospel of Peter* is quite differently portrayed. Immediately prior to the crucifixion, at 2.3-5 we read:

---

[8] Bauckham, *Jesus and the Eyewitnesses*, 45. So also R E Brown: 'The answer to … Matthew's description of Joseph lies in the great likelihood that after the resurrection Joseph did become a Christian and that is why his name was remembered in all the Gospel accounts.' From *The Death of the Messiah* (2 vols; Doubleday, 1994) 2.1223.

[9] Matthew and Luke have exactly the same Greek words for the whole of this last sentence (9 words in all) – an example of the occasional common agreements of the two against Mark. These occasional agreements have raised questions in the discussion of the so-called Synoptic Problem. I remain of the view that Matthew and Luke were separately dependent on Mark, and that their agreement here is co-incidental. The last five words are commonly given by all three evangelists.

[10] The literary relationship between John and the synoptics has been much debated in the last century. See D Moody Smith, *John among the Gospels – The Relationship in Twentieth Century Research* (Fortress, 1992).

[11] Matthew uses the verbal and John the noun form of 'disciple'.

> *But Joseph, the friend of Herod and of the Lord, stood there, and knowing that they were about to crucify him, came to Pilate and asked for the body of the Lord for burial. And Pilate sent to Herod and asked for his body. And Herod said, 'Brother Pilate, even if no-one had asked for him, we would have buried him, since the Sabbath is dawning. For it is written in the Law that the sun should not set upon one who has been put to death.' And he [Herod? Pilate?] delivered him over to the people before the first day of unleavened bread, their festival.*

Then follows the details of the crucifixion with the Jewish people presented as the sole actors against Jesus. The Roman soldiery fade into the background. At 6.23-24 we read:

> *But the Jews rejoiced and gave over his body to Joseph for him to bury it, since he had beheld how many good things he had done. And taking the Lord, he bathed and wrapped him in a shroud and carried him to his own sepulchre, called Joseph's garden.*

The *Gospel of Peter* is an intriguing second century document. Is it totally dependent on the written canonical gospels, or does it also make use of some oral traditions that have come down to the second century? There is no common mind among the scholars. What we can say is that the verses above are full of historical impossibilities: how did Joseph know that Jesus would die before sunset such that he asked for the body before he was crucified; Joseph could hardly have been a friend of Herod Antipas from Galilee; Herod had no jurisdiction in Jerusalem such that Pilate would make request to him concerning Jesus' body; the Romans, not the Jews, would have given over Jesus' body to Joseph. And there is nothing before us that could not be considered an elaboration based on the canonical gospels. The reference to Jesus' burial in Joseph's own sepulchre (*eis idion taphon*) in a garden known as Joseph's Garden would appear to be based upon Jn 19.41, with a possible link to Matt 27.60. Even the reference to the law in Deut 21.22-23 concerning the need for dead bodies to be removed by sunset would seem to be derived from Jn 19.31. In other words, there is nothing in this second century gospel that need interest us relating to Joseph of Arimathea.

Except for one important point that presents a huge hurdle for the Tabor thesis. We have just noted that *G Peter* 6.24 expands the earlier traditions derived from Jn 19.41 and Matt 27.60 about the burial place of Jesus, in a garden locality, in a tomb owned by Joseph, and gives the location a name, Joseph's Garden. This suggests that by the second century, at least in the traditions known to the *Gospel of Peter*, no other tomb or locality is associated with the burial of Jesus and the action of Joseph of Arimathea. It would not have been possible for the earlier traditions found in John and Matthew to survive and develop into the next century, as they did in the *Gospel of Peter*, if the Christians of Jerusalem knew that Jesus had been finally buried elsewhere in another tomb, also owned by the same Joseph.

So where do the gospels leave us in our understanding of Joseph? We come away with the following conclusions:

- At the time of the crucifixion, Joseph was a known member of the High Priest's Council.
- At the time of the crucifixion, Joseph had no associations with Jesus and his movement.
- Joseph made personal request to Pilate for the body of Jesus.
- There is no indication that Joseph consulted the family of Jesus or his disciples prior to his appeal to Pilate.

But these conclusions themselves leave us with questions:

- On what grounds did Joseph make appeal to Pilate for the body of Jesus? Did he come as an individual or as a representative of the Council?
- Are there reasons why Jesus' family members or disciples could not have made the appeal for the body?
- Matthew's and John's reference to Joseph's discipleship of Jesus: is it a fabrication without historical base, or does it reflect the knowledge that Joseph did at some point align himself with the Christian movement?

These conclusions and questions drive us forward to seek further information about both Roman practice and Jewish custom in relation to crucified prisoners.

4. Roman Crucifixions in the Time of Jesus

The first century AD author Petronius in his *Satyricon* 111-12, narrates a humorous story that tells us much about Roman practice relating to crucifixion in the Empire of Jesus' day. A Roman centurion at Ephesus was given responsibility for ensuring that the bodies of some crucified criminals were not stolen by relatives. Nearby, a grieving widow had been mourning her recently deceased husband, staying night and day in his tomb. The soldier, anxious to 'console' the widow, spent a night in the tomb with the widow, and during the night family members came and took away one of the crucified bodies. The centurion feared that he would be held responsible for the lapse in security and prepared to die in the tomb. But the widow, who was 'no less compassionate than chaste' offered her deceased husband to be hung on the cross, considering it far better to make use of a dead body than to string up one who is alive!

Two further quotes will add to the picture. The deterrent value of crucifixions is seen in this quote from the first century AD writer, Quintilian (*Declamations 274*) : 'Whenever we crucify the guilty, the most crowded roads are chosen, where the most people can see and be moved by this fear. For penalties relate not so much to retribution as to their exemplary effect.'

Finally, Josephus provides a gruesome account of the fate of Jewish fugitives in AD 70 seeking to flee from Jerusalem in its final hours:

> *When they were going to be taken (by the Romans), they were forced to defend themselves, and after they had fought they thought it too late to make any supplications for mercy; so they were first whipped, and then tormented with all sorts of tortures before they died and then were crucified before the wall of the city. Titus felt pity for them, but as their number – given as up to five hundred a day – was too great for him to risk either letting them go or putting them under guard, he allowed his soldiers to have their way, especially as he hoped that the gruesome sight of the countless crosses might move the besieged to surrender. So the soldiers, out of the rage and hatred they bore the prisoners, nailed those they caught, in different postures, to the crosses, by way of jest, and their number was so great that there was not enough room for the crosses and not enough crosses for the bodies.* (Jewish War 5.449-51)

Crucifixion, though not a Roman 'invention',[12] was certainly 'regularised' in the Roman Empire as the most severe form of punishment for a range of serious crimes against the state and the social order. Mass crucifixions were used against those who rose in revolt against Rome (as in the Josephus quote), but individual bandits and robbers could also suffer the punishment, and in many parts of the Empire this was seen by the populace as a necessary method of maintaining the *pax Romana* (Quintilian quote).

Were the bodies of the crucified to be given over to relatives for burial? The evidence here is not clear: texts from about AD 200 suggest that by that period relatives had such a right, but other evidence suggests that actual practice in the provinces would vary according to the whim of the governor in charge (Petronius quote). Certainly, in cases of treason (*maiestas*), the provincial authority would not have been willing to give way to public sympathy for the condemned. Rome could show no mercy in such cases. So then, in fact, 'it was almost proverbial that those who hung on the cross fed the crows with their bodies (Horace, *Epistle* 1.16.48) .[13]

---

[12] Martin Hengel, *Crucifixion* (SCM, 1977), 22, writes of its use by the Persians and even earlier barbarian peoples, as a form of execution.

[13] Brown, *Death of the Messiah*, 2.1208.

What, then, of Jesus, condemned as 'king of the Jews'?[14] There is no evidence that any of the family or disciples of Jesus made any request for his body; indeed, the bulk of the male disciples appear to have fled the scene, presumably fearing for their own safety. Apart from the reference to the Beloved Disciple at Jn 19.26, they are not mentioned in the crucifixion scenes. But if any of them *had* come to Pilate and asked for the body, would he have acceded? The most likely answer is, probably not. Whatever private opinion he may have had as to the security threat posed by Jesus and his movement,[15] in the Roman political climate of the post-Sejanus period, Pilate could not have been seen to be weak in the matter of state security. He could not afford to have false accusations against him getting back to Rome.[16]

And since this last paragraph also has great relevance for Joseph of Arimathea, we need to provide some historical background. On October 18, AD 31, the much hated Lucius Aelius Sejanus was killed in Rome. Commander of the Roman imperial bodyguard since AD 14, Sejanus had exercised almost complete power in Rome since the departure of the Emperor Tiberius to Capri in AD 26. Ambitious and ruthless, Sejanus was the *de facto* emperor. And Pontius Pilate, prefect of Judea, was said to have been a favourite of Sejanus and owed his appointment to this man! The murder of Sejanus would have made Pilate deeply sensitive of the need to show his loyalty to the emperor. He needed to ensure that Rome knew he was indeed 'friend of Caesar' (Jn 19.12).[17] In particular, as I have said, he could not allow any report to get back to Rome suggesting that he had treated leniently anyone who was a threat to Roman security and authority. The relevance of this for Joseph's request is obvious in two ways. Firstly, whatever his status in Jewish society, we can be confident that in coming to Pilate and requesting the body of Jesus, he did not appeal on the basis of any personal friendship with Jesus, nor did he come

---

[14] Martin Hengel has well established the historical credibility of the superscription hung over Jesus on the cross. See 'The Debate about the "Messianic Mission" of Jesus' in B Chilton and C Evans, *Authenticating the Activities of Jesus* (Brill, 1999), 336-339. See also my *Enigmatic Jew*, 293.

[15] And it is noteworthy that no attempt was made to round up the followers of Jesus.

[16] I am working on the presumption of a crucifixion date of AD 33, not AD 30 as proposed by Tabor. Despite his often overly simplistic reading of the biblical texts, I find convincing the astronomical and other evidence presented by Colin Humphreys concerning the date of the crucifixion. See *The Mystery of the Last Supper* (CUP, 2011).

[17] Behind the implied threat in Jn 19.12 lies the phrase *Caesaris amicus*, friend of Caesar. The phrase is found elsewhere in Roman literature and was a notable political term. See A H Sherwin-White, *Roman Law and Roman Society in the New Testament* (Oxford, 1963) 46-47. Also R Schnackenburg, *The Gospel According to St John* (3 vols; Seabury/Crossroad, 1980-82) 3.262-63.

seeking any special favour. There is no reason to think that Pilate would have acceded to any 'personal requests'. And secondly, in view of the fact that it was the Jewish authorities who handed Jesus over to Pilate and demanded his execution, it is unimaginable that Pilate would have granted Joseph's request unless he was satisfied that it had the backing of the Council. Having already granted their request to have the troublemaker punished, it would have been too politically dangerous for him to get offside with them by releasing him to his family or followers. In short, we can be as confident as history allows us to be that Joseph came before Pilate and requested the body of Jesus with the full knowledge and backing of the Jewish authorities.

And that takes us on to consider Jewish attitudes towards crucified bodies.

5. Jewish Attitudes Towards the Bodies of the Crucified[18]

In the time of Jesus, Judaism had to come to terms with the reality of crucifixion as the Roman punishment for rebellion and certain crimes. The biblical text that was relevant to the issue was Deut 21.22-23: *'When someone is convicted of a crime punishable by death and is executed, and you hang him on a tree, his corpse must not remain all night upon the tree; you shall bury him that same day, for anyone hung on a tree is under God's curse. You must not defile the land that the Lord your God is giving you for possession.'* This injunction, however, relates to the public display of those already dead from the punishment of stoning (e.g. Deut 21.21), not to hanging as the means of killing. But it was taken seriously, nonetheless. Thus, in contrast to Roman disregard for crucified bodies, we know from Josephus that even during the chaos of the First Revolt the Jews took seriously the injunction not to allow bodies to remain overnight: '... the Jews pay so much regard to obsequies that even those found guilty and crucified are taken down and buried before sunset.' (*Jewish War*, 4.317) As well, evidence from Qumran indicates that Deut 21.21 could be interpreted to apply not just to the public display of dead bodies, but also to crucifixion as a death penalty. The *Temple Scroll*, in a clear interpretation of Deuteronomy, instructs as follows:

> *If there were to be a spy against his people who betrays his people to a foreign nation or causes evil against his people, you shall hang him from a tree and he will die. On the evidence of two witnesses and on the evidence of three witnesses shall he be executed and they shall hang him on the tree.... Their corpses shall not spend the night on the tree; instead you shall bury them that day because they are cursed by God and man, those hanged on a tree; thus you shall not defile the land that I give you for an inheritance. (11QTemple Scroll 64.7-13)*

---

[18] In this section I am much indebted to Brown, *Death of the Messiah*, 2.1209-1211.

One other factor in Jewish tradition needs to be brought into the equation. From the evidence of a number of Old Testament texts it appears to have been common practice to deny honourable burial to those convicted and executed for their crimes. In other words, burial in a family plot was denied – at least for an initial period. Relevant texts are 1 Kings 13.21-22; Jer 22.19; 26.23; 1 Enoch 98.13. This tradition lies behind the later regulation in the Mishnah (at *Sanhedrin* 6.5-6). The wider text has to do with the regulations relating to the punishment of those deserving capital punishment. Deut 21.23 is quoted (at *Sanh* 6.4), and then follows: *'They used not to bury him in the burying place of his fathers, but two burying places were kept in readiness by the court, one for them that were beheaded or strangled, and one for them that were stoned or burnt. When the flesh had been wasted away, they gathered together the bones and buried them in their own place [i.e. the family tomb].'* This text helps to make sense of the discovery in 1968 in an ossuary at Giv'at ha-Mivtar of the ankle bone of the crucified man Yehohanan. This first century man, whatever his fate during the time of his decomposition, was certainly later gathered and given an honourable second burial in the family tomb.

It is true that as yet no archaeological evidence has been found for the 'two burying places' that the Mishnah refers to and, as a result, we cannot be certain that in first century Judea such a precise provision was made. But the literary evidence surrounding the Second Temple period, both before and after, should give us confidence that in the time of Jesus those condemned to death by Jewish courts would not be allowed to be buried with their ancestors in the family tomb. For the initial period of their decay, their first burial, they were to be set apart. Open family mourning at the family site was not permitted. Theirs was what has been classified as a shame burial.[19] But their identity was not lost, and upon decomposition, an honourable second burial was allowed.

6. What, Then, of the Burial of Jesus?

What would have been the attitude of the Jewish authorities to the burial of Jesus? Prof Jodi Magness has expressed the view that Jesus was not condemned by the Jewish Council for violating Jewish Law, but by Rome for crimes against Roman authority. She adds that the capital charges in the Mishnah do not allow for crucifixion of the living, and a charge of blasphemy against Jesus would have resulted in his stoning, as occurred in the case of Stephen (Acts 7) and James. Consequently, Magness rejects the 'shame burial' hypothesis.[20]

---

[19] See Byron McCane, *Roll Back the Stone*, especially chaps 1 and 3. See also Byron McCane, '"Where no-one had yet been laid": The Shame of Jesus' Burial', in Chilton and Evans (eds), *Authenticating the Activities of Jesus* (Brill, 1999) 431-452.

[20] Jodi Magness, 'Ossuaries and the Burials of Jesus and James,' *JBL* 124/1 (2005) 140-

During the 1960s and 1970s there was much scholarly debate and research on the trial/s of Jesus. The question of the accuracy of and conflicts in the gospel accounts of Jesus' appearances before the Jewish authorities was examined, especially in relation to known later Mishnaic legislation.[21] While some questions remain unanswered, and, in theory, no historical debate can be considered closed, I consider that the following can be said concerning the Sanhedrin and its attitude to the death of Jesus:

- Jesus was tried and condemned by a constituted gathering of the High Priest's Council;
- He was condemned on a charge of blasphemy;
- At the time, the Jewish authorities did not have the *ius gladii*, the right to capital punishment. The stoning of Stephen was a case of lynch mob violence, and the death of James in AD 62 occurred during a time of Roman political vacuum in Judea.[22]
- We have already noted that Jewish texts of the time could interpret Deut 21.22 to apply to crucifixion of the living.

In other words, as I have previously indicated, the Jewish authorities had a vested interest in ensuring that the body of Jesus, the body of a blasphemer, was treated according to their law and custom. Certainly later rabbinic tradition looked upon the death of Jesus as Yahweh's just judgement against him. The Babylonian Talmud *Sanhedrin 43a* says:

> On (Sabbath eve and) the eve of Passover Jesus the Nazarene was hanged. And a herald went forth before him for forty days heralding: Jesus the Nazarene is going forth to be stoned because he practised sorcery and instigated and seduced Israel (to idolatry). Whoever knows anything in his defence may come and state it. But since they did not find anything in his defence, they hanged him on (Sabbath eve and) the eve of Passover.[23]

144.

[21] See the important collection of articles in E Bammel (ed), *The Trial of Jesus* (SCM, 1970). Also still valuable is J Blinzler, *The Trial of Jesus* (Mercier, 1959).

[22] In AD 62 the Roman procurator Porcius Festus died suddenly, to be succeeded four months later by Lucceius Albinus. In the interregnum, the ardently patriotic Sadducean High Priest, Annus II, used the power vacuum to rid himself of other popular leaders, including James. But Roman control was soon restored, and when the Jewish authorities wanted to be rid of Jesus ben Ananias, a Jewish prophet who railed against the Temple, they 'brought him before the Roman governor' (Josephus, *War* 6.309).

[23] In fact, we don't need to go any further than Paul and Josephus in the first century as supports for the position that the Jewish authorities were actively responsible (along with Pilate) for the death of Jesus. See 1 Thess 2.15 ('the Jews, who killed the Lord

It is important not to be sidetracked by the obvious differences here from the gospel accounts. As Peter Schäfer points out, 'the rabbis were certainly aware that crucifixion was the standard Roman penalty, that Jesus was indeed crucified and not stoned and hanged.' What they have done is told their story according to the Mishnaic regulations (stoning as the due penalty for idolatry and blasphemy). And they have done this in order to emphasise their own control of the fate of that arch-heretic. As Schäfer writes, it is as if the tradition now says, 'Yes indeed, ... Jesus was a Jewish heretic, who was quite successful in seducing many of us. But he was taken care of according to Jewish law, got what he deserved – and that's the end of the story.'[24]

7. Conclusion: Joseph of Arimathea and the Burial of Jesus

We may dearly wish that we had more literary light to shed on the burial of Jesus. If only the Jewish records were clearer about contemporary practice; if only the gospels had given us the historical information we are seeking rather than the more biased post-Easter perspective. But we are not entirely in the dark, and even the evidence we do have allows us to draw the following conclusions:

- Jesus was formally condemned by the Jewish authorities as a blasphemer and heretic, and was handed over to Pontius Pilate for capital punishment (which meant the real possibility of crucifixion).
- Jewish custom for centuries past, and contemporary Jewish law, did not allow for the honourable burying of those condemned for blasphemy. Family and others were not to be granted the usual mourning privileges.[25]
- In view of the obvious urgency that accompanied the Jewish arrest, interrogation, trial and handing over of Jesus – in short, their desire to have him dealt with as quickly as possible before the Festival of Passover and Unleavened Bread commenced[26] - we can be confident that they would not have countenanced any attempt by friends and family to take his body for honourable burial.
- In other words, the Jewish authorities would have considered their responsibility in the matter of the divine judgement of Jesus of Nazareth

---

Jesus'). Also Josephus (*Ant.* 19.64): 'When Pilate, upon hearing him [Jesus] accused by men of the highest standing among us, had condemned him to be crucified.'

[24] Schäfer, *Jesus in the Talmud*, 64-72. The quotes are from pages 71-72.

[25] In the mid-second century, the body of the martyred Polycarp of Smyrna was denied to the local Christians upon the urgings of the local Jews who were opposed to his being granted an honourable burial. See *Martyrdom of Polycarp* 17.2.

[26] On the dating of the death of Jesus in relation to Passover, see my *Enigmatic Jew*, 257-264.

to be complete only once they had ensured that he received the burial proper for a heretic – that is, a shame burial.

- The disciples and family of Jesus would have been under no illusions as to their rights in respect of Jesus' body. They would have known that both Jewish law and Roman custom would have meant that they could never be granted direct access to his body.

- Ben Witherington has suggested that the family and disciples of Jesus avoided making request for the body out of a sense of shame ('they may have felt that Jesus did not deserve an honourable burial'; and they 'may have been too ashamed to hang around and watch Jesus die and then place him in the tomb').[27] True, this was an honour-and-shame culture, but there is no evidence that this was a factor in the behaviour of the family and disciples.

- There is no reason to doubt the historicity of the person known to us as Joseph of Arimathea and his role in the burial of Jesus. But in what capacity did he approach Pilate? In the light of the above, the one secure conclusion we can come to is that he came before Pilate as one authorised by the High Priest and the Council. He did not act unilaterally; he did not act without their knowledge; and he did not act as the proxy of Jesus' family and disciples. Only to one authorised by the Council would Pilate have been prepared to release this particular body, a body over which so much official fuss had been made.

- But did Joseph *offer* to act on behalf of the Council? Was it because he did indeed hold quiet but positive feelings about Jesus? Or was he *delegated* to act, and only became a convert well after the event? (And if the latter, was he delegated to negotiate with Pilate for all three bodies?) About these questions there can be no certainty. The fact of his later conversion to the Christian movement does not help us, and if Mark's Gospel were all we had, we could have no reason to believe that at this stage Joseph had any special sympathies for Jesus. But if the account of assistance provided by Nicodemus is historical, then it lends support to the position that Joseph knew of Nicodemus' sympathy for Jesus (as reflected in Jn 7.50-52) and invited this quiet 'fellow-traveller' to assist with the burial.[28] On the other

---

[27] Ben Witherington, *What Have They Done With Jesus?* (HarperCollins, 2006) 126-127, 172.

[28] Commentators and scholars will disagree on whether Nicodemus' role here is an historical recollection or a theological fabrication. See the major commentaries of Beasley-Murray and Carson (historical); Brown (non-committal); Barrett (non-committal); Schnackenburg (Johannine elaboration); Bultmann, Haenchen and Lindars (legendary addition).

hand, there are four interesting texts that speak of *Jewish* responsibility for the deposition and burial of Jesus: (i) Acts 13.29: '... they [the Jews] took him down from the tree and laid him in a tomb'; (ii) Jn 19.31: the Jews asked Pilate to have the bodies removed before Sabbath;[29] (iii) *G Peter* 6.21 reads, 'And they [the Jews] pulled out the nails from the Lord's hands and placed him upon the ground.' And (iv) Justin, the mid-second century apologist wrote, 'For the Lord also remained on the tree almost until evening, and towards evening *they* buried him.' (*Dialogue with Trypho* 97.1)[30] But I am not convinced we can rely too strongly on these references. Each can be explained as due in some measure to the literary or theological interest of the writer. But if there is something behind them, then they would provide support for the view that Joseph acted, perhaps with others, as representative of the Council.

So where does this leave us with the Tabor hypothesis that has Joseph, a definite convert to the Jesus movement (though perhaps a secret one), taking upon himself to approach Pilate, gaining release of the body, burying it hastily nearby, and intending, after the Sabbath, to give him an honourable burial in a dedicated Jesus family tomb on his own estate on the outskirts of Jerusalem? And all of this without any communication on his part with the family or disciples!

The response can only be: the hurdles are too high: Joseph has to be held in good standing by the Council; the Council would have to be satisfied of Joseph's burial plans for Jesus; and Jesus' guilt in Jewish eyes requires his burial be a shame burial. There is one further point that has been ignored. If Joseph intended to provide an honourable burial for Jesus after Sabbath was concluded, that would have had to include the option for the family to come and perform the normal mourning at the grave.[31] In other words, he would have included the family in his plans. The moving of the body would have been for *their* benefit, not just for the honour of Jesus, for proper burial and family mourning went hand in hand. And yet they are kept totally in the dark over what he has done. Not only do the family members not visit the grave (they are forbidden to mourn a heretic), but even the other women who risk a visit are in total ignorance of what has been done to Jesus.

---

[29] And a few ancient texts (including original Sinaiaticus and a few western texts) at Jn 19.38 have '... so they came and they removed his body.'
[30] See Brown, *Death of the Messiah*, 2.1219.
[31] On the importance of mourning at the family tomb, see McKane, *Roll Back the Stone*, 96-98.

No, from what we know of Roman practice, contemporary Jewish law and custom, and from the literary evidence available to us, the Tabor thesis just doesn't add up.

Excurses

1. Talpiot as the Location for Arimathea

One of the puzzling features of the Joseph tradition is that the location of Arimathea is historically uncertain. Apart from Luke, the other gospels simply refer to Joseph as coming from Arimathea.[32] Luke 23.51 adds the information that this was a 'city of the Jews'. This is an interesting note on Luke's part. Elsewhere in his gospel he is quite careful to distinguish towns and districts according to whether they are Galilean or southern Judean locations (see, for example 1.26, 39; 2.4). Tabor makes the sweeping statement that Luke's knowledge of the geography of Palestine is inaccurate (229 n38), but a careful examination of Luke and Acts does not back up this claim. To be preferred is the summary statement of Pixner: 'The author of Luke and Acts demonstrates an intimate knowledge of the topography of the Holy City and its surroundings, but this contrasts with the information he provides about the area in the north of the country.'[33] If the 'we' sections of Acts indicate the presence of the author, then Luke visited Jerusalem during Paul's final visit there (Acts 20-21). He would have travelled up to Jerusalem from the coast, perhaps from Caesarea Maritima, passing Judean towns. Galilee, by contrast, would have been foreign territory to him. So it is interesting that Luke, the cautious recorder, does not identify Arimathea more closely than to tell us that it was a Jewish (as opposed to a gentile) town.[34]

Why the lack of precision? I suggest that the answer lies in a combination of factors. As a wealthy and influential man, Joseph was now resident in Jerusalem and perhaps had been so for some years. Yet, just as today Middle Eastern dwellers in a large city like Beirut, Damascus or Cairo still have their links back to their home village, so Joseph and his home village were linked in the appellation given to him in early Christian memory. When Luke came to write his gospel he inherited that appellation, 'from Arimathea'. By this

---

[32] Mk 15.43, followed by Matt 27.57-58, has a clumsy double use of 'come' which could be read to suggest that Joseph came in from Arimathea on that day and then came to Pilate. But this is unlikely to have been Mark's intent, since *ho apo Arimathaias* can really only be understood adjectivally: 'who was from the town of'.

[33] B Pixner, 'Luke and Jerusalem' in his *Paths of the Messiah*, 423-432. Pixner also makes reference to an article, unavailable to me, by M Hengel, 'Der Historiker Lukas und die Geographie Palästinas in der Apostelgeschichte,' *ZDPV* 99 (1983) 147-83.

[34] Perhaps Luke also wants to tell us that it was not one of the towns of the Decapolis or of Samaria.

time Luke had departed from Judea and had no opportunity to make further enquiries (or perhaps was not interested in the question). All that he did know was that Joseph had impeccable Jewish credentials, and so he felt justified in claiming that Joseph came from a thoroughly observant Jewish village. This proposal of mine may be wide of the mark – but at least it makes sense of Luke's unusual and imprecise phrasing.

But where was it? The short answer is, we simply don't know. Possibilities that have been proposed are Rathamin (1 Macc 11.34), Ramathain (Josephus *Ant* 13.127), Rathamaim-Zophim (1 Sam 1.1). Is it possible that Tabor is correct in his suggestion that the name derives from the Hebrew *ramathaim*, meaning 'two heights'?[35] This was adopted in the early Christian Syriac Peshitta texts, and the name was later Hellenised as Remtis, a town north of Jerusalem.

All of this uncertainty is resolved for Tabor who informs us that from Jerusalem looking south towards Talpiot 'two prominent ridges are clearly visible' (127). Arimathea, therefore, refers not to a town but a location. But this solution will not satisfy, for the following reasons:

- Luke's carefully worded phrasing, that Arimathea was a Jewish town, should not be dismissed;
- Given Luke's eventual presence in Jerusalem, we would expect him to be more certain about the locality of a site if it was only a couple of kilometres from the city;
- 'Joseph from Arimathea', as given by the evangelists, can only have referred to a known and defined town or district, even though it may have derived its name from a geographical feature;
- There is no evidence that the Talpiot area was ever given the name Arimathea.

In short, the Talpiot/Arimathea proposal will not hold. Until we are given firm evidence that that area, a few kilomtetres south of the city, was known as Ramathaim (or the like) in the first century, we can only conclude that the suggestion is without foundation. Thus, the sole literary and historical claim linking Joseph of Arimathea to Talpiot falls away.

2. What Does Mark Mean by *Tolmēsas* (Mk 15.43)

Among the unsolved puzzles in the gospels is Mark's meaning when he says that Joseph 'went boldly/dared to go before Pilate' and ask for the body of Jesus. As Allison asks: 'Does it reflect the fact (or is it Mark's guess?) that

---

[35] A suggestion already proposed by C S Mann, *Mark* (Anchor Bible; Doubleday, 1986) 657.

because Jesus was executed for high treason the Romans would be expected to deny him burial altogether?'[36] My own suggestion is that it is pointless to ask whether this represents the fact of the case (for example, as later told by Joseph to the church); all we can ask is what Mark intended by this word. Matthew and Luke obviously found its meaning unclear and omitted it. Does it indicate that Mark considered that Joseph acted on his own initiative, and that Mark was unaware that Joseph acted on behalf of the Council? Coming directly after Mark's description of Joseph's moral and spiritual character, was it meant to highlight Joseph's willingness to act with integrity even before the Roman prefect? I suspect that Mark would give an affirmative response to both these questions. But we cannot be sure.

3. The Inevitable Cover-up

Consider the following details that are either part of, or implicit in, the Tabor thesis relating to Joseph of Arimathea:

- Joseph removed the body of Jesus to a dedicated tomb complex on his estate;
- Joseph's action was intended as a positive gesture of reverence for Jesus;
- The women (and then the disciples) found the original burial site empty;
- Soon after that, perhaps even on that Sunday, Joseph would have informed the family of Jesus of his actions, so that they could now mourn for him according to custom;
- Joseph eventually became a well known member of the Jerusalem community of followers of Messiah Jesus;
- Within the Jerusalem community, the story of Joseph's honourable re-burial of Jesus would have been told and retold – told at first by Joseph, and then by others;
- That story would have been passed on outside of Jerusalem as part of the narrative of the final days and hours of Jesus' life.

In other words, within the space of a few months, and certainly within a few years, at least the main details relating to the re-burial of Jesus by Joseph of Arimathea would have been known to the Christian communities in Jerusalem and in wider Palestine and Syria. That means that probably hundreds (and perhaps thousands) of people would soon have learnt of Jesus' re-burial on the 'Arimathea Estate'. More than that, we are entitled to presume that the 'truth' of Jesus' re-burial would also have come to be known among the Jewish population in general. And yet ….

---

[36] Allison, *Resurrecting Jesus*, 363 n 643. See also comments in Brown, *Death of the Messiah*, 2.1217.

As we scour the literary material available to us from early Christianity, from rabbinic texts, or from any other sources, there is total silence. Not a single text provides any hint that Tabor may have hit upon the truth about Joseph. In our chapter on Mary Magdalene we considered and rejected the few texts that Tabor brought forward to support his theses relating to her marriage to Jesus and suppressed knowledge of her status in the early days of the Christian movement. In the case of Joseph, however, Tabor presents us with not a single piece of evidence. On the contrary, we have already noted that in the second century *Gospel of Peter*, the only detail that is known is that the place of *original* burial became known as Joseph's Garden. No other tradition had found its way to that author.

That, I believe, leads us to only two possible conclusions: either Tabor has uncovered what can only be considered the most astounding cover-up by virtually every member of the early Christian movement in Jerusalem and beyond, or there is no story here at all!

Chapter Nine
RESURRECTION IN EARLY CHRISTIAN THINKING

The fourth and final hurdle that the Tabor/Jacobovici thesis must overcome relates to the traditional understanding of what the early Christian community believed about the resurrection of Jesus.

1. Rethinking Resurrection Belief

As we have seen, the Jesus tomb claims require us to accept the following reading of the historical data:

- The first, temporary, tomb of Jesus was found by Mary Magdalene/some women to be empty.
- Joseph of Arimathea had removed the body of Jesus some time after the conclusion of the Sabbath, and had placed it in a new tomb complex situated on his own estate.
- After the conclusion of the festival of Unleavened Bread, the disciples returned to Galilee.
- In due time Peter, followed by the others including James, had visionary experiences that convinced them that Jesus was not dead but alive. They began to speak of him as being resurrected.
- At no time did these disciples consider that their belief in Jesus' resurrection meant that his physical body was not interred in the tomb provided by Joseph. On the contrary: the 'early followers of Jesus would have visited the Jesus family tomb and declared their resurrection faith, while honoring and remembering their revered teacher, the one they believed was the Messiah.'[1]
- The apostle Paul supports this way of thinking about resurrection. Firstly, he knows nothing of the (later) empty tomb traditions; secondly, he likens his own visionary experience of the resurrected Jesus with those of the apostles before him (1 Cor 15.8); and thirdly, he speaks of a contrast between the old 'flesh and blood' and the spiritual body that is the focus of Christian hope (1 Cor 15.42-50).
- The resurrection appearance stories in Luke and John, in which Jesus appears bodily before the disciples, were created and written in the last decades of the first century AD, and have distorted the earliest Palestinian Christian beliefs about the resurrection of Jesus. As a result of the

---

[1] This quote comes from an article written by James Tabor and posted on his web site. See 'Why People are Confused about the Earliest Christian View of Resurrection of the Dead' at http://www.jamestabor.com.

legendary narratives in Luke and John, the resurrection of Jesus has come to be seen as the restoration to life of Jesus' physical body, something the first Christians did not hold to.

- All of the above is in line with contemporary Jewish resurrection beliefs. Those beliefs held that while God was expected to raise the dead to live again in an embodied form, that body will be a transformed one and would have 'nothing to do with the former physical body'. The old physical body, now turned to dust, and the hoped for future spiritual body, are entirely different from each other. *'That is why the presence of bones – even the bones of Jesus – next to statements of faith in resurrection, was not a contradiction'*.[2]

A detailed response to these claims would require a separate monograph.[3] Instead, I want to concentrate on the key points being made by Tabor. In Chapter 8 we have already discussed the role of Joseph of Arimathea, along with contemporary Jewish practice and regulations regarding the disposal of the bodies of condemned criminals and others.

At the outset, it needs to be recognised that much of what Tabor has written is not new. Both at the academic and the popular level others have gone before him in claiming that the disciples had certain visionary experiences and called it resurrection, that Paul was ignorant of empty tomb traditions and had no place for them, and that many of the gospel tomb and appearance stories are later legends.[4] Having said that, and without proceeding to a detailed response, we can consider the following questions:

2. What Did 'Resurrection' Mean in Contemporary Judaism?

Belief in resurrection was a long time coming to Judaism. In fact, it was not until the 2nd century BC that we find it being given clear and unambiguous expression. And when it does emerge, it is in the context not of individual but of corporate hope. In other words, resurrection hope is the developed expectation that when Israel's God establishes the rule of peace and plenty that he has always promised for his people, those faithful saints of old who would otherwise have missed out will be resurrected to enjoy the fruits of

---

[2] From the Tabor article cited above. Italics original.

[3] Such as I have covered in my *Jesus Resurrected? sifting the historical evidence* (Createspace, 2011). Though not written with the Tabor thesis in mind, it provides a detailed response to the issues it raises, especially in chapters 1, 2 and 7.

[4] At the academic level, see G Lüdemann, *The Resurrection of Jesus* (SCM, 1994); and AJM Wedderburn, *Beyond Resurrection* (SCM, 1999). At the popular level, Bp J S Spong, *Resurrection: Myth or Reality?*

their faithfulness. The first unambiguous expressions of this hope can be seen in Isa 26.19 and especially Dan 12.1-3.

But did this hope presuppose the raising of dead bodies? There is no Jewish treatise on resurrection that directly answers our question, but a combination of factors leads us to the conclusion that for any 1st century Jew, talk of resurrection could only imply the raising and transforming of a decayed body:

- The first thing to note is that in the Judaism of the times, resurrection hope did not hold universal sway. In fact, a range of attitudes could be found concerning what happened at death.[5] For some Jews, death was final, and from the grave 'there is no coming back' (Sirach 38.21; see also Sirach 14.18-19). As Mattathias charges his sons from his death bed, he recounts the glories of the faithful ancestors from Abraham on. But it is their memory that lives on, nothing more (1 Macc 2.49-70). For other contemporary Jewish writings, especially those influenced by hellenistic thinking, the language of the soul's immortality, separated from the body, is used to describe the post-death state. For example, the late 1st century AD text 4 Maccabees concludes at 18.23 with: 'But the sons of Abraham, together with their mother, who won the victor's prize, are gathered together in the choir of their fathers, having received pure and deathless souls from God, to whom be glory for ever and ever. Amen.' The point to be observed from this is that Judaism was not confined to resurrection language when it wanted to speak about what happened at death or what could be expected beyond the grave.

- Other texts from intertestamental Judaism, however, do indicate that resurrection is central to their beliefs. A good example is 4 Ezra 7.32-33a: 'The earth shall give up those who are asleep in it, and the dust those who rest there in silence; and the chambers shall give up the souls that have been committed to them. The Most High shall be revealed on the seat of judgement.' Other relevant passages are 1 Enoch 51.1; 62.14-16; 2 Baruch 50.2, 4; 2 Macc 7.1-23 (espec. verses 10-11).[6]

- As already mentioned, there is no systematic Jewish treatise on resurrection. But whenever we do find an attempt to describe resurrection, it is common for it to be portrayed in rather crude terms. For example, Rabbi Ishmael (AD 120-140) wrote: 'When the Holy One, blessed be He,

---

[5] A most useful and thorough survey of contemporary Jewish attitudes to death and post-death existence is given by N T Wright, *The Resurrection of the Son of God* (Fortress, 2003) 85-206.

[6] Though 4 Ezra and 2 Baruch postdate Paul, they nonetheless are relevant to our enquiry.

calls to the earth to return all the bodies deposited with it, that which has become mixed with the dust of the earth improves and increases and raises up all the bodies without water'.[7]

- The early second century AD document *2 Baruch* even writes of a two stage resurrection process. At first, on the day of resurrection 'the earth will surely give back the dead ... not changing anything in their form.... For then it will be necessary to show those who live that the dead are living again, and that those who went away have come back.' (50.2-3) Then 'after this day' each resurrected one will receive its due reward, and those who have proven to be righteous will be transformed: 'their splendour will then be glorified by transformation, and the shape of their face will be changed into the light of their beauty so that they may acquire and receive the undying world that is promised to them.' (51.1-3)

- There has been considerable debate as to whether bodily resurrection hope was integral to Essene theology. The reason for this is twofold: Josephus' report of the Essenes uses Hellenistic soul and immortality language to speak of their post-death hopes;[8] and the Dead Sea Scrolls provide little evidence of systematic consideration of the question. Nonetheless, in two Scroll fragments (4Q385 *frag* 2 and 4Q386 *col* 1) we find the dead bones vision of Ezekiel 37, which originally referred to the restoration of national fortune, unity and life after exile, now applied to the revivifying of mortals, so that they will rise up to bless the Lord.

This leads to the conclusion that in contemporary Judaism, when resurrection language was used, it was intended to be understood quite literally. It is just too simplistic to suggest that because the resurrection body was expected to be a transformed body, it therefore 'has nothing to do with the former physical body'. Nor does Jesus' dialogue with the Sadducees over the nature of resurrection existence (see Mk 12.18-27/Matt 22.23-33/Lk 20.27-40) establish that point. It is true that Jesus says that the resurrected ones will exist in a transformed world, where today's familial relationships will no longer apply. We can agree with Tabor that they will be in a transformed body. But this does not establish that there is no presumed link between the old, decayed body and the resurrected bodily life. In fact all of the evidence we have suggests the very opposite: though it was never systematically worked out, *when, in the Judaism of Jesus' and Paul's days, resurrection hope was spoken of, it always implied both continuity and discontinuity with the decayed mortal body.*

---

[7] *Pirkê de Rabbi Eliezer* 24.
[8] See *Jewish War* 2.154-158; *Antiquities* 18.18.

3. Did Paul Know of or Presume the Empty Tomb?

On this matter we can make the following points:

- It is illegitimate to argue that when Paul writes in 1 Cor 15.3-4 that 'Christ died for our sins in accordance with the scriptures, he was buried, and was raised on the third day in accordance with the scriptures', since he is silent on the emptiness of the tomb, he is thereby ignorant of it. As all scholars recognise, Paul is here quoting what was perhaps the earliest Christian credal formula, probably created in the earliest days of the new movement. Creeds are neat, repeatable statements, not wordy declamations. What we need to ask is: 'When the earliest believers repeated this creed, what did they presume about the body of Jesus?' In the light of what we know of Jewish belief about resurrection, I believe that J C O'Neill was correct when he wrote: if the credal formula had not presumed the tomb was empty, it 'would have omitted the words "he was raised" and have written "he was buried and on the third day appeared to Cephas"'.[9]
- In other words, the argument from silence leads us not to the conclusion that Paul and the earliest Christian community were ignorant of, or cared nothing about, the location of Jesus' body. On the contrary, we are entitled to presume that they took it for granted that the body of Jesus had been raised (and transformed) 'on the third day'.
- Whether Paul actually knew of the details of the discovery of the empty tomb we will never discover. On his first post-conversion visit to Jerusalem (Gal 1.18-19) he may well have made enquiries along those lines, but we will never know. In fact, we may be entitled to express surprise that when

---

[9] J C O'Neill

in 1 Cor 15 Paul writes a clear defence of the concept of resurrection,[10] he nowhere makes mention of the raising of Jesus' body and the emptiness of the tomb. Surely, it may be claimed, that would have clinched his case in opposition to the Corinthian doubters. And perhaps it would have – but we need to be careful not to presume to tell Paul what he should or should not have written.

4. Does Paul Believe the Future Spiritual Body is Unrelated to the Old Physical Body?

Tabor (and other scholars) make much of the clear distinction that Paul presents in 1 Corinthians 15 between the old, 'flesh and blood' body that he calls the physical body (the *sōma psychikon* – v 44) and the new spiritual body (the *sōma pneumatikon*). Indeed, the distinction between the two is so powerfully argued by Paul from verse 35 through to verse 50, that one is entitled to agree that Paul is arguing against those who want to dismiss the notion of resurrection, since they considered that it involves the crude belief in the resuscitation of dead bodies.[11] But did he draw a sharp distinction between the old and the new, such that they were essentially unrelated, as Tabor claims? Verses 51-55 give the lie to this suggestion, and it is noteworthy that these verses are never mentioned by Tabor. These verses need to be understood in the context of Paul's current expectation that Christ would return within his lifetime and in the lifetime of the majority of the Corinthians. Having spelled out the fundamental difference between the old body and the new, Paul now concludes by relating it to the existence of the Corinthians: '*Behold, I tell you a mystery: we shall not all sleep, but we shall all be changed. In a moment, in the twinkling of an eye, at the last trumpet call. For the trumpet will sound, the dead will be raised imperishable, and we shall be changed.*' Without doubt, there is both continuity and discontinuity here, for those alive at the coming of Christ will undergo bodily transformation. In no sense does Paul think of those believers who are alive at Christ's coming simply leaving their old bodies behind, as though they will be parked forever like old cars in a scrap metal yard, while they walk around in their transformed spiritual bodies. No, the old is taken up and transformed into the new. 'We will all be changed' can mean nothing less.

, 'On the Resurrection as an Historical Question,' in S Sykes and J Clayton (eds), *Christ, Faith and History* (CUP, 1972) 208.

[10] 1 Cor 15 is in fact the first systematic Jewish treatise on resurrection.

[11] The interpretation of the situation that prompted 1 Cor 15 has been the subject of much study. See the major commentaries; also N T Wright, *The Resurrection of the Son of God*, 312-361; Murray J Harris, *Raised Immortal – Resurrection and Immortality in the New Testament* (Eerdmans, 1983) espec chaps 4, 8.

Paul's theological presentation in 1 Corinthians 15 (along with what he writes later in 2 Corinthians 4-5) represents the most detailed contemporary Jewish defence of resurrection. And it is clear from it that Paul could never have come to faith in a resurrected Messiah of whom it was known that his decaying body was safely interred in a family tomb outside of Jerusalem.

5. Did Paul Consider His Visionary Experiences Matched Those of the Apostles?

I have dealt at length with this question in my *Jesus Resurrected?*[12] On three occasions Paul makes reference to his experience of the risen Christ (1 Cor 9.1; 15.8; Gal 1.16). On the surface, these verses look as though Paul is claiming that his and the apostles' visions of Christ were exactly the same in expression. But there are two problems with this line of reasoning. Firstly, what Paul is claiming, particularly in 1 Cor 9.1 and 15.8, is not that his vision of Christ had the same *form* as those of the apostles before him, but that it had the same *quality and value*. That is, in defending his apostolic credentials he wants it to be clear that the risen Christ has appeared to him also. Secondly, in the three accounts of Paul's Damascus Road conversion provided by Luke in Acts (9.1-19; 22.6-16; 26.12-18) it is clear that Luke considers Paul's experience as being quite different from that of the apostles, recorded in Luke 24. While Luke tells us that Paul saw the risen Jesus (9.17, 27; 26.16), what actually is recorded is the hearing of the voice of Jesus and the seeing of blinding light. Now, all are agreed that for Luke, Paul's apostolic status is in no way inferior to that of Peter and the other apostles. And yet he undoubtedly presents Paul's experience of the risen Christ as being different in expression from that of the apostles.

These two factors render it invalid for us to work back from Paul's claims of his visions of Christ (or the Lukan reports of Paul's visions in Acts) to the resurrection experiences of the apostles. If Luke can see no conflict between the different *form* of the apostles' and Paul's experiences and their equality of *status and value*, neither should we presume that Paul saw things any differently. That the risen Jesus appeared to him just as he appeared to Cephas, James and the Twelve was all that mattered.[13]

6. Luke 24 and John 20-21 – Are They Late First Century Legends?

The resurrection appearances in these two chapters have undoubtedly been shaped by the evangelists to suit their particular thematic and theological

---

[12] See *Jesus Resurrected?* 35-38.

[13] Against Tabor in *Jesus Dynasty*, 232: 'Also, Paul equates his own "sighting" of Jesus, which was clearly "visionary", with those of the original founders – possibly implying that their experiences were much like his.'

interests.[14] But are they simply late first century fabrications, and do they present a crude 'resuscitated body' view of the resurrection of Jesus, as Tabor insists? The evidence will not support these claims. The following points can be made, in brief:

- The Emmaus road incident (Lk 24.13-35), for all its Lukan shaping, appears to owe its origins to the memory of the family of Jesus. It is widely recognised that the Cleopas mentioned in the narrative is the brother of Jesus' father, Joseph, and whose son, Simeon, is chosen to replace James as leader of the Christian movement after the latter is killed in AD 62.[15] There is no reason to think that Luke would fabricate a narrative and introduce a relative of Jesus at a time when that relative was still living.

- The appearance stories in Luke 24.36-49 and John 20.19-23, for all their differences, have striking similarities: sudden appearance of Jesus; 'Peace be with you' spoken; Jesus shows his hands and side/feet as demonstration of his reality; commission to preach forgiveness of sins; bestowal of the Spirit. Beyond reasonable doubt, Luke and John are not the originators of these stories, but they have drawn upon a common tradition. That immediately pushes the origin of these stories back into the period of oral tradition – they can no longer be seen as 'legendary accounts written many decades after the events'.[16]

- But how far back can we go? It's impossible to say, but two points can be made. Firstly, if the earliest believers knew the early creed in 1 Cor 15.3-5, it is only reasonable to presume that they also had the details of that creed filled out in their catechetical teaching. In other words, you don't recite your belief that Jesu appeared to Peter and the twelve without wanting to know the details of those appearances. That would suggest that resurrection appearance accounts existed from the very beginning of the early church's life. Secondly, if we are to accept that Paul's companion, Luke, was the author of Luke-Acts, and if we are to believe him when he says that he accompanied Paul to Jerusalem (see Acts 21.3), then it is only reasonable to presume that he used his time there to gather details for his future writing.[17]

---

[14] See *Jesus Resurrected?* 73-86.

[15] See Bauckham, *Jude and the Relatives of Jesus,* chaps 1-2, espec. pp 79-94.

[16] Quote from article 'Why People are Confused' in James Tabor blog (see footnote 1 above). See also *Jesus Discovery*, 194-5.

[17] I recognise that the Lukan authorship of Luke-Acts is contested, as is also the question of whether the 'we' passages of Acts represent real autobiographical detail. On these see the introductions in major commentaries. The point I am making is simply that the case for regarding Luke as mere fabricator of his accounts has many

- And how crudely physical is the resurrected Jesus of Luke and John? He certainly is able to materialise, show his bodily parts, and eat. But he also appears and disappears suddenly, and is incapable of being automatically recognised. Surely what Luke and John give us is nothing more than what Paul is arguing for in 1 Cor 15, namely an expression of the continuity and discontinuity between the crucified Jesus and the risen Lord. It is too simplistic to suggest that Luke and John present us with a resurrected Jesus who comes back 'in the same body that had been placed in the tomb', as though he is merely resuscitated, for it fails to appreciate the subtlety of sameness yet difference that Luke, John and Paul all wish to convey.

- There is one final text that should be mentioned, Matt 27.52-53. Matthew records that as Jesus dies, an earth tremor cracks open the ground in Jerusalem, '*and the tombs were opened and many bodies of the saints who slept were raised, and came forth from their tombs after he was raised, entered the city, and appeared to many.*' The issue of the historicity of this detail is difficult to defend and, fortunately, need not concern us,[18] but its significance for our current discussion is important. We cannot say whether Matthew has inherited this tradition or is responsible for its creation, but what we can affirm is that it would have had no place in Matthew's gospel if he had not presumed that the resurrected Jesus was also bodily raised. Unlike Luke and John, Matthew may not have provided us with accounts of the risen Jesus revealing himself bodily to his disciples, but it is obvious that he shared the same outlook as those other two evangelists, and presumed that his readers did also.

Conclusion.

From the literary evidence available to us, the case that Tabor and Jacobovici present for the early Christians' beliefs about the state of the resurrected Jesus is unsustainable. We can say with confidence that no first century Jew could have visited the tomb of Jesus, knowing it held his decaying body, and at the same time rejoice in the belief that he had been resurrected. The two were mutually contradictory.

---

weaknesses, and is certainly not self-evident, as Tabor seems to suggest. It is also noteworthy that Luke's knowledge of Jerusalem and its physical environs appears to be much more exact than his flimsy knowledge of Galilee's geography. See Bargil Pixner, 'Luke and Jerusalem' in his *Paths of the Messiah*, 423-432.

[18] Even many conservative scholars are prepared to accept that Matthew may be making more of a theological statement than reflecting an historical event. See, for example, D Hagner, *Matthew 14-28* (WBC 33B; Word, 1995) 851.

Part C

Under the Microscope

The Talpiot Ossuaries and the Jesus Family Tomb Thesis

Chapter Ten
THREE TALPIOT B OSSUARIES – WITNESSES TO JUDAEO-CHRISTIAN FAITH?[1]

We turn now to the Talpiot B tomb and the three ossuaries within it that have some kind of inscription or marking. For Tabor and Jacobovici these three ossuaries provide all the evidence they need to establish their earlier claims about the Jesus Family Tomb. And the tomb itself 'provides the earliest archaeological evidence of faith in Jesus' resurrection from the dead, the first witness to a saying of Jesus that predates even the writing of our New Testament gospels, and the earliest example of Christian art'. (*Discovery* 1) Very strong claims indeed! When an historian uses phrases like 'clear and unambiguous' and 'the connection to Jesus is direct and explicit', (*Discovery* 184) one expects the interpretation of the evidence to be both universally acknowledged and unassailable. In fact, the opposite has been the case. In relation to the claims made both for Talpiot A and for Talpiot B, one can say only that the scholarly community worldwide has given an almost unanimous 'thumbs down'. Even a cursory websearch will reveal scores of responses from respected academics, liberal and conservative, religious and non-religious, who dismiss the Tabor claims as unjustified. Indeed, some of the responses have been quite scathing. And yet, from my reading of the various blog responses that he has provided, it appears that Tabor continues to hold to his essential claims.

1. Ossuary 5 – The Four Line Inscription

The four line inscription that is clearly discernible on ossuary 5 is interpreted by Tabor and Jacobovici as clear evidence that it contained the bones of a Jewish believer in Jesus. There are two indicators for this claim:

- The four letters of the second line are read as a Greek version of the Hebrew Tetragrammaton, the four letter divine name (usually anglicised as Yahweh). This indicates that the deceased was Jewish, but no ordinary Jew. For according to Tabor and Jacobovici, the writing of the divine name on an ossuary would be considered heretical, and this establishes that the deceased and his/her family has become liberated from some of the rigid controls of Jewish life. And someone from the new Judaeo-Christian movement, by reason of their new resurrection faith, would fit this description. (*Jesus Discovery* 127-128)

---

[1] The ossuaries in Talpiot B have no classification number either from the IAA or in Rahmani since they remain *in situ*.

- The three Greek letters of line three (ΥΨΩ) and which all agree are related to the Greek verb *hupsoon*, are interpreted to have something to do with resurrection: either faith in Jesus' resurrection or hope/prayer that the deceased will be resurrected – or both! (*Discovery* 93-94)

Unfortunately, the ossuary's inscription is not as unambiguous as Tabor and Jacobovici would have us believe.[2] We consider each line in order.

1.1 Line 1 – ΔΙΟΣ

It is possible that this word is being used as a noun (the possessive/genitive of Zeus), or as an adjective (meaning: divine, wondrous, majestic). Tabor and Jacobovici opt for the second possibility, and they may be correct. But another possibility has been suggested by Bauckham, whereby the first two lines are to be translated as 'belonging to Zeus Yahweh'. (What exactly belongs to Zeus Yahweh need not delay us now – we consider the question later.) There is plenty of evidence from the Greek world of altars and other sacred objects bearing the inscription ΔΙΟΣ + an additional epithet. If this were to be the background to our Ossuary 5, and if line 2 is read as referring to Yahweh (see below), it would be the only known example from the period where Zeus and Yahweh are identified together. The Maccabean Revolt of the 2nd century BC had put a stop to all Jewish hellenistic attempts to identify Yahweh with Zeus.

1.2 Line 2 – IAIO

There remains some doubt as to whether this is a reference to the tetragrammaton. The problem lies with the reading of the first letter – unlike the other two uses of 'I' in the inscription (letter 2 in line 1, and letter 3 in line 2) this 'I' has horizontal bars across the top and bottom. Rollston, an acknowledged epigrapher, says that in the use of the Greek script of the period, the upper case *iota* consistently lacks the horizontal bars. That leaves us with the obvious question: if not an *iota*, what is it? Unfortunately, Rollston does not commit himself, suggesting it may be a 'T' or a 'Z', but in any case 'there is no tetragrammaton here'. Bauckham comes to our assistance here, in providing evidence from ossuary inscriptions that counters Rollston's assertion: an *iota* with top and bottom horizontals is found on several ossuary inscriptions. Why, then, the horizontal bars on this *iota* and not the other two? Bauckham suggests that the horizontally barred *iota* is used at the commencement of the four lettered IAIO in order to mark out the word as special.

---

[2] In what follows I will be drawing from two helpful and detailed responses from Prof Christopher Rollston (dated 2.28.2012) and Dr Richard Bauckham (dated 3/8/2012), both from the ASOR Blog.

Where does this leave us with lines 1 and 2? It would be a bold scholar who is willing to assert with confidence that these two lines are unambiguously clear. Rollston may just be correct: the first letter of line 2 may not be an *iota* at all. The weakness of his claim is that no other contender strongly presents itself – the T (*tau*) and Z (*zeta*) suggestions do not commend themselves. Bauckham's evidence of the presence of the horizontally barred *iota* on ossuaries is impressive, but his suggestion for its presence at the beginning of line 2 and absence elsewhere will convince some but not others. On balance, I am inclined to agree with Bauckham (and hence with Tabor and Jacobovici) that line 2 does present us with a Greek version of the tetragrammaton.

Even if we accept line 2 as a reference to Yahweh, we are not out of the woods, for line 1 still puzzles. For the sake of the argument, let us consider both options and ask whether either could represent the theological outlook of a pious Jewish believer in the resurrected Jesus. As to Bauckham's proposal ('belonging to Zeus Yahweh'), this can only represent the outlook of a true Jewish hellenist, one who is prepared to invoke the language of Greek mythology and apply it to the god of Israel. This is a far cry from the picture we get of the first generation of Jerusalem-based Judaeo-Christians. For them, such was their commitment to the Law that they looked with deep suspicion upon the missionary practice of Paul in the gentile world. However much Luke has attempted to protect his presentation of the relationship between James and Paul, one cannot but see that Paul's Torah-free gospel to the gentiles was a real problem to large numbers of Jerusalem-based believers (see Acts 15; 21-26).[3] The naming of Zeus, the head of the Greek pantheon, alongside the god of Israel would have been unthinkable for any of the early Judaeo-Christians, of that we may be confident.

Nor does the adjectival option (ΔΙΟΣ = divine/marvellous/brilliant) sit much more comfortably. The problem here is that it is a poetic word, found only rarely once we get beyond Greek classical literature, and never in the Septuagint (LXX), the New Testament or early Christian writings. For a devout Judaeo-Christian who wanted to give praise to Israel's god, even one at home in the Greek language, *dios* would not be the natural choice to reflect the character of Yahweh. It does not form part of his normal vocabulary when thinking of Israel's god. Rather, he would search his Old Testament and the prayers taught him since childhood, and come up with something more appropriate, even if he had to abbreviate it. Adjectives such as holy (*hagios*) and faithful (*pistos*) would come to mind, but never *dios*.

---

[3] See also Painter, *Just James*, 42-102.

No, whichever way you look at it, even siding with Bauckham against Rollston, the first two lines of the inscription do not reflect the piety of anyone from the band of early believers in the resurrected Jesus.

Before passing to line 3, we need also to put to rest the other claim of Tabor and Jacobovici, namely, that the writing of the divine name, the tetragrammaton, was considered heretical by Jews and could only have been done by someone who had been liberated from some of the legalities of Jewish law. This, in fact, is incorrect. Rather, it is the pronouncing of the divine name that will exclude one from having any portion in the world to come. This is best articulated in the Mishnah at *Sanhedrin* 10.1: '*And these are the ones who have no portion in the world to come: he who says, the resurrection of the dead is a teaching which does not derive from the Torah ... Rabbi Aqiba says, "Also, he who reads in heretical books ..." Abba Saul says, "Also, he who pronounces the divine Name as it is spelled out."*'[4] In any case, the four Greek letters of our inscription are not the letters of the divine name but an attempted Greek transliteration.[5]

1.3 Line 3 – ΥΨΩ

In the light of the Tabor/Jacobovici interpretation of this line, two questions need to be put: are these three letters an abbreviation (of either *hupsōsei* ['he will exalt/raise up'] or *hupsōson* ['exalt/raise up']; and is the meaning related to resurrection hope? It is true that the verb *hupsoon* can be used to express resurrection hope, but that is not the primary sense in which the verb is used either in the Septuagint or in contemporary secular Greek, where it means either to lift up, raise up (in the literal sense) or to exalt or elevate. And in view of the possibility that lines 1 and 2 refer to Yahweh, it is worth pointing out that *hupsoon* is used in the LXX in reference to exalting the name of Yahweh – see Ps 34.3; 148.13; Isa 12.4; Jdth 16.1.[6] Nor need ΥΨΩ be read as an abbreviation, for the three Greek letters can stand on their own as the first person singular, present indicative active of the verb *hupsoon*, to be translated 'I exalt/raise up'. This is the natural reading of the line, particularly when we bear in mind that the abbreviation of verbs on inscriptions is rare. And where it does occur, it is

---

[4] Also *m Sanh* 7.5: 'The blasphemer is not culpable unless he pronounces the Name itself' - as everyone who has seen the Monty Python film *The Life of Brian* can testify!
[5] Discussion of line 2 and the writing of the divine name has been somewhat simplified, but is fundamentally true to the contemporary situation. One could, however, mention that Greek transcription of the divine name was more usually (but not always) given by three letters IAO; and that there is some evidence that, out of reverence, Jewish piety would sometimes vary the transcription of the divine name in non-biblical texts. See Harry Gamble, *Books and Readers in the Early Church* (Yale Uni Press, 1995) 75-76 + notes 120, 123.
[6] I owe these references to Bauckham.

almost unheard of for the abbreviation to consist of the first letters only – the reason being that the verb's number, mood, voice and possibly tense are left to be guessed. That is why Tabor and Jacobovici are unable to decide how they should translate the three letters. We can, I suggest, conclude with confidence that ΥΨΩ on the inscription should be read in its natural sense and simply as 'I exalt' - it has nothing to do with resurrection belief or hope.

1.4 Line 4 – ΑΓΒ

This line had proven to be the most difficult of all to make sense of. All acknowledge it is not a Greek word, and therefore it probably represents a Greek transliteration of a Hebrew word. But a transliteration of what? Tabor and Jacobovici suggested that it derives from the Hebrew verb *gabah*, which in its Hiphil form means to make high, exalt. In the Old Testament the verb can apply to things (trees: Ezek 17.25; nests: Jer 49.16 and Job 39.27) and people (the lowly: Ezek 21.26). On our inscription, then, the last line requests Yahweh to raise up the deceased (in resurrection) just as the deceased has metaphorically raised up Yahweh (in exaltation). As Bauckham neatly puts it: 'the writer proposes a kind of quid pro quo'. This option is certainly possible, but it raises the immediate question: why has the author chosen to use a Hebrew verb that is not otherwise associated with resurrection?

Bauckham has come forward with a further suggestion. He reminds us that the letters ΑΓΒ can be read as the family name of the deceased, Hagab. That name appears in Ezra 2.45, 46; and Neh 7.48, on some earlier ostraca and seals, and also in the LXX (1 Esd 5.30). We also meet it in the New Testament at Acts 11.28: Agabus is an early Jerusalem based Christian prophet, so we know that the name persisted into Late Second Temple times.[7] This proposal has the attraction of bringing onto the ossuary the name of the deceased, otherwise lacking in the Tabor/Jacobovici proposal.

1.5 Further Observations

Most ossuary inscriptions are haphazardly located and frequently poorly written. What is interesting about the four line inscription on ossuary 5 is that it is very carefully and centrally placed on a facing side. On either side of it and coming up into an arch shape are two columns. The whole face of the ossuary gives the impression of having been carefully designed to make the

---

[7] Bauckham further notes that the Hebrew word means 'grasshopper' or 'locust'. This suggests that what was once a nickname in time became a family name. Rahmani, at *CJO* 498, also lists an ossuary with the name *Ioulia trōksallis* inscribed on it. *Trōksallis* is the Greek for 'grasshopper'. Rahmani suggests that the deceased Julia was so called either because of a personal trait, or because she belonged to a family named Hagab.

inscription the centrepiece. This, along with the unique reference to Yahweh on an ossuary, calls for explanation.

Bauckham has an intriguing proposal which draws our attention to a similar arched pattern on some coins of the Bar Kokhba Revolt (AD 132-135).[8] On these also an object may be observed in the centre of the arch, and this is now taken by some to be an image of the ark of the covenant in the sanctuary of the Temple, which the Jewish rebels had vowed to rebuild. Similarly, suggests Bauckham, this inscription is a representation of the ark of the covenant and it is thus fitting that the divine name should have been written. It also explains what it is that can be considered as 'belonging to Zeus Yahweh' – it is the ark itself.

Figure 14. *Bar Kokhba Coin with Ark of the Covenant*

This is a fascinating proposal that merits careful consideration by the scholarly community. But questions will need to be answered, not least why an ossuary of the first century AD (that is, before the First Jewish Revolt and while the Temple was still standing) should take up the imagery of the ark and apply it to a dedicated ossuary. That there was no ark in the Second Temple makes it even more puzzling why this image should have been chosen. In respect of the Bar Kokhba coins, while I agree that they portray the façade of the Temple Sanctuary, it is not clear that the Ark of the Covenant is also portrayed. For my money, it is just a representation of the entry doors of the Sanctuary.[9] Thus, I remain impressed but unconvinced by the ark of the covenant hypothesis.

Perhaps of more assistance to us may be later tombstones that have engraved on them an arch or gate, inside of which is an inscription that names the

---

[8] An excellent example is at http://www.livius.org/a/1/judaea/bar_kochba_coin1.jpg.

[9] Three excellent reconstructions of the Sanctuary façade (including the Bar Kokhba coins and the Dura Europos fresco) are shown on p 27 of R Hachlili, *Ancient Jewish Art and Archaeology in the Land of Israel* (Brill, 1988).

deceased. An example of these was found near Kerak in southern Jordan (see Fig.15) and its Greek reads, 'Meteria of Mazabanus (died at) age four'.[10] Such a parallel would lend support to Bauckham's reading of line 4.

Figure 15. *Tombstone and Inscription from Kerak (B Bagatti)*

1.6 Conclusions

What conclusions may we draw from this inscription? I believe we can with some confidence round off our discussion as follows:

- There is a good chance that the first two lines are an invocation to Yahweh – though it is just possible that Rollston is correct and that line 2 does not refer to Yahweh.
- We must remain uncertain whether *dios* in line 1 is intended to be read adjectivally ('marvellous Yahweh') or as a reference to Zeus ('of Zeus Yahweh')
- The most natural reading of line 3, particularly coming after the invocation to Yahweh in line 2, is 'I exalt'.
- Line 4 is probably best taken as the name of the deceased, Hagab, rather than as an abbreviation of a Hebrew verb.
- It is highly unlikely that the inscription has anything to do with resurrection hope.
- Even if in the unlikely possibility that resurrection hope is being alluded to in lines 3 or 4, it cannot be an expression of Jesus-focussed resurrection hope. That is, this ossuary cannot have housed the remains of a first century Judaeo-Christian.

---

[10] I owe this detail to B Bagatti, *The Church of the Circumcision – History and Archaeology of the Judaeo-Christians* (Franciscan Printing, 1984) 198-199.

If I have to give my own judgement on the translation of the inscription, I will opt for the following: 'I, Hagab, exalt Zeus Yahweh', with another option coming a close second: 'I, Hagab, exalt marvellous Yahweh'.

In other words, for various reasons this ossuary is a valuable addition to our material relating to early Judaism, but it has no contribution to make to the study of early Christianity. The person whose bones it housed was certainly not a committed follower of the resurrected Jesus.

Postscript: Prof Bauckham's New Interpretation

Professor Bauckham has drawn my attention to the fact that he has now radically altered his interpretation of the four line inscription (see his paper in Mark Goodacre's NTBlog of 1 August, 2012). His new interpretation rests upon the following observations and judgements:

- The majority of ossuary inscriptions give only the name of the deceased;
- Unconventional spellings are not unusual on ossuaries;
- The 'O' in line one represents a correction of the previous Greek letter Υ;
- The first letter of line two is not the Greek *iota*, I, but *tau*: T;
- The first nine letters (i.e. down to the Y in line three) direct us to the name of the deceased, Dositheos. They should be read as the genitive form of the noun, namely, Dositheou – 'belonging to Dositheos'
- The final five letters, ΨΩΑΓΒ, direct us to the final (but one) and the first three letters of the Greek alphabet. This suggests the application of alphabetic magic to protect the bones from disturbance, for which evidence has been found in other Jewish tombs.

Bauckham concludes that the ossuary thus housed the remains of a Jew who went by the name of Dositheos, who employed magic arts to protect his bones from grave robbers.

This is an intriguing interpretation, one that departs radically from suggestions that have gone before. It deserves careful scrutiny by the academic community, especially the restricted league of recognised epigraphers. It matters not that the inscription's words are not confined to a single line (see Figure 15 above) Factors for consideration will include the reading of the letters – in line one, is the second letter an *upsilon*, Υ, and not an *iota*, I? And is the *omicron*, O, in line one a correction of the previous letter? As to the alphabetic magic in lines three and four, has Bauckham satisfactorily explained the presence of the *alpha*, A? We await the judgement of the experts.

In any case, if Bauckham's revised 'final solution' (as he modestly calls it – no doubt tongue in cheek!) does prove to be correct, we can with confidence conclude that far from expressing any hope in resurrection by Israel's God, or any hint of belief in the resurrected Jesus, the man in this ossuary was a thoroughly hellenised Jew who also believed in the power of the magic arts. This new interpretation, if correct, would take us even further away from providing any assistance to the Jesus Family Tomb thesis.

2. Ossuary 3 – MARA Inscription

Ossuary 3 has a faint and worn rosette, slightly off-centre, on one of its sides and above it are four Greek capitals: MAPA,[11] the same Aramaic word that appears on the Mariamene Mara ossuary in Talpiot A. Since this is a word found on only five ossuaries from the period, Tabor and Jacobovici felt able to conclude that it 'seemed to us beyond chance or coincidence' that this rare word should be found twice in tombs so close together. Surely this is an indication that the two tombs are 'related in content, not just in proximity'. (*Discovery* 67)

But whatever Tabor and Jacobovici wish to suggest from this concurrence (and it is never clear) the case falls apart on close examination. For a start, in the Aramaic of the period, including Dan 2.47; 4.16, 21; and 5.23, מרא means 'sir/lord/master', and when transliterated into Greek, it is normally written as *mara*. The feminine form of *mara* is *martha*, and in the late Second Temple period that word came to be used often as a personal name, as we find in the gospels (Jn 11 and Lk 10.38-42). Where things become complicated is that *martha* can also be found abbreviated to *mara* – with the result that *mara* can serve as both a masculine and a feminine.[12]

A good example of the interchangeability of *mara* and *martha* can be seen on the ossuary listed by Rahmani as *CJO* 468. On the rim of the chest is inscribed *mara*, and on the narrow side is inscribed *martha*. As to the possibility that *mara* could indicate a male body in the ossuary, it is worth noting that Bauckham has suggested that the *mara* on the so-called Mary Magdalene ossuary (*CJO* 701) could refer to a male, perhaps the husband of Mariame who had pre-deceased him.[13] While this is not impossible, I know of no other ossuary where the name of the wife is placed ahead of the husband.

The only conclusion that can be drawn from these details is that the presence of the same word *mara* on ossuaries found in tombs 60 metres from each

---

[11] Non-Greek readers should note that the Greek letter *rho* is written as P in the capital form. Thus MAPA is pronounced *mara*.

[12] A neat summary of the points in this paragraph are presented by Rollston in his ASOR blog of 28/2/2012.

[13] Bauckham, 'The Names on the Ossuaries' 94, 104.

other is pure co-incidence. Our *mara* inscribed on ossuary 3 in Talpiot B may refer to a male known in the family as 'the master', or, more likely, it may refer to a woman known as Martha. We have no grounds for thinking that the person had any association with the Christian movement.

3. Ossuary 6 – The 'Jonah' Ossuary

Without doubt, the markings on ossuary 6 and the interpretations given them by Tabor and Jacobovici, have caused the greatest stir. Before we examine the figure itself, we turn to two historical claims made by Tabor and Jacobovici.

3.1 Jonah and the Q Tradition

Several of the assumptions and claims made concerning the Jonah traditions found in the gospels need to be challenged.

(i) The material found in both Matthew and Luke which scholars refer to as Q cannot with certainty be spoken of as a 'lost gospel', as though it were necessarily a written body of Jesus tradition. It may have been, but equally it may have been a rather fixed body of oral tradition, consisting mainly of sayings of Jesus.[14] In fact, it may even be the case that Q never existed in either written or oral form, and that the agreements between Matthew and Luke are due to the one evangelist having drawn from the other.[15] I must confess that I have long been a 'Q sceptic', and tend to favour the line that for the most part, the so-called Q material is nothing more than evidence that Matthew drew upon Luke for some of his material.[16] But for our purposes, I will speak of Q or the Q tradition, without making any presumption as to whether it existed in oral or written form, or, indeed, whether it is simply that sayings material

---

[14] A whole body of scholarship has developed around the study of Q. For the beginner I recommend Ivan Havener, *Q – The Sayings of Jesus* (Michael Glazier, 1987). For our purposes it needs simply to be pointed out that Tabor's and Jacobovici's simplistic presumptions concerning Q are not justified. There is no scholarly consensus in relation to Q.

[15] Martin Hengel, for example, is a recent defender of Matthew's dependence on Luke, thus obviating the need for a separate Q tradition. See his *The Four Gospels and the One Gospel of Jesus Christ* (Trinity, 2000) 169-207. Mark Goodacre has also challenged the existence of Q in his *The Case Against Q. Studies in Markan Priority and the Synoptic Problem* (Trinity, 2002). Goodacre opts for Luke's dependence on Matthew, a position popularised by Austin Farrer in his article, 'On Dispensing with Q' in D E Nineham (ed), *Studies in the Gospels – Essays in Memory of R H Lightfoot* (Blackwell, 1967).

[16] I thus tend to side with Hengel on this matter.

common to Matthew and Luke such that one evangelist drew upon the other.

(ii) It is misleading to write of Q as 'an early collection of the sayings and deeds of Jesus', (*Discovery* 75) when in fact the Q material consists almost entirely of sayings, teaching and parables of Jesus. The only two 'deeds' of Jesus are the Q account of his baptism (Matt 3.13,16; Lk 3.21b, 22) and the healing of the centurion's servant (Matt 8.5-10, 13; Lk 7.1b-10).

(iii) More importantly, the assertion that the 'resurrection' of Jonah tradition found in Matt 12.40 derives from Matthew's version of Q will not stand up to careful scrutiny.[17] The two accounts in Luke 11.29-31 and Matthew 12.39-40 read as follows:

Matthew	**Luke**
An evil and adulterous generation	This generation is an evil generation;
seeks a sign,	it seeks a sign
and no sign will be given it	and a sign will not be given it
except the sign of Jonah the prophet.	except the sign of Jonah.
For as Jonah was	For as Jonah became a sign to the Ninevites
in the belly of the sea monster for three days and three nights	
so will the son of man be	so will the son of man be to this generation.
in the heart of the earth for three days and three nights.	

The explicit reference to death and resurrection is absent from Luke and found only in Matthew. But the hint is there – for Luke's 'so will the son of man be to this generation' already provides the forward look to the coming events in Jerusalem. We can be confident that Luke himself has understood it this way, locating it in his 'Travel Narrative' – that part of his gospel that commences at 9.51 and in which Jesus sets his face for Jerusalem and death. But there is nothing explicit – not until we get to Matthew, where the forthcoming death and resurrection of Jesus

---

[17] Tabor has, in fact, been very careful in his wording on pages 76-77 and 85 of *Jesus Discovery*, and he may wish to deny that he and Jacobovici are asserting that Matt 12.40 was part of Q rather than a Matthean elaboration of the Q tradition. But, especially for most readers, that is the clear impression given by their wording.

are unambiguously referred to. What Matthew, therefore, has done is to spell out clearly for his readers what lies implicit in Luke.[18]

There is one other observation to be made. Luke's tradition continues to locate Jesus' words in the immediate context of Jesus' own generation – 'this generation' is used twice, at the beginning and at the end of the saying. Matthew, writing late in the first century and well after the death of Jesus' generation, removes the references to 'this generation'. He thereby makes Jesus' response applicable to every generation, including that of the churches for whom he is writing his gospel: Jesus' death and resurrection is the sign that speaks to every generation, and to seek for more is a sure indicator of unbelief.

The conclusion to be drawn from this is that there is *no evidence that an explicit narrative that links the Jonah story with the death and resurrection of Jesus found its way into the gospel traditions until Matthew put it there*! Luke, also writing after AD 70, only knew the tradition in its parabolic form, and from that we can confidently conclude that Matthew's version did not originate in an already existing Q tradition. It is simply incorrect for Tabor and Jacobovici to write that 'it is in Q that we learn one of the earliest interpretations of the mysterious "sign of Jonah"'. If, as seems likely, Luke represents the earlier tradition,[19] the resurrection interpretation of the sign of Jonah is only implicit. It only becomes explicit in Matthew's gospel, and in all likelihood it is Matthew himself, who likes to make Jesus' teaching clear and unambiguous (as a careful comparison of Mark's parable chapter [Mark 4] with Matthew's [Matthew 13] reveals), who is responsible for bringing to the surface the Jonah-son of man comparison.[20]

---

[18] My reading of Lk 11.29-31 is supported by I H Marshall, *The Gospel of Luke* (Paternoster, 1978) 484-486. I remain unpersuaded by other commentators, along with Simon Chow, *The Sign of Jonah Reconsidered* (CB NTS 27; Almqvist & Wiksell, 1995) 117-8, 139-41, who interpret the sign as the preaching of repentance to Luke's generation. Lk 16.30f and Acts 1.3; 17.31 support the claim that Luke understood 11.30 as a reference to Jesus' coming resurrection.

[19] It is very difficult to imagine that Luke has stripped away the explicit resurrection details from the Jonah reference (as we find them in Matthew) and that he has changed Matthew's generalised time reference to the more specific 'this generation'.

[20] Matt 12.40 also has three common Matthean words (*hōsper*; *gar*; and *gē*) adding weight to the claim that Matthew himself is responsible for expanding the original Q saying. For a list of common or characteristic Matthean terms see Davies and Allison, *Saint Matthew*, 1.75-79.

If this analysis is correct, the implications for the Tabor/Jacobovici thesis are profound. Matthew 12.40 did not form part of a pre-existing Q tradition, as Tabor and Jacobovici will have us understand. In fact, we can have no confidence that the Jonah story formed part of the Christian narrative until Matthew wrote his gospel, well after AD 70. Even Luke, who also wrote after AD 70, did not draw out the association.[21] Certainly, it was not such a familiar part of the Christian story of Jesus' death and resurrection that a Jerusalem-based Christian would have a fish etched on his ossuary, expecting others to understand its meaning. As Snyder wrote, '… signs have social origins and implications rather than private, mystical meaning.' So then, early Christian art has an 'important communal meaning'.[22] If that is the case, we can be confident that no such social and communal meaning had been attached to the Jonah tradition in the pre-70 life of the early Christian community. One swallow does not make a summer – and when that swallow arrives 100 years ahead of the others one can justifiably begin to question whether it is in fact a swallow at all!

3.2 Jonah in Jewish Tradition and Early Christian Art

Before passing to the ossuary itself, I need to make a few comments on what appears to be some confused logic relating to the Jonah narrative and its use in Jewish and Christian thought and art.

(i) The first point of note is that Tabor and Jacobovici tell us that Jonah plays an insignificant role in (pre-Christian) intertestamental Jewish thought. In particular, we are advised that Jonah is never mentioned in the Dead Sea Scrolls. I am puzzled as to what the authors want to make of this point. They then proceed to tell us that in later rabbinic writings Jonah is rarely mentioned, and then suggest that this is due to the fact that by the 4th and 5th centuries Christians had taken over the Jonah narrative for their resurrection claims – and this explained the Jewish avoidance of Jonah. But this line of reasoning won't take. Quite apart from the fact that Jonah references are more prevalent

---

[21] Nor does the Jonah/Jesus parallel find any echo in the rest of the New Testament or in early Christian thought until Justin Martyr (*Dialogue with Trypho*, 107-108) in the mid-second century. Even there, Justin's emphasis is not on Jonah as a type of Christ in relation to his deliverance from the fish, though he does mention it. Rather, Justin's emphasis is on Jonah as preacher of repentance. This in itself suggests that the Jonah-Jesus link relating to resurrection was not prominent in the early church. See 3.2 (ii) below.

[22] Graydon Snyder, *Ante Pacem – Archaeological Evidence on Church Life before Constantine* (Mercer, 1985) 14.

in rabbinic writings than is admitted,[23] it is difficult to put the blame on the Christians for any Jewish avoidance of Jonah when it has been readily acknowledged that Jonah received only scant attention in the pre-Christian period of intertestamental Judaism.

(ii) There is one more problem. Tabor and Jacobovici write that the reason that Jews of later centuries avoided reference to Jonah was because 'Christians had claimed and co-opted him as foreshadowing the resurrection of Christ'.[24] Again, we read: 'Christians saw the Jonah story not only as a powerful image of Jesus' resurrection from the dead, but also as a way of affirming their own faith in the resurrection of the faithful at the end of days.' (*Discovery* 79-80) The problem is that the physical evidence from early Christian art will not bear out this claim. True, the Jonah narrative is the most frequent depiction on Christian art (sarcophagi, mosaics and frescos) until the time of Constantine (early 4th century). Especially on sarcophagi, depictions of Jonah being cast out of the boat into the sea, Jonah being spewed from the clutches of the sea monster, and Jonah at rest, naked and lying under a vine – these elements of the Jonah narrative[25] are found more frequently than all other biblical scenes.[26] But none of the Jonah scenes is a representation of Jesus resurrected! Why representations of Jonah were so popular, and what exactly they were meant to suggest, are questions that have occupied scholars, and we need not be detained by them.[27] Perhaps the clue may be found in this observation by Snyder: '*After the peace of Constantine, the Jonah cycle waned sharply in popularity. When the environment was no longer hostile to the Christian, when the Christian community was no longer harassed qua Christian, then the pictorial*

---

[23] Chow, *Sign of Jonah* 25-44, has a helpful discussion of the pre- and post-Christian Jewish references.

[24] Simon Chow, *Sign of Jonah* 26, makes the same claim: '… it is unlikely that Jewish writers would invent anything elaborate in praise of Jonah in Christian times, when the Christians had appropriated him as a prototype of Jesus' resurrection (Matt 12:40)'. In fact, we will see below that Jonah as a prototype of Jesus' resurrection receives no emphasis in Christian art and only minimal attention in Christian writings.

[25] Jonah at rest under a vine is, in fact, a distortion of Jonah 4.6-11, and is probably influenced by the mythical story of Endymion, given eternal sleep by Zeus. See Chow, *Sign of Jonah* 198.

[26] Snyder, *Ante Pacem* 43, provides a useful statistical chart. Of 182 representations, 108 are of parts of the Jonah cycle. Where a panel has all three elements of the Jonah cycle, Snyder lists each part separately – but even so, the Jonah numbers are impressive.

[27] See the discussion in Snyder, *Ante Pacem* 46-49; Chow, *Sign of Jonah* 202-208.

symbol of a peaceful Orante [someone standing, arms outstretched, in prayer to God] *amidst critical (biblical) situations no longer served a useful purpose.*'[28] What is important for our study is that there is nothing in early Christian art that suggests that Matt 10.40 had any influence upon the depiction of the Jonah story.

As to early Christian writings, the situation is more mixed.[29] Some early fathers (notably Irenaeus, Tertullian and Origen) are explicit in drawing attention to Jonah as a type of the dying and resurrected Christ. Even they, however, will also use the Jonah narrative as an encouragement to Christians to remain confident in God's deliverance or as a defence of the Christian hope of resurrection. Several other writings only make use of Jonah either to encourage believers (*Acts of Paul*; *Apostolic Constitutions*) or to urge repentance (1 Clement; *Kerygmata Petrou*). The second century apologist Justin makes a brief allusion to Jesus' resurrection, but concentrates on Jonah as a preacher of repentance (see *Dialogue with Trypho* 107-108).

Where does all this leave us? While Christian writers were not reluctant to draw the link between Jonah and Christ, it is clear that the association was not a dominant concern for them. The writings of Irenaeus, Tertullian and Origen run into many volumes, and yet interest in Jonah as a type of Christ occupies little of their attention. The overwhelming impression we get both from early Christian art as well as from early Christian writings, is that Jonah primarily served the pastoral need of providing assurance to Christians living in a hostile environment. Nor should we ignore the fact that after the peace of Constantine (early 4th century), interest in the Jonah narrative waned significantly.

Returning to Tabor and Jacobovici, *we can with confidence assert that even if, from the 4th century on, there was any Jewish avoidance of the Jonah story, it was not because the Christians had taken it over as a symbol for Jesus' resurrection.*

(iii) Our authors claim that the Jonah and the fish ossuary in Talpiot B is unique to Jewish art. (*Discovery* 79-80) Even after the 3rd and 4th centuries, when Jews began to represent living beings in their art, there is no known representation of Jonah. (Again, blame for this absence in Jewish art is laid squarely at the feet of the Christian monopoly of the Jonah tradition.) The point that is easily missed is that Tabor and

---

[28] Snyder, *Ante Pacem* 49.
[29] Chow, *Sign of Jonah* 177-193, provides a useful analysis of the relevant writings.

Jacobovici have made a presumption here that is yet to be established, namely, that the etching on the ossuary is indeed a fish, and indeed represents Jonah being spewed from the mouth of the fish. If it is not, then the observations about later Jewish art are irrelevant. Also to be noted, if contemporary Jewish art strictly avoided the representation of living objects, especially humans,[30] as our authors presume, how can we explain its presence here? In fact, a few instances of fauna representation have been noted from this period (see note 30), and we shall soon note that a few crude representations of fishes have been found on ossuaries. Nevertheless, nothing compares to the brazen depiction of a fish spewing out a human. Now, this tomb certainly belonged to a Jewish family, as ossuaries 3 and 5 testify. Even if it were a Jewish family now committed to Messiah Jesus, were they so liberated that they could radically break the current convention with its narrow interpretation of the second commandment? I am aware of no developed Christian iconography earlier than the late 2nd century, and certainly not in the Jewish world of Palestine. Among the many ossuaries at the Dominus Flevit site on the Mount of Olives there are possible Christian symbols and markings, but these are primitive and esoteric, quite unlike our 'Jonah fish'.[31]

(iv) It is worth pointing out that, even if ossuary 6 does have a representation of a fish and Jonah, it had no impact upon later Christian art. Matthew 12.40 is an exact quote from the LXX of Jonah 1.17, and in place of the Hebrew's *dag gadol* (great fish), it has *kētos mega*. This Greek word *kētos* is the term used for a dragon-like mythical sea monster, sometimes sent by Poseidon, and usually depicted as serpentine in appearance with long rows of sharp teeth. This is exactly how the *kētos* is depicted in early Christian art. Our fish on ossuary 6 is certainly a tame antecedent for such a monster.

---

[30] Rachel Hachlili's *Ancient Jewish Art* is an authoritative study. Part One covers Jewish Art in the Second Temple Period. On p 65 she agrees that 'neither figurative nor symbolic representations were depicted' in Jewish art of the period. On p 81, however, she identifies a few exceptions to this rule, including birds among vine branches on a stucco wall in the Goliath family tomb in Jericho. Unfortunately, in fig. IV.21 of the book it is difficult to detect the birds.

[31] See Jack Finegan, *The Archaeology of the New Testament* (Princeton University Press, 1978) 243-249.

Figure 16. *Jonah and Sea Monster on Sarcophagus (Museo Pio Cristiano)*

3.3 Is it the Jonah Fish?

For Tabor and Jacobovici the engraving on ossuary 6 is unquestionably meant to represent Jonah and the fish. They recognise that the pattern is 'crude and homemade', indicating that it was carved not by a professional mason but by the family that owned the ossuary. This point is supported by the presence of an incomplete engraving of the same symbol found on the end of the ossuary – only half of a 'fish' is engraved, suggesting that the engraver did not plan well and ran out of space.

Figure 17. *Reproduction of the 'Jonah' Ossuary*

As to the engraving in question, the observations offered to support the fish interpretation are as follows:

- It looks like a fish, with a large, clearly defined tail, a head narrowing to a mouth, with scales etched on the body, and with two fins on the sides.

- Though no mouth is well-defined, it could be argued that the straight vertical line at the base of the figure may be intended to represent the mouth of the fish.
- The fish appears to be regurgitating something. At this point vivid imagination is applied, and the various lines towards the base of the carving are understood as a stick figure with arms and legs. As to the stick figure's head, it is emerging from the mouth of the fish wrapped in something. This, we are told, can be understood as a reminder of Jonah 2.5, where Jonah speaks of weeds that were wrapped around his head.
- The representation of a fish on an ossuary of this period is claimed to be unique. The engraver was involved in a 'daring and heretical move' making a clear 'affirmation of faith' in violation of 'the biblical prohibition of making images'. With no precedent to guide, the engraver/family is seeking to make a statement of faith that relates the 'oral tradition reflected in Q' to the hope of resurrection from the dead based upon Jesus' conquest of death.[32]
- One other scholar of international repute has given partial support to the Jonah thesis. Prof James Charlesworth has come forward to suggest that the lines of the stick figure, which Tabor and Jacobovici proposed were the body of Jonah, can be read as the four Hebrew letters of the name Jonah.[33]

The Jonah thesis, along with the later Charlesworth reading, has not gone unchallenged. In fact, a host of archaeologists and others competent in the field, have entered the fray to point out the weaknesses in the Jonah proposal.[34]

- The fish is engraved vertically on the ossuary, with the mouth at the base. If a fish is to disgorge Jonah one would expect that it would be presented horizontally.

---

[32] The quotes are from pages 85-86 of *Jesus Discovery*. We have already dealt with the claims made about Q and the Jonah tradition in Matt 12.40.

[33] See the article by Charlesworth, 'What is the Message of "the Patio Tomb" in Talpiot, Jerusalem' at www.bibleinterp.com/articles/cha308011.shtml/. See also Charlesworth's interview with Ben Witherington on www.patheos.com/blogs/bibleandculture/2012/05/14/dr-jim-charlesworth-on-the-talpiot-tomb-b/.

[34] The blogs of the following scholars present valuable responses: Mark Goodacre; Ben Witherington; James McGrath; Robert Cargill. In my judgement, the most damaging response has been that of A Lombatti, 'Observations on the "Jonah" Iconography on the Ossuary of Talpiot B Tomb' at www.bibleinterp.com/articles/lom368026.shtml. Apart from Charlesworth's contribution, I am not aware of a single scholar who provides any support for the Jonah thesis.

- The supposed scales look nothing like scales. The lines are too patterned, neat and geometrical for scales. They more naturally resemble the lines on an amphora or some other physical object.
- It is simply not true that no other fish designs are to be found on ossuaries of the period. Lombatti has drawn our attention to up to twelve examples of fish, or fish-like, figures on ossuaries or sarcophagi of the period. But far from being a support to the Jonah thesis, this proves to be damaging evidence. As Lombatti demonstrates so clearly, the other fish engravings bear no resemblance to the Jonah ossuary. (See the comparisons below at Fig. 21.) If the Jonah ossuary was intended to represent a fish, it was done in ignorance of the other dozen fish-like drawings.
- Lombatti reminds us that the fish had a symbolic meaning in several cultures of the Ancient Near East. Within Judaism it was related to the hope of immortality and the future resurrection of the deceased. In that context of Jewish expectation, certainly, our Jonah ossuary may have a place.
- The original claim to see the lines towards the base of the figure as representing a human stick figure is far from convincing. Careful observation reveals that there are many lines – far too many to make the arms and legs of a stick figure. As to the ball and scratchings at the base, there is no justification for seeing in them a human head covered in weed.
- A further point against the Jonah claim is that everything is so unbalanced for it to be credible. If the central theme is Jonah as symbol of resurrection hope, he has been overwhelmed by the fish itself. Jonah himself is represented by a mere few small stick lines and an unclear blob, while the fish itself occupies all our attention.
- Charlesworth's claim that the lines towards the base can be read as the four Hebrew letters of Jonah also fails the test of careful scrutiny. For a start, he also has to ignore several of the scratchings in order to identify just four. Moreover, the long Hebrew letter *nun* turns out not to be a single stroke but two separate lines, as Cargill identifies (see strokes within his oval marking at Figure 18).
- Other common sense questions also come to mind. What was the purpose of hiding the name 'Jonah' within the lines that make up the stick man? Was it some sort of secret only for the initiated? It certainly would suggest a level of sophistication not matched by the quality of the engraving. Nor should we forget that ossuary markings were not made for public display, but were identifiers for the benefit of the family. What other evidence do we have from Jewish engravings to suggest that Jews of the Second

Temple period were willing to inscribe human images, even if only stick images?

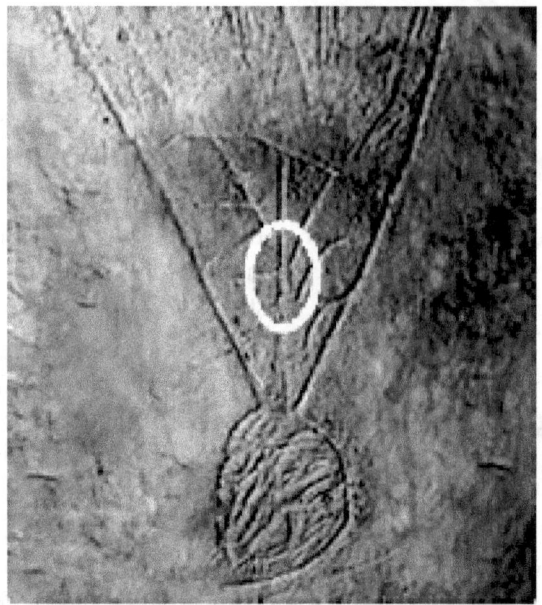

Figure 18. *Lines of 'Stick Man Jonah'* (R Cargill)

So then, is the engraving meant to represent Jonah emerging from the fish? It has to be said that the odds are heavily stacked against the claim. In fact, one can conclude that the *only* argument in support of the claim is the point that at first sight the figure looks like a fish. Closer examination, however, quickly throws up a host of counter arguments. As to the association with Jonah, one is led to respond that this claim appears to be nothing more than the figment of a fertile imagination.

3.4 Is it an Amphora?

If not a fish, what is it? Two other proposals have been submitted to explain our engraving on ossuary 6. Even before comparing it with other known examples, it has the appearance of a rather crudely drawn amphora.

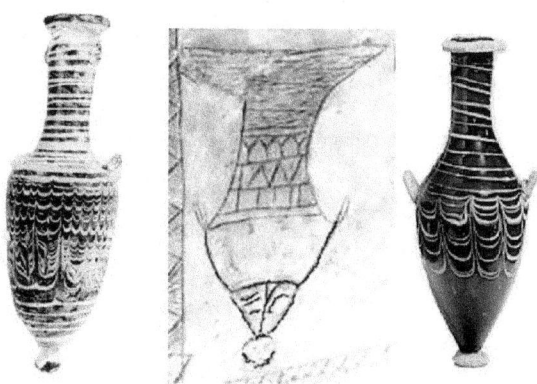

Figure 19. *'Jonah Fish' Engraving and Hellenistic Amphoras Compared (A Lombatti)*

What the Jonah thesis takes to be scales can be seen to be typical design markings on an amphora; and what are taken to be fins can be seen as the two handles of the jar. As to its vertical positioning on the ossuary, that also well suits the amphora claim. It is true, the blob at the base of the engraving looks clumsy and hardly suitable for an amphora, but there are contemporary examples not far removed. For example, *CJO* 213 in Rahmani has a carefully inscribed amphora with a base equally delicate as that on our ossuary. In fact, while Lombatti acknowledges that 'vase-like graffiti' are not very common on ossuaries, neither are they so rare that our ossuary 6 stands out as an oddity. Five ossuaries with amphoras are shown in Rahmani.[35] Lombatti claims to have found 20 vase-like images on ossuaries.

There is something else about the amphoras on the published ossuaries that supports this interpretation. All but one (CJO 815) of the ossuaries with amphoras in Rahmani (i) are delicately drawn, (ii) have a common shape, and (iii) are centrally placed between two rosettes (see Fig. 20). In other words, they have the appearance of having been professionally carved according to a standard pattern. The amphora on our ossuary 6 contrasts with these on all counts. It is crudely drawn, such that its shaping is not even uniform. It does not conform to the normal amphora design. Rather, one gets the impression that the engraver has sought to replicate the pattern of real amphoras he/she has seen elsewhere. The amateurish skills of the engraver are on display not only here but also on the side of the ossuary where another attempt to engrave an amphora was misjudged – resulting in only half of an image because he/she ran out of space on the surface. Finally, our amphora is located to the left side of the front panel of the ossuary, with another design occupying the right

---

[35] Rahmani, *Catalogue of Jewish Ossuaries*, numbers 120, 183, 213, 325, 815.

side. No delicate rosettes here! All of this gives the distinct impression of a 'no brand' ossuary bought on the cheap, with the engravings performed not by a skilled artisan but by a 'family friend'!

Figure 20. *Ossuary with Amphora Design*

3.5 Is it a *Nefesh*?

The only other suggestion that has any claim to credibility is the claim that the engraving is meant to represent a Jewish *nefesh*.[36] A *nefesh* was the name given to a stone obelisk erected above a grave. Several of these remain today, including some in the Kidron and Hinnom Valleys at Jerusalem. Such replicas of *naf'shot* have also been noted on ossuaries, as shown in Figure 22 below. There is a certain resemblance between the engraving on our ossuary and the *naf'shot* that Meyers draws our attention to. But there is one major problem, as Tabor points out in his response to Meyers' review: the supposed *nefesh* on ossuary 6 is upside down! If it is a *nefesh* representation, it is the only known example of one in this orientation.

3.6 Conclusion

The so-called Jonah ossuary has occupied much of our attention – and that is because its interpretation is so critical to the claims made for it by Tabor and Jacobovici: this modest ossuary, originally jam-packed with bones and located in the first niche of the burial tomb, was quite possibly the humble ossuary of Joseph of Arimathea. Through the depiction of the Jonah narrative, it expressed the confidence of the deceased not only in the Jonah-like resurrection of Jesus but also in his own future resurrection. In its own way, it brought forward by over 100 years the later Christian use of the Jonah narrative to express both these beliefs.

Our study has led us to the conclusion that very little of this thesis has any merit. In particular, we may now assert with some confidence:

---

[36] This suggestion was made, for example, by Prof Eric Meyers in his review of *Jesus Discovery* published in the ASOR blog on 28/2/2012.

(i) The link between Jonah and the resurrection of Jesus, as found in Matt 12.40, cannot be seen to pre-date AD 70, and certainly was not part of the early Christian mindset until made explicit by Matthew late in the first century.

(ii) Later Christian art of the third and fourth century owes nothing to depictions of fishes on Jewish ossuaries of the first century.

(iii) Use of the Jonah story in Christian art avoided any link to the resurrection of Jesus, and in early Christian writings any such association was limited. Jewish attitude to the Jonah story would not have been negatively influenced by Christian usage.

(iv) When it comes to the question of what is being represented on ossuary 6, there are serious flaws in the Jonah/fish proposal. So serious are those flaws that they make it all but impossible that any allusion is intended to the Jonah story. They also make it highly improbable that an ordinary fish is intended.

(v) The proposal that has the strongest claim is that which sees in the engraving a rather amateurish representation of an amphora.

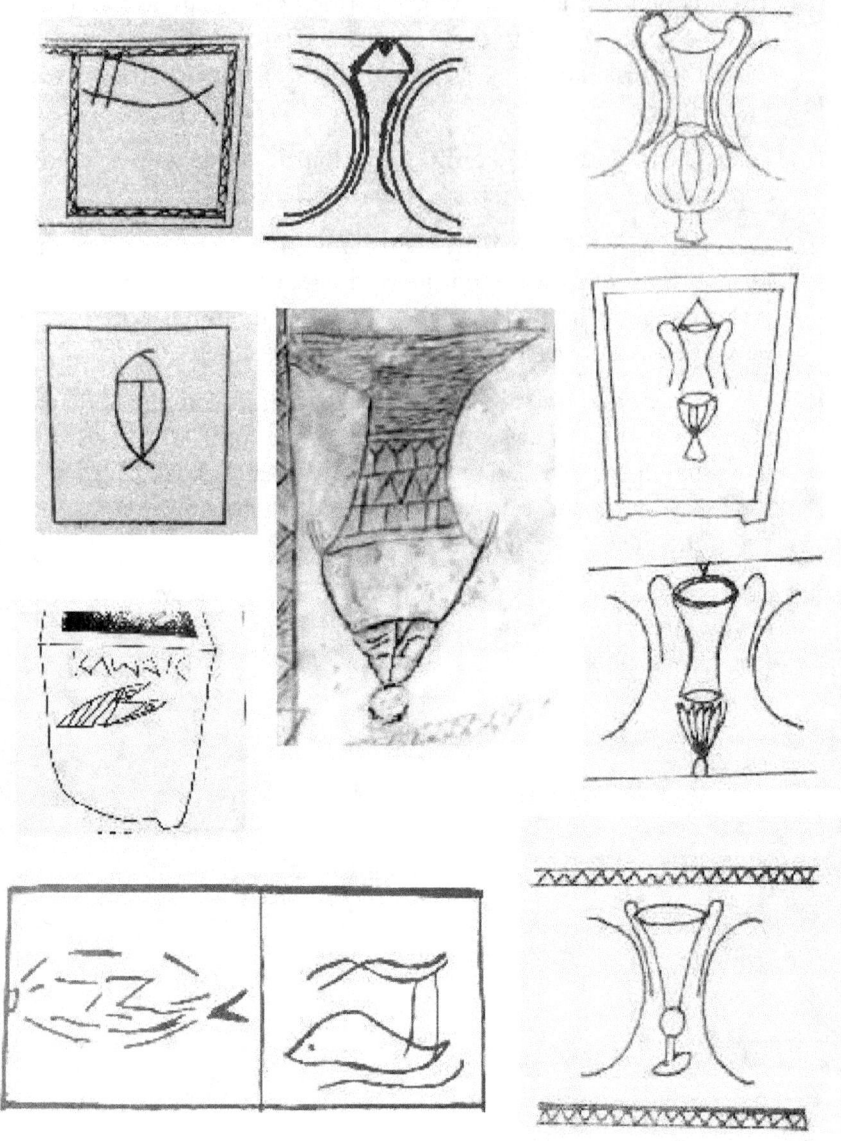

Figure 21. *Fish or Amphora? Talpiot B 'Jonah Fish' Engraving Compared with Fish and Amphora Ossuary Engravings (Adapted from A Lombatti)*

Postscript

In an attempt to establish the credibility of his interpretation of the representation on ossuary 6, Tabor has posted the following comparisons.

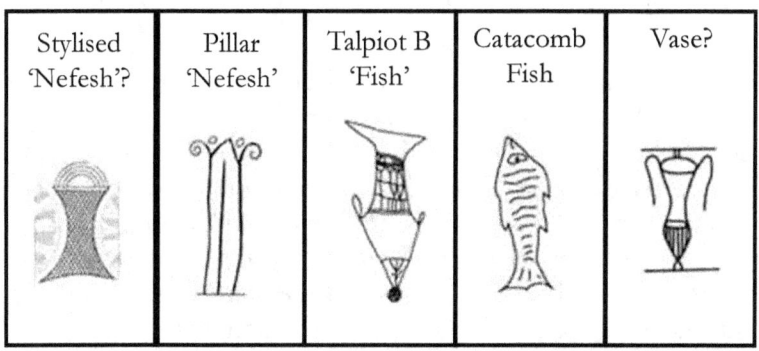

Figure 22. *Ossuary Images: A Comparison (J Tabor)*

I agree that the comparisons establish that the nefesh hypothesis will not take. But the hoped for fish comparison also fails the test. The fish does not come from a Jewish ossuary but from a Roman catacomb. It is 180 degrees inverted, and it does not have anything to do with the Jonah story.

4. Concluding Thoughts on Talpiot B and its Ossuaries.

A four line inscription, an ossuary with a single name, *mara*, and a fish-like engraving. These provided ample material to convince Tabor and Jacobovici that the Talpiot B tomb, a mere 60 metres distant from Talpiot A, provided all the evidence they needed to support their already strong conviction that Talpiot A was the Jesus Family Tomb. The four line inscription was a prayer to Yahweh, arising from faith in the resurrected Jesus, and crying out for a like resurrection. The *mara* ossuary provided some unclarified pointer to the *mariamene mara* ossuary just 60 metres away. And the fish-like engraving was the icing on the cake: for it signified Jonah being disgorged from the large fish – and that itself was a direct pointer to the saying of Jesus in Matt 12.40. It was a Christian affirmation of faith in Jesus' resurrection after 'three days and three nights', and of the consequential hope of sharing in the same destiny. Here was a family tomb, probably that of Joseph of Arimathea, deliberately located near to that of the resurrected Lord Jesus.

But on closer examination it all falls apart. There is nothing about these ossuaries that suggests early Christian association. More to the point, one of the ossuaries, the four line inscription ossuary, could not have come from the pious and conservative community of Jewish believers in Jesus Messiah. Whichever way we are to read it, it breathes the spirit of liberal hellenised Judaism. The *mara* ossuary tells us nothing other than that the deceased was Jewish – whether male or female we cannot tell. As to the so-called Jonah ossuary, the odds are overwhelmingly stacked against its being a fish, let alone Jonah's fish.

We commenced this chapter with two confident quotes from *Jesus Discovery*. They are worth repeating: The findings in Talpiot B provide '*the earliest archaeological evidence of faith in Jesus' resurrection from the dead, the first witness to a saying of Jesus that predates even the writing of our New Testament gospels, and the earliest example of Christian art*'. In Talpiot B '*the connection to Jesus is direct and explicit*'. A more careful analysis of the evidence can only lead to a conclusion directly at odds with these claims: there is nothing about the contents of Talpiot B to suggest any association with the Talpiot A tomb. Its contents add to our data relating to Second Temple Judaism, but have nothing to do with the early Christian movement.

We turn now to the contents of Talpiot A, unassisted by anything that its near neighbour has revealed.

CHAPTER 11
THE 'JESUS TOMB' OSSUARIES

In Chapter 4 we considered the merits of the claims made for the so-called James ossuary. We did not enter the debate as to whether that ossuary had once housed the remains of James the brother of Jesus of Nazareth. Rather, we concentrated on the proposal of Tabor, Jacobovici and Cameron that the ossuary came from Talpiot A, concluding that the scientific evidence goes against the claim. In our last chapter we decisively rejected any proposals that the three marked ossuaries in Talpiot B demonstrated any Judaeo-Christian associations. On the contrary, we concluded that the four line inscription excluded the possibility of its representing the piety of the conservative early Jerusalem church.

Having cleared the deck in relation to the James ossuary and the Talpiot B tomb complex, we thus now turn to the ossuaries in Talpiot A. Six of the nine (originally ten) ossuaries have named inscriptions, and our task is simple: we want to ask whether the names on those ossuaries refer to Jesus of Nazareth and known members of his family. That in a nutshell is the thesis of Tabor, Jacobovici and Cameron. Reaction and response to the claims was fast, furious and at times quite heated in the early years. Much of it was conducted in personal blogs, and it was not unusual for scholars to make the same point in criticism.[1]

We will tackle the issue by addressing certain key concerns and questions.

1. Are All the Names Clearly Identifiable?

Most of the names inscribed on the ossuaries are clearly identifiable. However, serious doubts exist concerning the two key ossuaries.

1.1 The Jesus Ossuary (*CJO* 704)

As we indicated in Chapter 3, the inscription on the Jesus ossuary is both poorly written and in part, nearly illegible. The inscription itself appears as follows:

---

[1] For this reason, footnoting in this chapter will be kept to a minimum, but at the end of the chapter I will add a list of articles and web sites that are useful. Some blogs may no longer be available.

Figure 23. ישוע בר יהוסף

As all agree, the final seven letters (reading right to left) are reasonably clear and identifiable: *bar jehoseph* = son of Joseph. But what do the preceding markings indicate? After much consideration, Rahmani opted for *jeshua* = Jesus. But this is far from certain. The scratches are rough and uneven, so that Charlesworth is able to claim that what we have is more like 'sloppy graffiti' than a formal inscription. As Rahmani himself admits: 'The first name, preceded by a large cross-mark, is difficult to read, as the incisions are clumsily carved and badly scratched.' What seems to persuade him in favour of *'jeshua'* is that this would allow this person to be the same as the one listed as 'father of *jehuda*' (*CJO* 702). Many others are not convinced, and would see no justification for bringing in the *'jeshua* father of *jehuda'* ossuary in support. One or two have offered different options to *'jeshua'*. Thus Stephen Pfann of the University of the Holy Land has suggested *hanun* as a possibility. Others are unwilling to give a guess, simply saying that 'Joseph' is the only part of the inscription they can be certain of. For example, Steve Caruso, an Aramaic specialist, has suggested he cannot be more than 10% certain of anything in the inscription other than 'Joseph'.[2] He has even mooted the possibility that the X mark may in fact be the first letter of the Hebrew alphabet, *aleph* (א).

Now, these are pretty damaging judgements concerning one of the most critical ossuaries for the Jesus Tomb argument. Indeed, even Tabor is willing to acknowledge that the inscription is 'quite difficult to read' (*Discovery* 29), and yet the case presented in the various publications proceeds on the presumption of Rahmani's tentative reading. In fact, Tabor and Jacobovici go even further and assert: 'That a tomb contains an ossuary inscribed in Aramaic *Yeshua bar Yehosef* ... is not in dispute.' (*Discovery* 105) This betrays a confidence that is in no way justified and is surprising for an academic like Tabor, with such experience in the field of archaeology. It may be 'Jesus', but there's a healthy chance it is something else.[3] In the face of such widely acknowledged doubts,

---

[2] Steve Caruso's *The Aramaic Blog* for March 29, 2007 offers a lengthy study of the Jesus son of Joseph ossuary.

[3] Hershel Shanks in his editorial comment in *Biblical Archaeology Review* for July/August 2007 was certainly overconfident when he wrote: 'What seems clear to almost

one is bound to admit that to build a case on such an insecure reading of an inscription is a very risky enterprise. It does not destroy the case altogether, but what it does require is other powerful and persuasive support that pushes the interpretation in a given direction. That is what we will need to find in the rest of our enquiry. Uncertainty with respect to the name on the so-called Jesus ossuary means that we need to be strongly convinced about the others.

1.2 The Mary Magdalene Ossuary (*CJO* 701)

This ossuary presents us with a different set of problems. The rather clearly identifiable Greek lettering is as follows:

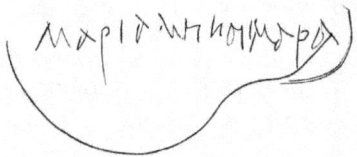

Figure 24. *The Disputed 'Mary Magdalene' Inscription*

In his editing of the text, Rahmani (*CJO* 701) took these letters as reading MARIAMENOU'MARA, and this he translated as 'of Mariamene who is (a.k.a.) Mara', and this is the reading adopted by Tabor and Jacobovici. It is this reading of the name Mary, unknown until it surfaces in the third century and is used of Mary Magdalene both by Hippolytus and in the *Acts of Philip*, which convinces Tabor and Jacobovici that the ossuary is that of Mary Magdalene. In Chapter 7 we have already considered the historical and literary evidence relating to Mary Magdalene and need not revisit it. But Rahmani's interpretation of the ossuary's text has been challenged. In particular, Stephen Pfann has provided a careful and persuasive critical re-appraisal of the ossuary.

The first point to be noted is that the inscription neatly divides into two parts. The first seven letters are written in fairly standard formal Greek script, and can be read as MARIAME, the usual Greek way of writing the Hebrew name Miriam. There is then a slight spacing and then follow the rest of the letters, but this time written in a cursive hand. Pfann suggests that the following letters should read as KAI MARA, meaning 'and Martha'. We thus have a

all expert observers (*pace* Stephen Pfann ...) is that one of the bone boxes in the cave is inscribed "Jesus son of Joseph". (p 4) He was corrected by Pfann in his letter to the editor in a later edition: 'True, the experts almost unanimously consider the "bar Yehosef" part of the inscription to be clear. But they likewise almost unanimously consider the "Yeshua" part of the inscription to be "messy" (Frank Cross), or "difficult to read" ... (L Y Rahmani)' (*BAR* November/December, 2007; p 12). Pfann also quotes Joseph Naveh, Emile Puech and Ada Yardeni as agreeing that the 'Yeshua' part of the inscription is highly doubtful.

situation where a second person was later interred in the ossuary, possibly Mary's daughter or her sister. More to the point, we have a reading that raises none of the problems that the original given by Rahmani does.

What are the difficulties with Rahmani's reading of the text? Pfann lists up to ten grammatical and stylistic problems. Among them are:

- Rahmani understands *mariamenou* as the genitive of the diminutive *mariamenon*. However, the expected ending should have been *mariameniou*, derived from *mariamenion*.
- In order to arrive at *mariamenou*, the eighth letter is read as a backwards written N, rather than a normal K which is the natural reading of the letter.
- For *mara* to be a further descriptor of the first name, it should be in the same grammatical form, but it is not.
- Where two names refer to the same person, it is normal for them to be foreign to one another – for example, one should be Hebrew and the other Greek (as in *CJO* 868: *alexas mara*). But here we have two Hebrew names.
- There is a vertical scratch just before *mara*, which Rahmani takes to signify *hē kai*, meaning 'she who is also/who is also known as'. But no such marking is known elsewhere as an abbreviation for *hē kai*.

The fact that the writing shows clear evidence of having been written by two hands, and the fact that both scribes show evidence of being 'both practiced and comfortable in writing Greek' is at odds with the grammatical and stylistic problems that Pfann detects in Rahmani's interpretation. Those problems fall away when the two names solution is adopted.

Pfann's solution has won considerable support, including from Shimon Gibson, Ben Witherington and Richard Bauckham.[4] It may not be correct, but at least it can be said that it appears to hold fewer problems than the translation supported by Tabor and Jacobovici.

Where does this leave us? The *Jesus Discovery* authors hesitantly and reluctantly acknowledge the possibility that the inscription may refer to two women, Mary and Martha, though they are not personally persuaded. (*Discovery* 157) They are open to this option only because they think that the gospel writers may have got themselves confused when they present Mary Magdalene and Mary of Bethany as separate women. Thus, as a second best, they concede the

---

[4] R Bauckham, 'The Names on the Ossuaries' 93. Bauckham also cites two well reputed epigraphers, Emile Puech and Tal Ilan, who independently have come up with solutions similar to that of Pfann.

possibility that Mary Magdalene, wife of Jesus, may have been buried in the same ossuary as her sister Martha who (presumably) died after her. But their choice remains with Rahmani's one person reading of the inscription to which they add the particular twist of reading *mara* as a term of dignity and status. The problems with Rahmani's reading, however, are significant, and one feels bound to suggest that the case for seeing here the work of two scribes referring to two women has the stronger claim.

The significance of this for the Mary Magdalene claims of Tabor and Jacobovici will occupy us in Section 3 of this chapter. Nor have we concluded our examination of *mara* on this ossuary and on the ossuary in Talpiot B. For the moment our concern has been to highlight the difficulties associated with the reading proposed by Rahmani and adopted by Tabor and Jacobovici.

1.3 The Other Inscribed Ossuaries

Four other of the nine ossuaries have names inscribed. These are listed by Rahmani as 702: *jehuda bar jeshua* (= Yehuda son of Jesus); 703: *matya* (= Matthew); 705: *yoseh* (= Joseph); 706: *maria* (= Mary). All four are clearly discernible. There is a further observation that is ignored by Tabor and Jacobovici: the scripts of 705 (Joseph) and 706 (Mary) are very similar and Rahmani suggests that this, along with the similarity in the ossuaries themselves (unfortunately no photos are given), may suggest that these two are the parents of the proposed *jeshua* of 704. This, of course, is pure conjecture (as Rahmani acknowledges) but certainly no more unreasonable than that of the Jesus Family Tomb thesis (*yoseh* = brother of the Jesus in ossuary 704) If accurate it would be a further stumbling block to the Jesus Family Tomb thesis, for it is widely acknowledged, even by Tabor and Jacobovici, that Jesus of Nazareth's father, Joseph, died much earlier.[5] Hence the silence about him in the gospel records and Acts. Tabor and Jacobovici are convinced that *yoseh* is the brother of Jesus, an interpretation we will consider later in the chapter.

---

[5] See *Jesus Dynasty* 76; *Jesus Discovery* 122. In speaking of Joseph as Jesus' father, we are making no judgement on the question of Mary's virginal conception. Jesus was adopted into the family of Joseph, and the gospels freely speak of Jesus as the son of Joseph (Lk 2.48; 3.23; 4.22; Matt 13.55; Jn 1.45; 6.42).

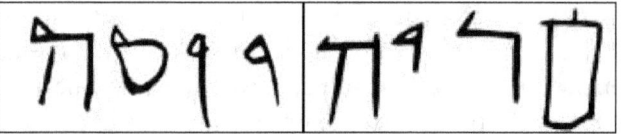

Figure 25. *Joseh and Maria Inscriptions – Husband and Wife?*

We are left with the intriguing result that the two most important ossuaries for the success of the Jesus Family Tomb thesis have serious problems with their interpretation. It is not at all clear that on ossuary *CJO* 704 the son of Joseph should be read as *jeshua*. And as to the reading of *CJO* 701, there is a very strong case for holding that two separate hands wrote the names of two separate people, Mary and (possibly) Martha.

2. Are Any Family Members Missing?

If we are to accept the proposition that Talpiot A is the family tomb of Jesus of Nazareth, then two consequences follow. We should be able to associate all of the named ossuaries with Jesus' family; and at the same time we should be able to justify the absence of any family members.

2.1 Missing Family Members – General

As to the absence of family members, Tabor and Jacobovici are correct: the sisters of Jesus (referred to in Mk 6.3) will presumably have married, settled in Galilee rather than transfer to Jerusalem, and would have been buried in the tombs of their husbands. (*Discovery* 121-122) Jesus' father, Joseph, also seems to have died before the ministry of Jesus commenced, and so would have been buried in Galilee. There is one other body of relatives that we know existed, namely, the wives (and presumably children) of Jesus' brothers. In 1 Cor 9.5 Paul explicitly refers to wives of Jesus' brothers, who travelled (or were entitled to travel) with their husbands. Where did they travel and where were they based? In the following section, we will propose that apart from James, Jesus' brothers were not necessarily based in Jerusalem. If this proposal is correct, then the absence of the wives and children of Jesus' brothers may not be a problem – though one could well respond by questioning why any senior family member of Jesus would want to have their remains (and hence their ossuary) housed anywhere other than in the tomb where Jesus the Messiah lay buried. In other words, ten ossuaries does seem a small number considering both the size and the importance of the family of Jesus.

2.2 Two Missing Brothers? – Simon and Jude

Let us stay with the brothers of Jesus. We have no reason to doubt the reports of Mark 6.3 and Matt 13.55 that Jesus had four brothers – James, Joseph, Jude and Simon. Nor need we doubt that all four were active members of the Christian movement, as Paul affirms in 1 Cor 9.5. Tabor's take on these brothers was summarised in Chapter 3. It runs as follows: Upon the death of Jesus' father Joseph, Mary married Joseph's brother Clopas, and from that marriage were born the four brothers. The departure of Messiah Jesus resulted in a dynastic succession. First, James led the movement, and upon his death in AD 62 Simon (known as Symeon in Eusebius) was elected to lead the community. Tradition from Eusebius and Epiphanius records one named Jude as third in line of leadership after Symeon, and there is good reason to believe this is a reference to Jesus' brother. Yet, if Jude had been born before Simon, we would expect him to have been elected to lead the movement. So all of this suggests two things: (i) that Matthew's listing of the four brothers, which places Simon ahead of Jude, is to be preferred; and (ii) that Joseph, the second brother, had died before James.

What are we to make of this? For our purposes, we do not need to enter into discussion on Mary's possible re-marriage to Clopas. There are no firm historical grounds for the conjecture, though Tabor is not the first to suggest it. On the other hand, there are reasonable grounds for the claim that at least some of the children mentioned as Jesus' brothers and sisters were born to Joseph by a previous wife.[6] As to the Symeon appointed to lead the Jerusalem church after the death of James, he was only ever remembered as the son of Jesus' paternal uncle, Clopas, never as a brother of Jesus. In this he is clearly distinguished by Eusebius, and by Hegesippus on whom Eusebius was dependent, from James, who was recognised as brother of Jesus.[7] In other words, nothing in the earliest Christian sources gives us any confidence to treat Symeon, second bishop of Jerusalem, as the brother of Jesus. Cousin, yes, but not brother.

As to Jude, Tabor draws our attention to a list of fifteen Jewish leaders of the Jerusalem Church, presented independently by Eusebius and Epiphanius

---

[6] For a thorough discussion of the relatives of Jesus see Bauckham, *Jude and the Relatives of Jesus* 5-44. See also my *The Enigmatic Jew* 42-45.

[7] See Eusebius, *HE* 3.11; 3.22; 3.32.6; 4.22.4. For example, at 3.11 Eusebius describes Symeon as 'son of Clopas ... cousin of the Saviour, for Hegesippus tells us that Clopas was Joseph's brother.' At 3.22 the contrast between Symeon and James is even more stark: 'Symeon was similarly the next after our Saviour's brother to be in charge of the church at Jerusalem.'

(both 4th century).[8] Both writers list as numbers 14 and 15 the names Joseph and Judas; but at number 3, succeeding James and then Symeon, Eusebius lists Justus while Epiphanius lists another Judas. Tabor suggests that it is 'conceivable' that Judas, the brother of Jesus, succeeded his brother Simon as third bishop of Jerusalem, who died some time early in the second century. Bauckham, however, presents a strong case for transcriptional error on the part of Epiphanius. In his judgement, it is far more likely that Justus was the successor to Symeon.[9] Tabor agrees with Bauckham and others that the list of 15 men provided by Eusebius and Epiphanius most likely comprised the first three Jewish-Christian bishops of Jerusalem until the Second Jewish Revolt (AD 132-135) along with a list of twelve supporting elders. We might also add that it seems unlikely that the last two elders named (Joseph and Judas) would be brothers of Jesus – one would expect any brothers of Jesus to be placed at the head of the list.

Where does this leave us in respect of Jesus' two brothers Simon and Jude? Did they succeed their brother James as leaders of the Jerusalem church? The case for such a claim receives no support from Eusebius and other early Christian writers. Can we assert that had they been alive in AD 62 (when James died) the elder of the two would have been appointed to succeed? In other words, does the appointment of a cousin of Jesus (Symeon) to succeed James rather than any brother indicate that his three other brothers (Joseph, Simon and Jude) were no longer alive? At 4.22 of his *Ecclesiastical History* Eusebius quotes Hegesippus (2nd century):

> When James the Righteous had suffered martyrdom like the Lord and for the same reason, Symeon the son of his uncle Clopas was appointed bishop. He being a cousin of the Lord, it was the universal demand that he should be second.

This could (though need not) be read to indicate that had a brother been available he would have been appointed, and so Symeon was the next best choice. But even if this is the case, does it necessarily follow that the other three brothers were no longer alive? I think not. Consider the following:

- James died in AD 62. Yet only about seven or eight years earlier Paul was writing to the Corinthian church and mentioning the brothers of the Lord as though all were still alive (1 Cor 9.5). Did all three other brothers die in those intervening years? Of course it's possible, but one would hardly suggest it is likely, especially since there is no hint of other martyrdoms in the immediate years before James' death.

---

[8] See Eusebius *HE* 4.5; and 5.12; and Epiphanius, *Panarion* 66.21-22).
[9] See Bauckham, *Jude and the Relatives of Jesus* 45-94, especially 70-79.

- Paul's reference to the brothers of Jesus who travelled would seem to exclude James, for we get the clear impression that he did not travel outside of Jerusalem. Both from Galatians and from Acts not only does Paul meet with James every time he visits/returns to Jerusalem (Gal 1.19; 2.9; Acts 15.13; 21.18), but James sends emissaries to Antioch rather than himself travel (Gal 2.12). In other words, James saw his leadership role as involving permanent residence in Jerusalem.
- Where were these other brothers? We have no reason to presume that they had permanently relocated to Jerusalem from Galilee. Nothing in Acts provides any support for that presumption. It is true that Acts 1.14 refers to the presence in Jerusalem of Jesus' brothers and mother in the earliest days, but after that there is total silence. Apart from later church tradition that locates the death of Mary on Mt Zion (western catholic tradition) or at Gethsemane (eastern orthodox tradition), we really have nothing reliable to link these other family members with Jerusalem.
- The 3rd century writer Julius Africanus can perhaps come to our assistance. In a document aimed at reconciling the two genealogies of Jesus (in Matthew and Luke), he refers to an ancient tradition that speaks of descendent relatives of Jesus (called *desposinoi*) who travelled around preaching, and who were based in the north of Palestine, in Nazareth and Cochaba. As given in Eusebius (*HE* 1.7.14) it reads as follows:

    A few careful people ...took pride in preserving the memory of their aristocratic origin. These included the people mentioned above, known as Desposynoi because of their relationship to the Saviour's family. From the Jewish villages of Nazareth and Cochaba they passed through the rest of the country, expounding the genealogy discussed above, quoting from the books of Chronicles as far as they could trace it.

    While it cannot be firmly established, I believe it is reasonable to suggest that this later travelling activity of descendents of Jesus owed its origin to the initial missionary travels of his three brothers (i.e. those other than James). In other words, these three brothers eventually returned to their home base in the north, and from there they travelled the area (perhaps as far afield as Antioch and Damascus) with the message that their brother was the Messiah. Paul knows of their activity, though we have no reason to think he has ever met them in person.[10]

- Thus, when it came to the election of a successor to James, one of the unsaid presumptions was that the leader must be based in Jerusalem. The

---

[10] Though he does not develop the idea, Witherington, *What Have They Done With Jesus?* 219, agrees that apart from James, the rest of Jesus' family probably returned to Galilee after Easter.

three other brothers did not meet this qualification and for that reason alone were not considered. Symeon, however, was ideally suited. He was a close relative of Jesus, he and his family were well known and respected in the church (his father Clopas' memory was still preserved – Jn 19.25; Lk 24.18),[11] and he came from nearby Emmaus[12] – in fact, perhaps he had already relocated to Jerusalem.

This has been a long but necessary treatment of Simon, Jude, and, by implication, Jesus' third brother, Joseph. I believe that we must remain agnostic on whether they may have been alive at the time of the First Jewish Revolt. One or more of them may have died, but they may well have survived beyond AD 70. But even if any of them had died before AD 70, if they were resident in Galilee, we are in no position to expect that they would have been buried in a family tomb located in Jerusalem. They may have expressed a wish to be reunited with their brothers Jesus and James (and mother Mary?), but equally, they may have wished to be buried with their father Joseph (in Nazareth?).

So then, are Simon and Jude to be considered as missing from the Jesus Family Tomb at Talpiot A? I don't believe the evidence permits us to make that call. There is a more than likely chance that they were still alive in AD 70, and there is a reasonable chance that they were not resident in Jerusalem.

2.3 The Missing Brother – James

There is, of course, one other family member who is missing from the tomb, and we know that he died in Jerusalem. That person is James, the eldest of the four brothers of Jesus, and the leader of the Jerusalem based movement. We have already dealt with the questions relating to the provenance and authenticity of the 'James son of Joseph brother of Jesus' ossuary. What needs to be re-iterated is that if (and it's a big if) the so-called James ossuary housed the bones of Jesus of Nazareth's brother, then its absence from the Talpiot A tomb is a major negative against the Jesus Family Tomb thesis. Little wonder that Tabor and Jacobovici go to great lengths in seeking to establish the link between the ossuary and Talpiot A. Conversely, if the co-called James ossuary has nothing to do with Jesus of Nazareth's brother, because it is either a fraud or refers to someone else, then the question remains: where was James buried if not in Talpiot A? It is almost impossible to believe that James, the Lord's brother, who we know died in about AD 62, would not have been buried in

---

[11] In this I agree with Bauckham, *Jude and the Relatives of Jesus* 17, against Tabor, *Jesus Dynasty* 81 and 346 n11 who views Lk 24.18 as referring to someone else.

[12] The exact location of Emmaus is unknown, though a strong case can be made for its having been the now abandoned Arab village of Qoloniya, about 6 km from Jerusalem. See Peter Walker, *In the Steps of Jesus* (Zondervan, 2006) 204-205.

the family tomb, if such a tomb existed.[13] We can safely conclude that the absence from Talpiot A of an ossuary dedicated to James, brother of Jesus, is a major setback to the Jesus Family Tomb thesis.

3. Are All the Names in the Tomb Linked to Jesus' Family?

3.1 Matthew (*CJO* 703)

Rahmani's ossuary 703 is inscribed *matya*. Here is another problem, for no-one in the known family connections of Jesus went by that name. However, as we saw in Chapter 3, the name Matthew is fairly common in the family tree of Joseph recorded by Luke in Lk 3.23-38, where variants of the name Matthew are found six times, and two of these Matthews are sons of Levi. We also noted in Chapter 3 that Tabor abandoned his earlier proposal that the Matthew/Levi tax collector who becomes a disciple of Jesus was none other than Jesus' brother Joseph/Yoseh. Rather, the Matthew in Talpiot A is now an unknown member of Jesus' immediate family: 'He might be a son of one of Jesus' brothers. We just can't know.' (*Discovery* 107) With this statement we cannot but agree, but we also need to remind ourselves that such a thought is pure speculation lacking any evidence to support it. We can conclude that the presence of this ossuary does not help the thesis, but neither does it damage it, *unless* .... And the proviso is this: the thesis may be able to accommodate one puzzling ossuary without too much damage. But the presence of two or three begins to create real credibility problems. And this is where we now are headed.

---

[13] Early Christian tradition held to the view that James' burial place was not far from where he was killed (i.e. not far from the Temple site). This was affirmed by the 4th century scholar Jerome who lived nearby in Bethlehem. As well, the 2nd century Christian Hegesippus reported that the tomb of James was visible in the Kidron Valley (which runs alongside the Temple mount). Painter, *Just James* 314-324, provides extensive discussion of the traditions relating to the burial place of James. He regards the traditions relating to his burial within sight of the Temple as being a factor against support for either the James ossuary claims or the Talpiot burial claims.

3.2 Judah Son of Jesus (*CJO* 702)

Figure 26. *Judah Son of Jesus Ossuary with Inscription Clearly Visible (Rahmani)*

Ossuary 702 in the Rahmani catalogue is delicately ornamented with two six petalled rosettes, and bordered round its edges and down the centre with what is described as a zig-zag frame. The wording in formal text is clear and unambiguous. It is an adult sized ossuary though slightly smaller than others in the tomb,[14] and this is an important factor in considering its relevance to Jesus of Nazareth. If this mature age person named Judah was the child of Jesus and Mary Magdalene, then he would have been born at least 12 months after the commencement of Jesus' Galilean ministry. Let us make a few assumptions: (i) that Jesus died in AD 33; (ii) that Jesus' Galilean ministry lasted no more than a year;[15] and (iii) that Judah lived to be at least 15 years of age. If we grant these assumptions, then Judah's bones were placed in his ossuary no earlier than about AD 48. Let us now add one further presumption: (iv) that Judah's mother (Mary Magdalene) and father (Jesus) are also interred in the tomb. In the light of these presumptions we are surely entitled to ask why there is no hint of his existence either in the records and traditions of the New Testament and the early church fathers, or in the gnostic writings that, according to Tabor, preserve the memory of Mary Magdalene and her relationship to Jesus? After all, this is the Jesus Family Tomb, so this Judah was obviously *persona grata* with the family! In fact, his ossuary is inscribed with far more delicacy than that of his putative father!

[14] It is 55 x 23 x 27 cm. Others in the tomb vary from the large Mariamene ossuary (68.5 x 26 x 32.5), to 52 x 27 x 33 (Marya). On the basis of the size of the ossuary, Tabor suggests Judah son of Jesus died as a child. (*Jesus Dynasty* 328). But this is not the ossuary of a pre-pubescent child.

[15] This is the position I defended in my *The Enigmatic Jew* 123.

3.3 The Mariamene Mara Ossuary (*CJO* 701)

This ossuary is a problem to the Jesus Family Tomb thesis whichever way you look at it. We have already noted that the case is very strong for its being wrongly interpreted by Rahmani, and that there is a strong likelihood that it contained the bones of two persons, possibly two sisters or mother and daughter. Be that as it may, even the one person option can go no further, for we have already demonstrated that there is absolutely no historical justification for concluding that Mary Magdalene was married to Jesus of Nazareth. It is an unjustifiable series of jumps to leap from *mariamene mara* to Mary Magdalene to wife of Jesus. Whoever this Mary was, there are no justifiable historical grounds for concluding that she was Mary Magdalene, that is, that Mary Magdalene had married into the Jesus family. Remove Mary Magdalene and what are we left with? An ossuary that refers to either a Mary, or a Mary and a Martha. Either way, that's too many Marys for the family of Jesus!

3.4 Summary

The questions posed in the last two sections have resulted in damaging findings for the Jesus Family Tomb thesis. The all-important James, senior brother of Jesus, is missing from the tomb. His absence is a real problem for the claim that Talpiot A housed the Jerusalem-based family of Jesus. If his ossuary were to have been found (as some scholars assert) and if it were established that it did not originate from Talpiot A (see Chapter 4 and the summary of arguments from Krumbein and Cox), the headache for Tabor and Jacobovici would appear to be insurmountable. And we are also somewhat surprised that so few ossuaries were present for such an important family tomb.

Furthermore, in the tomb are three ossuaries whose 'owners' are not known to have any connection (by blood or marriage) with Jesus of Nazareth: Matthew, Judah son of Jesus, and Mary and Martha (or possibly just Mary). Justification for these persons involves leaps of presumption that have no historical base.

4. Other Factors for Consideration

4.1 Further Notes on the Jesus Ossuary

There are three further problems with the claim that *CJO* 704 is the ossuary of Jesus of Nazareth. I list them in ascending order of difficulty.

- We know from the ossuaries that have been catalogued by Rahmani that it was not uncommon for outside residents to Jerusalem to have their origin listed on the ossuary. This applies not only to those from foreign parts (Cyrenaica, Alexandria, Bithynia, Cilicia, Syria) but even to places within greater Judea. Thus Beth Shean (*CJO* 139), Sokho (*CJO* 257), Bet Alon (*CJO* 293) and Bethel (separately quoted but not in the catalogue) are known. Does this not suggest that an ossuary that housed Jesus from Nazareth would draw attention to his place of origin? Possibly, but what we don't know is how many people from elsewhere in Judea did not have their home town inscribed on their ossuary. In other words, we are simply not in a position to place this kind of expectation on the ossuary of Jesus of Nazareth. Having said that, neither does the evidence permit Tabor and Jacobovici to make this claim: '... a survey of ossuary inscriptions indicates that towns of origin are rarely given at all unless one is from outside the land of Israel ...'. (*Jesus Discovery* 108-109)

- A more nuanced approach is that of Prof. Jodi Magness, who indicated that 'If the Talpiot tomb is indeed the tomb of Jesus and his family, we would expect at least some of the ossuary inscriptions to reflect their Galilean origins'. Thus we might expect either Jesus son of Joseph from Nazareth; or Mary of Magdala and so on. This is a reasonable assumption, and I am inclined to agree with her conclusion that 'the inscriptions provide no indication that this is the tomb of a Galilean family and instead point to a Judean family'. But the absence is not conclusive proof.

- A further matter of note is the simplicity of ascription: nothing more than 'Jesus son of Joseph'. It is true that this is the way Jesus is referred to in the gospels (Lk 3.23; 4.22; Matt 13.55; Jn 1.45; 6.42), and it is also true that reference to one's father is quite common on ossuaries. But are we confident that this 'is precisely the ossuary inscription we would expect for Jesus'? (*Discovery* 107) Might we not have expected that in the case of Jesus, since his resurrection honoured as Lord (*mara*) and now the long awaited Messiah soon to return, some kind of honorific title would have been ascribed? After all, Tabor and Jacobovici are very quick to assert that Mary Magdalene was honoured in death as *mara*, so why not her husband? It's not sufficient to claim that inscriptions on ossuaries 'are not intended as public proclamations, but rather as private, intimate identification "tags" to help the family who is burying their dead over several generations keep straight which loved one's bones were put in which ossuary'. (*Jesus Discovery* 107-108) There is much truth in this, but it doesn't say everything. Many ossuaries were delicately embroidered, obviously as a sign of respect; some ossuaries were carelessly inscribed, some were inscribed with great care, and others were left uninscribed. It would seem that identification, though important, was not the only factor at work.

- That leads us to the major problem with the Jesus inscription. Look carefully again at the six inscriptions on the ossuaries. What is obvious is that the so-called Jesus inscription is in a class of its own – but not the right class! Four of the six are neatly inscribed in formal Hebraic script, suggesting considerable care was taken. Even the Mariamene inscription, the only one in Greek, shows that some care has been taken by the two hands that inscribed it. The line is straight and the letters clearly separated. All five are in stark contrast to the sloppy, semi-literate, and seemingly hasty style of the Jesus inscription. I am prepared to say that whoever wrote this inscription was showing no respect to Messiah Jesus. It is difficult to accept that if we are discussing the ossuary of Jesus of Nazareth the inscription was made by a family member (as Tabor and Jacobovici claim) or anyone else who honoured him as resurrected Lord. Nor will the informal cursive style of writing on the so-called Caiaphas ossuary serve as a comparison, as is suggested. For a start, the inscription is far more carefully written (as the photo on p 15 of *Jesus Discovery* reveals). As well, we are not at all confident that the Caiaphas referred to is the High Priest in office at the time of Jesus' death.[16] There is a world of difference between the Messiah and a member of the famous Caiaphas family.

All of the above comments have elements of subjectivity to them, but they are not unreasonable. The last observation in particular has been made by several respected scholars. *In my judgement, especially when contrasted with the other Talpiot inscriptions, it is almost impossible to imagine that Rahmani's ossuary 704 is making reference to Jesus of Nazareth.*

4.2 The Yoseh Ossuary (*CJO* 705)

As we noted in Chapter 3, the wording on this ossuary is important for the Jesus Family Tomb thesis. The argument of the thesis goes as follows:[17]

- Both Mark 6.3 and Matthew 13.55 refer by name to the four brothers of Jesus, and among them is a Joseph.
- Mark's gospel, however, uses an abbreviated nickname, *Iōsēs*, which is the Greek equivalent to the Hebrew, *Yoseh*.
- Matthew knows only the full name Joseph, and so he corrects Mark at this point.
- Mark, written earlier than Matthew, presents us with the 'earliest New Testament gospel tradition'.
- Mark's early tradition corresponds to what we find on the *Yoseh* ossuary.

---

[16] Tabor and Jacobovici (*Jesus Discovery* 15-16, 108) are too hasty in their presumption that the *Jehosef bar Qafa* ossuary refers to the son of the High Priest See my discussion in Chapter 1, and also note 9 for the reference to Bauckham's recent article.

[17] See *Jesus Discovery* 110-112.

- While *Yehosef* (= Joseph) is quite common on ossuaries, *Yoseh* is found only on our ossuary, and the Greek equivalent on six others.
- This conjunction of early gospel testimony and unique ossuary inscription provides support for the possibility that the *Yoseh* ossuary is that of the brother of Jesus by that name.

More recently, Eldad Keynan furthered the debate with an article published on the Bible and Interpretation web site.[18] Keynan makes the following claims:

- In the time of Jesus, *Yoseh* (the name on our ossuary) is virtually unknown and non-existent and it is not to be considered a variant of the more frequently found *Yosey*.
- The claims that *Yoseh* and *Yosey* were the same name, interchangeable, and pronounced the same, are incorrect. Keynan acknowledges that in 'day-to-day life' the same person may have been called *Yoseh* or *Yosey* by different people, but their formal birth name would have been clear and unambiguous.
- Jewish funerary inscriptions required that formal birth names should be inscribed. Rarely is a nickname inscribed without the formal name also being indicated. The reason for this is that in order to establish land ownership (and funerary ownership was linked to land ownership) 'formal birth names were crucial and irreplaceable'.

How shall we respond to these claims? We deal firstly with the biblical evidence relating to Jesus' brother.

- First, an important general comment. The mere fact that Mark was written first and that other evangelists made use of his work as a basis for their own, does not necessarily mean that where the earlier evangelist differs from the later, the earlier is more historically reliable. All sorts of reasons may explain the difference and the later gospel may well have corrected his written source because he knows another tradition. And that other tradition may well be more ancient and more reliable. Standing where we are, two thousand years later, we need to recognise that we simply cannot be certain which tradition is the earlier. Reading A, located in the earlier written record, is not necessarily more ancient than Reading B, located in the later document.[19] Tabor and Jacobovici were prepared to

---

[18] See http://www.bibleinterp.com/articles/key368019.shtml. The article is titled, 'Yoseh/Yosey – Heavyweight Names at Talpiot'. As at 10/30/2012 there were 23 items of correspondence.

[19] The recent writings of Dale Allison have done much to dispel the myth that modern scholarship can trace with accuracy the historical trajectory of the traditions that have

acknowledge this when they presumed that Matthew's ordering of the list of Jesus' brothers is a proper correction to that of Mark.[20]

- When we examine Mark carefully, we note that he refers to someone called Joseph on five occasions. Joseph of Arimathea is mentioned twice (15.43, 45). The other three references are at 6.3 (Jesus' brother) and 15.40, 47 ([probable] son of a Mary who witnessed Jesus' death and burial).[21] What is striking is that only Joseph of Arimathea is given the full spelling for Joseph – the other two Josephs are both written as *Iōsēs*.

- This observation raises the distinct possibility that for Mark his normal spelling for this name is *Iōsēs* (after all, it is capable of being declined in Greek, whereas *Iōsēf* is not).[22] Perhaps he breaks his rule in the case of Joseph of Arimathea only because this person's name is so fixed in the oral tradition he has received.

- It is also noteworthy that Matthew changes Mark's *Iōsēs* to *Iōsēf* not only at 13.55 (Jesus' brother) but also at 27.56 (women at the crucifixion scene).

- Is the Greek *Iōsēs* the equivalent only to the Hebrew/Aramaic *Yoseh* and to nothing else? The so-called 'fit' between the biblical text of Mark and the ossuary inscription requires this, but the point has not been established. In fact, with the Hebrew/Aramaic *Yosey* being overwhelmingly more common than *Yoseh*, and with the Greek spellings *Iōsēs*, *Iōsē*, *Iōse*, and *Iose* occurring with more or less equal frequency, it is more than likely that they were used to express *Yosey* more often than *Yoseh*.

- The only sound conclusion we can draw from all of this is that on the basis of the *literary* evidence available to us we have no grounds for concluding that one of the brothers of Jesus was normally called *Yoseh* rather than *Yosey* or *Yosef*. He may have been, but we would need more than what Mark has given us to have confidence on this matter. A simple transfer from Mark's Greek *Iōsēs* to the ossuary's Hebrew/Aramaic *Yoseh* will not do the trick. There are too many unknowns in between. All that we can

---

come down to us in the gospels. See, in particular, his *Constructing Jesus – Memory, Imagination and History*.

[20] On pages 110, 121 and 122 of *Jesus Discovery* Matthew's sequence of the brothers' names (James, Joseph, Simon and Judas) is adopted (and required for the thesis) rather than Mark's (James, Joseph, Judas and Simon).

[21] In Chapter 7 we rejected the proposal that Mark considers this Mary to be Jesus' mother. Hence, the *Iōsēs* at Mk 15.40, 47 is not Jesus' brother but someone else.

[22] In Ilan's *Lexicon* she lists nine variant Greek spellings of Joseph, and *Iōsēpos* is overwhelmingly dominant, occurring 47 times our of 69 listings. For this data I am dependent on Bauckham, 'The Names on the Ossuaries' Table 4 on p 109. Interestingly, this Greek spelling of Joseph is never used in the New Testament.

be reasonably confident of is that this brother was named after his father, Joseph, and that for some reason Mark chose to give to us an abbreviated Greek version, *Iōsēs*. [23]

Before considering the ossuary, we need to correct Jacobovici and Tabor in their reference to *Yoseh* as a nickname for the fuller *Yehosef*. 'Nickname' is not the appropriate term for this abbreviation. Real nicknames like 'the dour', 'the grasshopper', 'the mute', do occasionally turn up on the ossuaries. Much more frequent are short forms of fuller names (called hypocoristics).

- This leads us to the first observation on Hebrew names and ossuaries. Keynan's claim that formal birth names will have been inscribed on ossuaries fails to take account of two facts. Firstly, there are plenty of instances of shortened names (hypocoristics) being inscribed on ossuaries (for example, Mattai for Mattathiah; Liezer for Eliezer; Mara for Martha). Second, the irregular and slipshod character of some of the inscriptions supports the claim that such markings were not intended for public demonstration or to establish legal rights but simply for identification within the family. The evidence simply does not support Keynan's claim that what was inscribed, and what needed to be inscribed, was the formal birth name of the deceased.

- It needs also to be noted that nearly 75% of ossuaries listed in Rahmani have no inscription. Again, this weakens Keynan's argument for the importance of formal names to establish legal rights.

- Finally on Keynan's article, the claim that *Yoseh* and *Yosey* are quite different names and not at all interchangeable, appears to be contradicted by the (admittedly later) Talmudic evidence where Rabbi *Yoseh* and Rabbi *Yosey* are written of the same person in the same sentence.

- Turning to the ossuary, it is interesting to note that on the ossuaries catalogued by Rahmani there are eight variant spellings for Joseph, five in Hebrew/Aramaic and three in Greek. The full and 'normal' spelling of *yehosef* is the most frequent, found twelve of the nineteen times inscribed. Each of the other variants occurs once. Thus, while Tabor and Jacobovici are correct when they inform us that *yoseh* is found only on our ossuary, the fact that six other variants from the norm are found helps to put this information in perspective.

---

[23] Bauckham, 'The Names on the Ossuaries' 85, suggests as a possibility that this brother was formally named Joseph, but was commonly called Joses to distinguish him from his father. Again, this is possible, but we will never know.

- This amount of variation in spellings is not unusual. For example, Judah/Judas is represented by six variant spellings on twenty three ossuaries, five of them Hebrew/Aramaic and one Greek.

- The last two comments on spelling variants in names raise another important consideration. We need to recognise that, unlike in our own age, most people in ancient times rarely either spelled their name or saw it written. Thus, a person called *Yose* might have his name spelled in a variety of ways, and not always in the same way. Thus, the claims made for the relative uniqueness of *Yoseh* on our ossuary, while technically correct, are misleading. The one name could be spelled several ways in Hebrew script, all with the same (or almost the same) pronunciation, and likewise in Greek. It follows that to make a case on the basis of a particular spelling of a name is to fall into the trap of interpreting past practice in the light of our own times.

- When we ask why our ossuary has the shortened form of the name we are again faced with several possible reasons. As noted earlier, Rahmani has directed our attention to the similarity in inscription style between *Yoseh* and *Marya*. As well (though photos are not given), we are informed the ossuaries themselves are similar, and this suggests to Rahmani that we have a husband and wife set, both carefully and formally inscribed, and that the husband may well be the parent identified on the so-called Jesus ossuary that reads [*Yeshua???*] *son of Yehosef*. Otherwise this *Yehosef* remains unidentified, and the interrelationships within the tomb are blurred. Thus, Rahmani's proposal that links the three ossuaries (mother, father and son) appears to be the natural interpretation, but it is by no means certain. If this conjecture is correct, *Yoseh* may have been written by the professional engraver without consulting the family. Equally, however, it may have been the family that directed the choice of the name. But as to who dictated the spelling, we will never know.

- Even if we reject Rahmani's proposal that the *Yehosef* of *CJO* 704 ('[*Yeshua??*] son of *Yehosef*) is the same person as the *Yoseh CJO* 705, we should take seriously his suggestion that the similarity of script and of ossuary presents a strong case for *Yoseh* and *Marya* being husband and wife. It is certainly more natural to go down that path than to try to forge a linguistic and historical link between the *Yoseh* of the ossuary and the *Iōsēs* of Mark's gospel.

- One final challenge we need to put to Tabor and Jacobovici runs as follows: if the *Yoseh* on *CJO* 705 is the brother of Jesus of Nazareth, why does one ossuary (the so-called Jesus ossuary) make reference to the father (Joseph) while the other has no patronymic? And while we are comparing the two ossuaries, we return to the matter of the script on the so-called Jesus ossuary and that on the *Yoseh* ossuary. Why is the Messiah's brother's name inscribed so carefully, whereas, as we discussed earlier, the Messiah's name is inscribed in such a slipshod manner? It just doesn't add up.

What do we conclude from these various observations? It cannot be denied that *Yoseh* may have been the name by which the Joseph in *CJO* 705 was known in his family. But that is as far as we can go. As for Jesus' brother, Mark's choice of *Iōsēs* does not assure us that this brother was known in the family as *Yoseh*. Consequently, we cannot claim that 'there appears to be a complete "fit" between text and artifact'. (*Discovery* 112) There are just too many unknowns for such a claim.

4.3 The DNA Analysis

Finally, we return to the question of the DNA analysis performed on the fragments found in two of the ossuaries, the Mariamene and the Jeshua ossuaries.[24] The results established that the two persons tested bore no maternal blood relationship. They could not be brother and sister, nor mother and son. Tabor and Jacobovici are cautious in the conclusions they draw from this:

> *There is much more we would like to know from such tests, but even to be able to say that the Jesus son of Joseph in the tomb was not a brother or son of the woman called Mariamene Mara does nonetheless contribute to our understanding. It also correlates with the evidence that we have presented in this book that she is very possibly Mary Magdalene, the mother of Judah, the son of Jesus. (Discovery 202)*

Guarded as this conclusion is, it goes beyond the evidence. Consider the following:

- Ossuaries quite frequently contained the bones of more than one body. For example, the so-called Jonah ossuary in Talpiot B, as photographed in 1981, can be seen to be full of the bones of more than one person.[25] We have no way of being able to confirm whether the bone fragment in either tomb belonged to the person whose name is inscribed on the ossuary. For example, the fragment in the so-called Jesus ossuary may be the son of Joseph, or it may be that person's wife or his child. Indeed, it may even be the remains of someone placed in the ossuary in a later generation!

---

[24] The earlier tests, conducted in a laboratory in Toronto in 2006, are reported in *Jesus Family Tomb*, Chapter 13. The tests, repeated at the University of California in 2011, confirmed the earlier results. See *Jesus Discovery* 196-202.

[25] See the photo on p 89 of *Jesus Discovery*.

- We can make no presumptions as to the gender of the bone fragments being tested. The DNA analysis has not revealed to us the gender of the bone fragments, and it must not be assumed that the bones tested have been those of a male and a female correspondingly from the relevant 'Jesus' and 'Magdalene' ossuaries.
- Nor do we know the generational link between the two fragments. They may be separated by two, three or more generations. For example, the fragments in the Mariamene ossuary may be those of someone who died in 15 BC, while the fragments in the so-called Jesus ossuary could be the remains of someone who died just before the outbreak of the First Jewish Revolt – say, in AD 63. On that score, they could be separated from each other by three or four generations.

In other words, the DNA analysis has told us nothing more than that the two persons tested bore no maternal blood relationship to each other. If we had had fragments from all of the ossuaries in the tomb, the results may have been illuminating, but that luxury has not been granted to us. I venture to suggest that the results from the DNA analysis can provide absolutely no comfort to those who wish to espouse the Jesus Family Tomb thesis. Some may even dare to suggest it has been a waste of time and money.

5. Concluding Summary

The questions raised in this chapter have resulted in answers that are far from promising for the Jesus Family Tomb thesis. We can summarise them as follows:

- There is major doubt as to the names on the two most important ossuaries. The ossuary listed as 704 by Rahmani is so poorly inscribed that the first name cannot be clearly identified. *Yeshua* can be ranked as an outside possibility, but that is the most we can say for it. And yet the whole thesis of Tabor and Jacobovici rests upon an unambiguous *Yeshua* for this inscription.
- As to the Mariamene ossuary, the odds are heavily in favour of the correct reading being *Mariame kai Mara*. In other words, not one but two persons are remembered, a Mary and (probably) a Martha. There are no grounds for associating this ossuary with Mary Magdalene.
- The so-called Jesus ossuary is so clumsily inscribed, especially when compared with the others in the tomb, that it is almost impossible to believe that the bones of Messiah Jesus would have been notified in such a disrespectful manner.

- The absence from Talpiot A of an ossuary housing remains of James, brother of Jesus, is damaging to the thesis. After Jesus, the most senior member of the family was James and he certainly died in Jerusalem. A Jesus Family Tomb would certainly have housed his remains.
- The Judah son of Jesus ossuary faces the insurmountable difficulty that there is not a shred of evidence from early Christian sources that Jesus had a son. As Tabor and Jacobovici agree, the 'silence is ... quite deafening'. (*Discovery* 46) But not for the reasons they go on to suggest, namely, a conspiracy of silence by the male-centred church leadership that squashed all reference to Mary Magdalene, her leadership role and her marriage to Jesus, until it re-emerged in the faith of later gnostic groups. Rather, the silence is due to the absence of any historical support.
- Other claims can be seen to lead us nowhere. The *Yoseh* ossuary has no demonstrable link with the brother of Jesus; and the DNA analysis on the contents of ossuaries *CJO* 701 and 704 revealed nothing relevant.

In the Preface to Part B, attention was drawn to the need to find secure prosopographic fits when considering archaeological and literary evidence. In relation to the ossuaries in Talpiot A one can only conclude that there is not a single case of such a fit. Tabor and Jacobovici may wish to respond by claiming that though no single piece of evidence is a 'deal clincher', the cumulative evidence supports the Jesus Family Tomb thesis. Our analysis, on the contrary, concludes that (i) there is nothing of a positive nature in the Talpiot A tomb that supports any link back to Jesus of Nazareth, and (ii) there is much that argues against a link with Jesus.

To this negative assessment may be added the conclusions drawn from the four studies in Part B. The literary and historical evidence relating to (i) Jesus' marital status, (ii) Mary Magdalene, (iii) Joseph of Arimathea and the burial of Jesus, and (iv) the first Christians' view of Jesus' resurrection body – these four issues were found to be major road blocks for the Tabor/Jacobovici thesis.

6. What About the Statistical Analysis?

With all of the conclusions from Chapters 6-11 behind us we are now in a position to give the appropriate attention to the famous claims made about the names in the Talpiot A tomb and the statistical probability that they support the Jesus Family Tomb thesis. I have kept the statistical question to the very end, for as we shall see, the conclusions reached so far cannot be left out of the statistical equation.

6.1 The Case from Statistical Analysis[26]

As we noted in Chapter 3, statistical analysis has played an important supporting role in the case for the Jesus Family Tomb. Early in the piece, Jacobovici and Pellegrino were convinced that statistical analysis would provide confirmation of their conclusions about the Jesus Family Tomb. Writing in 2007 they affirmed: 'The proof of this cluster of biblical names would be revealed in the numbers.' By 2012 that confidence had become more measured: 'We do not believe that statistics alone prove one way or the other that the Talpiot Jesus tomb is that of Jesus of Nazareth …'.[27]

I will not repeat what has already been presented in Chapter 3, but the following points should be noted concerning the methodology applied:

- The question asked has always been: 'What is the statistical likelihood of the following list of names being found in the one family tomb?'
- Over several analyses the input data varied from being quite specific (e.g. *Yoseh* rather than Joseph; Mariamene rather than Mary) to being quite generic (*Yoseh* treated as Joseph; Mariamene treated as Mary)
- In its most generic or open listing, the names usually included the following: Jesus, son of Joseph, Mary, a second Mary, and Joseph.
- Some names were treated as neutral and were not included in the analysis: Matthew; Judah son of Jesus.
- Surprise or negative factors were also brought into the calculation: the absence of Jesus' brothers James and Jude were given negative probability values.

When all of the above were taken into consideration, including the generic listing for Mariamene and *Yoseh* and the application of negative factors, a probability result of 600:1 was arrived at. As we noted in Chapter 3, once the input data was changed (for example, include Jude son of Jesus; change Mary to Mariamene), the probability result expands considerably. Add the names on the James ossuary and you have a result that runs into the millions to one.

6.2 Asking the Right Question

The case from statistical analysis has provoked considerable response from the scholarly community. Many pointed out that the names on the ossuaries were so common that nothing of significance could be drawn from their presence together. The response from the Jesus Family Tomb community was to point

---

[26] Details of the use of statistics by Jacobovici, Pellegrino and Tabor are found in *Jesus Family Tomb* 69-83, 112-115; *Jesus Discovery* 323-329; and *Jesus Discovery* 116-119.

[27] *Jesus Family Tomb* 70; *Jesus Discovery* 118.

out that such a combination of names in the one tomb *was* unusual, as the statistics made clear. I have sympathy with this response as far as it goes. But a more helpful way forward was offered by Dr Randy Ingermanson. His critique of the statistical process involved was that it asked the wrong question. Instead of asking about the statistical likelihood of certain names being found in the one family tomb, Ingermanson insists that the correct question should be: *what is the probability that the Jesus of this tomb is Jesus of Nazareth?*

I believe that Ingermanson is correct for the following reason: the original question put to the statisticians ('What is the statistical likelihood of the following list of names being found in the one family tomb?') takes us only so far. It ignores all of the historical and other considerations that have been discussed in Part B and Part C. These considerations, which in the main have a negative impact upon the Jesus Family Tomb thesis, cannot be ignored. They also need to be brought into the equation. To this end, I have listed some of these factors, and in brackets offered my own arbitrary (and, I believe, generous) evaluation of the probability of each.

- There is a strong possibility that the son of Joseph named on Rahmani's ossuary 704 is not named *Yeshua* (probability factor: x 0.50).
- To my knowledge, no scholar of any repute believes that the historical and literary evidence supports the notion that Jesus of Nazareth was married (probability factor: x 0.10).
- The possibility that Jesus of Nazareth had a child named Judah receives no support from the evidence of early Christianity, including Christian debates with Judaism (probability factor: x 0.05)
- Ossuary *CJO* 704 is so poorly and clumsily written, that even if the first name is *Yeshua* it is unlikely to refer to someone honoured in death as Messiah (probability factor: a very generous 0.75)
- The Mariamene Mara ossuary quite likely refers to two persons and not one (probability factor: x 0.40).
- There is no evidence that Mary Magdalene was the wife of Jesus. Thus the presence of an extra Mary and as well as a Martha in this family tomb is problematic for they are not members of Jesus' family (see next dot point).
- Once you have factored in non-family members named Mary and Martha, should we not also give a negative value to the Matthew ossuary? The original statisticians gave it a neutral value and did not take it into account. That is probably acceptable for the presence of only one name unknown to the family of Jesus. But once you get three (Mary, Martha [or

a male, Mara]), it is difficult to ignore them. For this reason, I have given a negative valuation for the combined three names (probability factor: x 0.40).

- The absence of James, brother of Jesus, from the tomb is extremely damaging to the Jesus Family Tomb thesis. Feuerverger gave it a negative probability factor of 0.50. In the light of the important critiques of Krumbein and Cox, it should have a higher negative valuation (x 0.20).
- What negative value do we place on the undoubted and consistent early Christian conviction that Jesus had been physically raised, that is, that his body did not remain in a tomb? The matter cannot be ignored (probability factor: x 0.60).
- Do you give any valuation to the absence on all the ossuaries of any reference to Nazareth? Or is it a neutral consideration?
- In contrast to Feuerverger, and in line with our discussion earlier in this chapter, I see no reason to consider the absence of Jesus' brother Judas as a negative factor.

We could have brought forward other negatives, but this will do for the purpose of the exercise. Commencing with the 600:1 likelihood that Feuerverger arrived at, and multiplying it by the above 7 factors given a numerical valuation, we arrive at the figure of 0.0216:1 – that is, rather than being 600% likely to be the tomb of Jesus, the chance has reduced to 2.1%. The ratio has changed from 600:1 to 0.0216:1. Of course, the probability valuations I have given to these factors are subjective since there is no objective rule that one can apply. Others will give differing valuations, some more negative, some more generous. For example, one may be tempted to give a 0.0 valuation to the chance that Jesus had a son, and thus destroy the whole statistical exercise altogether! But historians do not deal in absolute certainties at either end of the spectrum, so it is best to give it some positive value, however small.

I suspect that the Jesus Family Tomb promoters will reject the above exercise altogether. Reading both *Jesus Dynasty* and *Jesus Discovery* one is left in no doubt that the archaeological findings must not be held to ransom by the traditional judgements of historians. Now, we can all agree that history must always be prepared to be re-evaluated in the light of new findings in other fields, especially archaeology. In theory one can only agree with this point. As I wrote a moment ago, history does not deal in certainties but only in degrees of probability and improbability. But there comes a time when the evidence from historical documents and tradition is so powerful that it would take a monumental and virtually unchallengeable discovery to overthrow the virtually unanimous judgement of history. However, when that discovery is itself fraught with its own problems of authenticity (for example, the readings on the Mariamene Mara and the Jesus ossuaries), one is justified in advancing only with extreme caution.

One further comment. What I have done in factoring in the force of historical and literary judgements is nothing more than following through with consistency what Feuerverger had already done in giving a negative probability value to the absence of James and Jude.

6.3 Concluding Comments

No doubt there will be many who wonder about the whole exercise of applying a mathematical approach to historical questions. As an historian, I sympathise with such scepticism. The factors involved in coming to historical judgements are complex. I would venture to add that giving a mathematical value to an historical consideration is an almost impossible task. Coming to historical judgements is difficult enough as it is!

Be that as it may, if we must apply ourselves to a statistical judgement, it is important that the correct question be asked. Ingermanson's approach does just that, for it allows established historical judgements, doubts and problems to be brought into the equation. As far as this exercise goes, the result is far from promising: on statistical grounds alone, there is little to encourage us to believe that Talpiot A is the family tomb of Jesus and that his own bones were placed there in his own ossuary.

7. Bibliographic Listing

The list of responses to the Jesus Family Tomb thesis is almost endless, particularly those on personal blogs and web sites. The following list is in no way intended to be exhaustive. Other relevant works/articles will be found in the general bibliography.

Bauckham, Richard, 'The Alleged "Jesus Family Tomb"' at http://www.christilling.de/blog/ctblog.html

Gibson, Shimon, 'Is the Talpiot Tomb Really the Family Tomb of Jesus?' from *Near Eastern Archaeology (= NEA)*, vol 69, No. 3/4 (Sept-Dec, 2006) 118-124; available at http://www.jstor.org/stable/25067661

Habermas, Gary R, *The Secret of the Talpiot Tomb* (Holman Reference, 2007)

Ingermanson, Randy: 'Statistics and the "Jesus Family Tomb"' at http://www.ingermanson.com/jesus/art/stats.php

Keynan, Eldad, 'Yoseh/Yosey – Heavyweight Names at Talpiot' at http://www.bibleinterp.com/articles/key368019.shtml

Magness, Jodi, 'Has the Tomb of Jesus Been Discovered?' in SBL Forum, 2007, available at http://www.sbl-site.org/Article.aspx?ArticleId=640

Meyers, Eric, 'The Jesus Tomb Controversy: An Overview' from *NEA*, Vol 69, No. 3/4 (Sept-Dec, 2006) 116-118, available at http://www.jstor.org/stable/25067660

Pfann, Stephen, 'Mary Magdalene Has Left the Room: A Suggested New Reading of Ossuary CJO 701' from *NEA*, Vol 69, No. 3/4 (Sept-Dec 2006) 130-131; available at http://www.jstor.org/stable/25067664

Quarles, Charles (ed), *Buried Hope or Risen Savior?* (B&H Publishing, 2008)

Rollston, Christopher, 'Prosopography and the Talpyot Yeshua Family Tomb: Pensees of a Palaeographer' in SBL Forum 2007, available at http://www.sbl-site.org/Article.aspx?ArticleId=649

Scham, Sandra, 'Trial by Statistics' from *NEA*, Vol 69, No. 3/4 (Sept-Dec, 2006) 124-125, available at http://www.jstor.org/stable/25067662

Web sites of: James Tabor, Mark Goodacre, Ben Witherington, Steve Caruso, James Charlesworth, Jesus Dynasty blog, University of the Holy Land (Stephen Pfann articles)

CONCLUSION

We commenced this study with a bold statement from James Tabor: "This promises to be one of the greatest and most controversial archaeological finds in history." This he wrote in 2007, well before the re-opening of the Talpiot B tomb in 2010, which gave even further support to the Jesus Family Tomb thesis. Here, just a stone's throw from Talpiot A, was another family tomb, and three of its ossuaries had inscriptions which, so the thesis goes, provided virtual proof that a wealthy Judaeo-Christian (probably Joseph of Arimathea) had established his family tomb as close as possible to that of Jesus.

So then, according to Tabor and Jacobovici, these two tomb complexes and the ossuaries they hold/held,[1] have opened up a whole new perspective on our understanding of Jesus of Nazareth, his disciples, and the early Judaeo-Christians of Jerusalem. Among other things, we now know:

- After his crucifixion, Jesus was removed from his temporary burial site on the edge of Jerusalem, and was honourably buried in Talpiot A.
- This deed was performed by Joseph of Arimathea.
- The bones from his decayed body were eventually gathered and placed in his own marked ossuary.
- His family and disciples came to know of this burial site, and yet proclaimed and worshipped him as the risen Messiah and Lord. Resurrection for them did not require that Jesus' body no longer be in the tomb.
- The appearance traditions in Luke and John which, they claim, suggest that Jesus' resurrection state was as a resuscitated body are a late first century fabrication.
- Talpiot A was granted to the Jerusalem-based family of Jesus by a wealthy benefactor, most likely Joseph of Arimathea, and over the years until the First Jewish Revolt (AD 66-70) it came to house the bodies of deceased members of Jesus' family.
- Among the bodies housed in Talpiot A were those of Mary (mother of Jesus), and of Mary Magdalene.
- Jesus was married to Mary Magdalene, as evidence from later gnostic and rabbinic writings supports.

---

[1] The Talpiot A ossuaries are all now held in the Rockefeller Museum under the care of the Israel Antiquities Authority; the Talpiot B ossuaries remain *in situ*. The so-called James ossuary, has not, as far as I know, been returned to its owner Oded Golan, and is still held by the IAA.

- Remnants of gospel traditions, especially in John's gospel, also point to a close physical relationship between Jesus and Mary Magdalene, traditions that were either suppressed or misunderstood by the evangelists.
- Jesus and Mary Magdalene produced a son who died before AD 66-70 and was buried in Talpiot A.
- Mary Magdalene exercised an apostolic and leadership role in the early Jerusalem-based church, the memory of which was suppressed by the male leadership, especially Peter, and the gospel writers.
- The ossuary inscribed 'James son of Joseph brother of Jesus' originally came from Talpiot A.
- Statistical analysis of the names on the ossuaries in Talpiot A overwhelmingly supports the conclusion that they are the names of members of Jesus of Nazareth's family.

Here is indeed a thesis that has the potential to be a 'game-changer' when it comes to our understanding of Jesus and early Christianity. But it has one major problem: it doesn't pass the test! In fact, it doesn't pass any of the tests that we both want and need to put to it.

1. The Test of Historical and Literary Coherence.

There is much that is unknown and uncertain about Jesus and the early Christian community. At the same time, there is also much that is known and about which the scholarly community can be confident. Among these are:

- There is no evidence, either from the New Testament or from the literature of the early centuries (Christian, pagan, Jewish) that provides any support for the claims that Jesus was married and fathered a son. In fact, the evidence suggests the very opposite: like his mentor, John the Baptist, Jesus foreswore marriage and devoted himself to a life of celibacy in the cause of prophetically preaching the coming Kingdom of God.
- Even the early gnostic literature provides no support for the claim that Mary Magdalene was the wife of Jesus or had a sexual association with him.
- There is no evidence from any early Christian literature that Mary Magdalene exercised any role of apostolic dignity or authority in the early Jerusalem based Christian community.
- There is no evidence that the early Christians knew of a second burial of Jesus away from the place of his first burial, and certainly not a second burial on a property owned by Joseph of Arimathea. In fact, from *G Peter* 6.24 we know that tradition knew of only one burial, in 'Joseph's garden'.

- The Jesus Family Tomb thesis requires the family of Jesus, the disciples, and eventually the whole Christian community, to have known that Jesus remained buried and decomposing in a second tomb. Yet those same people boldly preached that the resurrection of the dead had commenced on Easter Day. We have seen, however, that Luke and John were not the only two early Christian writers who stood in opposition to this presumption that a risen Jesus could at the same time be decomposing in a nearby tomb.

As we saw in Part B, these confident judgements of the overwhelming majority of scholars serve as hurdles that the Jesus Family Tomb thesis needs either to clear or to remove altogether from the track. And yet it can do neither – not because the thesis threatens entrenched and dogmatic positions,[2] but because the consensus scholarly conclusions are so cogent. To change the metaphor, the hurdles, in fact, become road blocks, stopping the thesis dead in its tracks.

In short, as we saw in Chapter 5, the Jesus Family Tomb thesis involves such a radical restructuring of the narrative of Jesus and the early Judaeo-Christian movement, that one of the two needs to be rejected. In the light of the many flaws and weaknesses in the Tabor/Jacobovici thesis, the choice is not difficult.

2. The Test of the Nearby Tomb Complex

When the optic fibre cameras revealed the contents of the Talpiot B tomb and managed to reveal the inscriptions on three of the ossuaries, their interpretation by Jacobovici and Tabor was quickly seen to provide the icing on the cake for the Jesus Family Tomb thesis. Here, a mere stone's throw from Talpiot A was 'reliable archaeological evidence' (*Discovery* 1) of (i) faith in the resurrection of the Jesus who lay buried nearby [the four line inscription + Jonah delivered from the sea monster]; (ii) testimony to a saying of Jesus that predates any of our gospels [Jonah as witness to the Q tradition behind Matt 12.40]; and (iii) the earliest example of Christian art [Jonah and the fish] predating by over 100 years later Christian adoption of the Jonah cycle, especially on sarcophagi.

But again, on close examination the promised yield proves to be totally elusive. The four line inscription conveys no allusion to Jesus, nor can we have any confidence that at line 3 the use of the verb *hupsoon* (to exalt, lift up) is intended to affirm any hope of resurrection. The one thing that can be said with confidence is that lines 1 and 2, which probably combine the divine name of Jewish faith with a derivative of Greek Zeus, could not have been written by an early Judaeo-Christian. For the early followers of Jesus Messiah, such

---

[2] For example, there is no dogmatic or theological reason why Jesus of Nazareth could not have married. A married Jesus would not be a threat to any aspect of Christian theology.

a blending would have been a compromise to the purity of Jewish faith – a purity which faith in Jesus in no way diluted.

As to the so-called Jonah ossuary, everything stands against the interpretation that Tabor and Jacobovici give to it: (i) The Jonah saying of Matt 12.40 is a late development of an earlier more cryptic saying of Jesus. It thus arrives too late into the gospel tradition, well after AD 70, to influence us in the interpretation of this ossuary. (ii) The engraving itself only superficially looks like a fish – an upside down one! On closer inspection it looks more like a rather crudely drawn amphora. (iii) Attempts to see the carving of a stick man, along with his name 'Jonah', are quite unconvincing – there are too many lines. And (iv) later Christian art, using the Jonah cycle, bears no resemblance to what is seen the on the Talpiot B ossuary.

So then, Talpiot B and its ossuaries, far from being a positive support to the Jesus Family Tomb thesis, is not even a neutral onlooker. Tabor and Jacobovici affirm that the two tomb complexes a mere 60 metres from each other were both part of the one private estate (belonging to Joseph of Arimathea). If this conjecture were correct, then the openly hellenistic Jewish faith that Talpiot B seems to demonstrate, at least on one of its ossuaries, does not bode well for what one may wish to say about the other complex.

Of course, 60 metres is a fair distance in Jerusalem and its environs. Remove the Joseph of Arimathea Estate hypothesis, and there is no reason to associate the two tombs. Even less when we recall that a third tomb complex (now destroyed and built over) was also found nearby. In conclusion, there is no good reason to associate Talpiot B with Talpiot A.

3. The Test of the Original Tomb Complex and its Ossuaries

When we turned to the Talpiot A complex, with its nine (originally ten) ossuaries, six of them inscribed, the Jesus Family Tomb thesis initially looked like an open and shut case. So many names crop up, names known to be associated with Jesus of Nazareth. Even the original statistical analysis supported the conclusion: this must be the family tomb of Jesus.

But again, the case quickly falls apart:

- The two key players, Jesus and Mary Magdalene, cannot with any confidence, be identified on the ossuaries. For different reasons, the identification of their ossuaries is dubious, to say the least.
- Even if the name 'Jesus' is read on the so-called Jesus ossuary, the quality of the inscription makes it virtually impossible to imagine that it held the bones of the revered Messiah Jesus.

- Too many names are present that are unknown to us from the narrative of Jesus' family: Matthew, Jude son of Jesus, a second Mary.
- The most important Jesus family member in the early Christian community, James, brother of Jesus, is absent.
- When the question posed for statistical analysis is reconfigured, the statistical likelihood of its being the Jesus Family Tomb suddenly evaporates.

The interpretation of the ossuaries in Talpiot A is, or course, the key to the whole Jesus Family Tomb thesis. This is where it began. And this is where it ends! The thesis fails the very first of the tests put to it: the ossuaries in Talpiot A simply will not bear the weight of interpretation placed upon them.

4. The Tests of Methodological Soundness and Consistency

As we analysed the Tabor/Jacobovici thesis, we made occasional comment on some of the critical presuppositions that have been applied in order to support the thesis. We made reference to what we can only describe as a measure of selectivity when it came to making critical judgements. Among them are:

- Argument from Silence Applied Arbitrarily. For example, the silence of the New Testament on the post-Easter leadership role of Mary Magdalene is taken to be evidence that the male leadership quickly took steps to suppress memory of her (and her child), and that the evangelists were either ignorant of her true status, or joined in the suppression. (*Discovery* 129-130) Or again, the 'quite deafening' silence (*Discovery* 46) of the New Testament on whether Jesus was married and had children becomes the grounds for looking more suspiciously at the texts, in the attempt to find traces of suppression and cover up. Not surprisingly, the evidence is found (as we saw, in John 20). The problem is, the silence only becomes evidence if you are already determined to read it as such. The evidence itself is silent.
- Lateness of Dating Indicates Greater Ignorance. This 'rule' is frequently applied without any justification. For example, the gospels, 'removed five or six decades from the events, know nothing (*sic!*)' of the life of the earliest community in Jerusalem. (*Discovery* 195-6) No justification is given for this claim, nor do Tabor and Jacobovici consider the possibility that the evangelists drew heavily on early traditions, and that the author of Luke-Acts may well have been Luke, the travelling companion of Paul, who spent time in Jerusalem. Nor is any thought given to the possibility that the author of Mark's gospel may well have had contact with Peter (as tradition from the second century affirms). As to the Fourth Gospel, no

consideration is given to the possibility that underpinning this gospel is the witness of a former disciple of Jesus resident in Judea.

- The Earliest Written is the Earliest Known. Conversely to the last rule, when it suits, this principle is applied. For example, on the question of the name of Jesus' brother Iōsēs/Joseph, Mark is to be preferred ahead of Matthew, as he is earlier. But the rule can be ignored, however, when convenience demands otherwise – for example where Matt 13.55 rather than Mk 6.3 is taken to present the correct birth order of Jesus' brothers. Again, John's (and Luke's) accounts of the resurrection appearances are deemed to be late, and therefore unhistorical, and yet John's account of the appearance to Mary Magdalene is taken to offer clues to the real marital relationship between Jesus and Mary.

- Possibilities become Presumptions of Fact. On many occasions one reads a claim that a certain text or reading may well be the correct reading or interpretation. This suggestion will often be repeated more than once, and in no time at all either the possibility has become a presumption of fact, or the reader is being told 'we are convinced' of the correctness of the case. The most damaging example is the reading of the so-called Jesus ossuary (Rahmani's *CJO* 704) – recognised as difficult to read, and yet almost in the next breath presumed without doubt to read 'Jesus son of Joseph'. Again, the suggestion that 'Magdala' and a Talmudic tradition *may* shed light on Mary's being the bearer of Jesus' son becomes a 'we are convinced' – as if that settled the matter.

- Q was an Early Gospel. This scholarly hypothesis is accepted without question as fact. Q is taken to have been written earlier than the four canonical gospels; its traditions are therefore earlier and enable us to 'go behind the gospels as they now stand and see an earlier time when the Jesus movement was young.' (*Discovery* 75) While many scholars may agree with these sentiments, others do not. We have seen how they have been applied to the interpretation of the Jonah ossuary.

Proper treatment of the critical methodology applied by Tabor and Jacobovici calls for a separate study – perhaps even a research thesis! A faulty, questionable or inconsistent methodology does not in itself guarantee incorrect conclusions. What it does suggest is that the researcher knows the conclusion he/she wants to arrive at, and will conveniently apply the critical tools which suit the desired conclusion. I have to say that this is the impression one gains while reading *The Jesus Discovery*. This means, of course, that when a more sound use of the tools of critical analysis is applied, the risk is great that the original conclusion drawn will collapse. Time and again, in our analysis of the Tabor/Jacobovici readings of the historical data, we have seen this to be the case.

5. The Test of the Prosopographic Fit

In the Preface to Part B, we introduced the concept of the prosopographic fit, whereby the evidence derived from texts, epigraphy and other data can be brought together to create a composite picture of a known historical personage. We saw that great caution needs to be exercised lest *faux* evidence be wrongly applied.

In the course of their investigations, Tabor and Jacobovici have presented the case that the two Talpiot tombs assist in our creating prosopographic fits for a range of names known to us from early Christianity. Among the names thrown up by the two tombs are: Jesus of Nazareth, Mary Magdalene, Joseph of Arimathea, James the brother of Jesus, Judah the son of Jesus and Mary Magdalene, and Mary the mother of Jesus. But it doesn't work. Three of the above names are not even identified on any ossuary from the tombs (Mary Magdalene, Joseph of Arimathea, James the brother of Jesus). No Judah, son of Jesus, is known from any early Christian records. And an ossuary, whose inscription may just possibly identify a certain Jesus, has been shown to have little chance of being a reference to Jesus of Nazareth.

In other words, against the strict standards that are applied in the scholarly community, nothing from the Talpiot tombs provides any prosopographic fit with any person known to us from early Christianity.

Conclusion

So, where does the Jesus Family Tomb thesis leave us? Certainly no closer to our understanding of Jesus of Nazareth, his disciples and the early Christian movement. What we have are two tomb complexes, reasonably close together, but with no demonstrable association with each other. One of the tombs (Talpiot B) provides interesting data (via the four line inscription) on the theological outlook current in 2nd Temple Judaism. The other tomb (Talpiot A) adds nothing new to our understanding of contemporary Judaism, and certainly has nothing to do with Jesus and his movement.

According to the Gospel of Mark, an angelic young man greeted the women on Easter Day with the words, 'You are seeking Jesus the Nazarene who was crucified. ... He is not here!' (Mk 16.6) I know of no angelic presence guarding the Talpiot A tomb, but if there were one, I am confident his message would be the same, though, just to make the point clear, he may well add: 'He is not here – he never has been!' Whether, as he did on Easter Day, he would also affirm, 'He is risen!', is a matter for each of us to decide.

BIBLIOGRAPHY

Albright, W F 'Recent Discoveries in Palestine and the Gospel of St John' in Davies and Daube (eds), *The Background of the New Testament and its Eschatology* (CUP, 1964)

Allison, Dale *Jesus of Nazareth, Millenarian Prophet* (AugsburgFortress, 1998)

Allison, Dale *Resurrecting Jesus: The Earliest Christian Tradition and its Interpreters* (T&T Clark, 2005)

Allison, Dale *Constructing Jesus – Memory, Imagination, and History* (SPCK, 2010)

Bagatti, B *The Church of the Circumcision – History and Archaeology of the Judaeo-Christians* (Franciscan Printing, 1984)

Bammel, E (ed) *The Trial of Jesus* (SCM, 1970)

Barrett, C K *The Gospel According to St John* (SPCK, 1978)

Batey, R 'Jesus and the Theatre,' *NTS* 30 (1984) 563-574

Batey, R *Jesus and the Forgotten City* (Baker, 1991)

Bauckham, Richard *Jude and the Relatives of Jesus in the Early Church* (T&T Clark, 1990)

Bauckham, Richard 'James and the Jerusalem Church' in Bauckham (ed), *The Book of Acts in its Palestinian Setting* (Eerdmans, 1995).

Bauckham, Richard *Jesus and the Eyewitnesses – the Gospels as Eyewitness Testimony* (Eerdmans, 2006)

Bauckham, Richard 'The Names on the Ossuaries' in C Quarles (ed), *Buried Hope or Risen Savior?* (B&H Publishing, 2008) 69-111

Bauckham, Richard 'The Caiaphas Family,' *Journal for the Study of the Historical Jesus* 10 (2012) 3-31

Beasley-Murray, G *John* (WBC 36; Word, 1987)

Blinzler, J *The Trial of Jesus* (Mercier, 1959).

Brown, R E *The Gospel According to John* (Anchor Bible; 2 vols; Doubleday, 1966)

Brown, R E *The Birth of the Messiah* (Geoffrey Chapman, 1977)

Brown, R E *Community of the Beloved Disciple* (Geoffrey Chapman, 1979)

Brown, R E *The Death of the Messiah* (2 vols; Doubleday, 1994)

Bultmann, R *The Gospel of John* (Blackwell, 1971)

Byrne, Ryan and McNary-Zak, Bernadette (eds) *Resurrecting the Brother of Jesus – the James Ossuary Controversy and the Quest for Religious Relics* (Uni of North Carolina, 2009)

Carson, D A *The Gospel According to John* (Eerdmans, 1991)

Charlesworth, James H (ed) *Jesus and Archaeology* (Eerdmans, 2006)

Chow, Simon *The Sign of Jonah Reconsidered* (CB NTS 27; Almqvist & Wiksell, 1995)

Collins, J J *Beyond the Qumran Community – The Sectarian Movement of the Dead Sea Scrolls* (Eerdmans, 2010)

Crossan, J D *The Historical Jesus: The Life of a Mediterranean Jewish Peasant* (CollinsDove, 1991)

Crossan, J D *Who Killed Jesus?* (HarperCollins, 1995)

Crossan J D and Reed, J *Excavating Jesus* (HarperCollins, 2001)

Culpepper, R A 'John 21:24-25: The Johannine *Sphragis*' in P N Anderson, F Just and T Thatcher (eds), *John, Jesus, and Histor, Volume 2 – Aspects of Historicity in the Fourth Gospel* (Society of Biblical Literature, 2009)

Davies, W D and Allison, Dale *Matthew* (ICC; 3 vols; T&T Clark, 1998-1997)

Dodd, C H *Historical Tradition in the Fourth Gospel* (CUP, 1963)

Ehrman, Bart and Pleše, Zlatko *The Apocryphal Gospels* (OUP, 2011)

Eusebius *History of the Church* (Penguin edition, 1989)

Evans, Craig *Jesus and the Ossuaries* (Baylor Uni Press, 2003)

Evans, Craig *Jesus and his World: the Archaeological Evidence* (SPCK, 2012)

Farrer, A M 'On Dispensing with Q' in D E Nineham (ed), *Studies in the Gospels – Essays in Memory of R H Lightfoot* (Blackwell, 1967).

Finegan, Jack *The Archaeology of the New Testament* (Princeton University Press, 1978)

Funk, R and Hoover, R et al, *The Five Gospels* (Polebridge, 1993)

Funk, R et al *The Acts of Jesus* (Polebridge, 1998)

Gamble, Harry *Books and Readers in the Early Church* (Yale Uni Press, 1995)

Gärtner, Bertil *The Theology of the Gospel of Thomas* (Collins, 1961)

Goodacre, Mark *The Case Against Q. Studies in Markan Priority and the Synoptic Problem* (Trinity, 2002)

Goodacre, Mark *Thomas and the Gospels. The Case for Thomas' Familiarity with the Synoptics* (Eerdmans, 2012).

Gundry, R H *Matthew: A Commentary on his Literary and Theological Art* (Eerdmans, 1982)

Gundry, R H *Mark* (Eerdmans, 1993)

Habermas, Gary *The Secret of the Talpiot Tomb* (B&H Publishing, 2007)

Hagner, D *Matthew 14-28* (WBC 33B; Word, 1995)

Hachlili, Rachel *Ancient Jewish Art and Archaeology in the Land of Israel* (Brill, 1988)

Hachlili, Rachel 'The Qumran Cemetery Reassessed' in *The Oxford Handbook of the Dead Sea Scrolls* (Lim and Collins [eds]; OUP, 2010)

Haenchen, E *John* (Hermeneia; 2 vols; Fortress, 1984)

Harris, Murray J *Raised Immortal – Resurrection and Immortality in the New Testament* (Eerdmans, 1983)

Hengel, Martin *Judaism and Hellenism* (SCM, 1974)

Hengel, Martin *Crucifixion* (SCM, 1977)

Hengel, Martin *The 'Hellenization' of Judaea in the First Century after Christ* (SCM, 1989)

Hengel, Martin *The Four Gospels and the One Gospel of Jesus Christ* (Trinity, 2000)

Horsley, R A *Jesus and the Spiral of Violence* (Harper and Row, 1987)

Horsley, R A *Bandits, Prophets and Messiahs* (Harper and Row, 1988)

Horsley, R A *Galilee – History, Politics, People* (Trinity, 1999)

Humphreys, Colin *The Mystery of the Last Supper* (CUP, 2011)

Ilan, Tal *Lexicon of Jewish Names in Late Antiquity* (Mohr Siebeck, 2002)

Jacobovici, Simcha and Pellegrino, Charles *The Jesus Family Tomb* (HarperCollins, 2007)

James, M R *The Apocryphal New Testament* (Oxford; Clarendon, 1924).

Jeremias, Joachim *The Unknown Sayings of Jesus* (SPCK, 1964)

Jeremias, Joachim *Jerusalem in the Time of Jesus* (SCM, 1969)

Josephus *The Jewish War* (Penguin edition)

Kloner, Amos "A Tomb with Inscribed Ossuaries in the East Talpiot," *Atiqot* 29 (1996) 15-22.

Lemaire, André 'A Burial Box of James the Brother of Jesus,' *BAR* 28/6 (2002)

Lemaire, André 'Israel Antiquities Authority Report Deeply Flawed,' *BAR* 29/6 (2003)

Lemaire, André 'Engraved in Memory – Diaspora Jews Find Eternal Rest in Jerusalem,' *BAR* 32/3 (2006) 53-57

Lindars, B *The Gospel of John*, (Marshall Morgan and Scott, 1972)

Lüdemann, G *The Resurrection of Jesus* (SCM, 1994)

Lührmann, D *Das Markusevangelium* (HNT 3; Herder, 1987)

McCane, Byron '"Where no-one had yet been laid": The Shame of Jesus' Burial,' in Chilton and Evans (eds), *Authenticating the Activities of Jesus* (Brill, 1999)

McCane, Byron *Roll Back the Stone – Death and Burial in the World of Jesus* (Trinity, 2003).

Mack, Burton *A Myth of Innocence: Mark and Christian Origins* (Fortress, 1988)

Magness, Jodi 'Ossuaries and the Burials of Jesus and James,' *Journal of Biblical Literature 124/1* (2005) 121-154

Mann, C S *Mark* (Anchor Bible; Doubleday, 1986)

Marshall, I H *The Gospel of Luke* (Paternoster, 1978)

Martyn, J L We Have Found Elijah', in his *The Gospel of John in Christian History* (Paulist, 1979)

Moule, C F D 'The Individualism of the Fourth Gospel,' *Novum Testamentum* vol 5 (1962) 171-190

O'Neill, J C 'On the Resurrection as an Historical Question,' in S Sykes and J Clayton (eds), *Christ, Faith and History* (CUP, 1972)

Painter, John *Just James – the Brother of Jesus in History and Tradition* (Uni of South Carolina, second edition, 2004)

Pixner, Bargil 'Luke and Jerusalem' in his *Paths of the Messiah* (Ignatius Press, 2010) 423-432

Pryor, John W *The Enigmatic Jew – in quest of the historical Jesus* (Createspace, 2011)

Pryor, John W *Jesus Resurrected? Sifting the Historical Evidence* (Createspace, 2011)

Quarles, C (ed) *Buried Hope or Risen Savior?* (B&H Publishing, 2008)

Quast, K *Peter and the Beloved Disciple – Figures for a Community in Crisis* (JSOT Press, 1989)

Rahmani, L Y *A Catalogue of Jewish Ossuaries in the Collections of the State of Israel* (Israel Antiquities Authority, 1994)

Reed, Jonathan *Archaeology and the Galilean Jesus* (Trinity Press, 2000)

Robinson, J M (ed) *The Nag Hammadi Library* (Brill/Harper and Row, 1988).

Schaberg, Jane *The Resurrection of Mary Magdalene* (Continuum, 2002)

Schaberg, Jane *Mary Magdalene Understood* (Continuum, 2006)

Schäfer, Peter *Jesus in the Talmud* (Princeton Uni Press, 2007)

Schnackenburg, R *The Gospel According to St John* (3 vols; Seabury/Crossroad, 1980-1982)

Shanks, Hershel and Witherington III, Ben *The Brother of Jesus – The Dramatic Story and meaning of the First Archaeological Link to Jesus and His Family* (HarperCollins, 2003).

Shanks, Hershel 'Fudging with Forgeries – A Closer Look at Professor Yuval Goren's "Scholarship"' in *BAR* 37/6 (2011) 53-58, 71

Shanks, Hershel '"Brother of Jesus" Inscription is Authentic,' *Biblical Archaeology Review* 38/4 (2012) 26-33, 62, 64-65

Sherwin-White, A H *Roman Law and Roman Society in the New Testament* (Oxford, 1963)

Shoemaker, S J 'Rethinking the "Gnostic Mary": Mary of Nazareth and Mary of Magdala in Early Christian Literature,' a paper delivered at the 2000 annual conference of the Society of Biblical Literature

Smith, D Moody *John among the Gospels – The Relationship in Twentieth Century Research* (Fortress, 1992)

Snyder, Graydon *Ante Pacem – Archaeological Evidence on Church Life before Constantine* (Mercer, 1985)

Spong, J S *Resurrection – Myth or Reality?* (HarperCollins, 1994)

Tabor, James *The Jesus Dynasty* (Simon and Schuster, 2007 edition)

Tabor, James and Jacobovici, Simcha *The Jesus Discovery* (Simon and Schuster, 2012)

Taylor, Joan *The Immerser: John the Baptist within Second Temple Judaism* (Eerdmans, 1997)

Walker, Peter *In the Steps of Jesus* (Zondervan, 2006)

Wedderburn, A J M *Beyond Resurrection* (SCM, 1999)

Wilson, R McL *Studies in the Gospel of Thomas* (Mowbray, 1960)

Witherington, Ben *What Have They Done With Jesus?* (HarperCollins, 2006)

Wright, N T *The Resurrection of the Son of God* (Fortress, 2003)

Zias, Joe 'The Cemeteries of Qumran and Celibacy: Confusion Laid to Rest,' in *Dead Sea Discoveries* 7.2 (2000) 220-253

Index of Passages Cited

I. Old Testament

Genesis
25.8 —7
25.17 —7
49.29-33 —7

Deuteronomy
21.21 —104
21.22 —100, 104, 106
21.22-23 —100, 104
21.23 —105

Judges
2.10 —7

1 Samuel
1.1 —111

2 Samuel
21.12-14 —7

1 Kings
13.21-22 —105
13.22 —7

2 Kings
2.1-18 —83
4 —84
4.42-44 —84
5 —84
9.28 —7

Ezra
2.45 —131
2.46 —131

Nehemiah
7.48 —131

Job
39.27 —131

Psalms
34.3 —130
148.13 —130

Isaiah
8.19 —8
12.4 —130
26.19 —117
29.4 —8
53.9 —95

Jeremiah
22.19 —105
26.23 —105
49.16 —131

Ezekial
17.25 —131
21.26 —131

Daniel
2.47 —135
4.16 —135
4.21 —135
5.23 —135
12.1-3 —117

Jonah
2.5 —36, 144
4.6-11 —140

II. Apocrypha

Judith
16.1 —130

Sirach
14.18-19 —117
38.21 —117

1 Maccabees
2.49-70 —117
11.34 —111

2 Maccabees
7.1-23 —117

1 Esdras
5.30 —131

4 Ezra
7.32-33a —117

III. New Testament

Matthew
3.1-12 —62
3.2 —61
3.13 —137
3.16 —137
4.17 —61
5.17-20 —86
8.5-10 —137

8.13 —137
11.2 —61
12.39-40 —37, 137
12.40 —137, 138, 144, 149, 151, 183, 184
13.55 —52, 157, 159, 166, 186
16.17-19 —86
16.18 —29
19.10-12 —64
19.12 —62, 63, 64
19.29 —64
20.20 —72
22.23-33 —118
26.57 —11
27.52-53 —123
27.56 —67, 71
27.57-58 —99, 110
27.60 —51, 95, 100
27.61 —67, 71
28.1 —67, 71
28.8-10 —69
28.9 —70
28.9-10 —68, 85
28.15 —77
28.17 —69
28.19-20 —86

Mark
1.15 —61
3.16 —77
3.17 —29, 77
3.21 —62
3.31-34 —62
6.1-6 —63
6.3 —52, 158, 186
10.29 —64
10.51 —69
12.18-27 —118
15.40 —67, 71, 72, 169
15.40-41 —28
15.43 —110, 111
15.47 —28, 67, 71, 72
16.1 —28, 54, 67, 71, 72
16.1-8 —54
16.6 —187

16.9 —67, 85

Luke
1.26 —110
1.39 —110
2.4 —110
2.25 —98
2.36-37 —98
2.48 —157
3.1-9 —62
3:15-17 —62
3.21b —137
3.23 —157, 166
3.23-38 —24, 163
4.22 —157, 166
6.15 —29
7.1b-10 —137
7.36-50 —86
8.1-3 —78, 86, 93
8.2 —67
8.3 —65, 72
9.51 —137
10.38-42 —135
11.1 —61
11.20 —62
11.29-30 —37
11.29-31 —137, 138
16.30f —138
18.29 —64
20.27-40 —118
23.49 —71, 87
23.50-52 —98
23.51 —96, 110
23.55 —71, 87
24 —87
24.9 —87
24.10 —67, 71, 72, 87
24.11 —87
24.12 —87
24.13-35 —122
24.18 —162
24.34 —85, 87

John
1.45 —157, 166
3.25 —61

3.26 —62
4.1-3 —62
4.27 —93
6.42 —157, 166
6.66-71 —89
7.3 —52
7.50-52 —108
11 —135
11.5 —93
12.32 —35
18.13 —11
19.12 —103
19.25 —67, 70, 71, 72, 74, 162
19.26 —53, 103
19.26-27 —53
19.31 —100, 109
19.38 —109
19.41 —100
20 —84, 85
20.1 —67, 68, 71
20.1-2 —68
20.2 —74
20.11-18 —29, 68
20.14-17 —85
20.17 —84
20.18 —67
20.31 —88
21 —88, 89
21.24-25 —88
Acts
1-2 —83
1.3 —138
1.14 —19, 23, 52, 161
2.32-33 —35
7 —105
11.28 —131
12.17 —80, 81
13.29 —109
15.13 —19, 80, 161
17.31 —138
20-21 —110
21.3 —122
21.18 —80, 81, 161
23.3-8 —12

1 Corinthians
1.12 —89
7.10 —65
7.25 —28, 65
9.1 —121
9.5 —52, 65, 158, 159, 160
14.34-35 —30
15 —54, 88, 120, 123
15.3-4 —119
15.3-5 —54, 122
15.3-7 —81, 88
15.3-8 —53
15.5 —85, 89
15.5-7 —79
15.5-8 —30, 54
15.8 —115, 120
15.42-50 —115
2 Corinthians
4-5 —121
Galatians
1.16 —121
1.18-2.14 —79
1.18-19 —119
1.19 —19, 161
2.9 —81, 161
2.12 —161
Phillippians
2.9 —35
1 Thessalonians
2.15 —106
IV. Jewish Pseudepigrapha
1 Enoch
51.1 —117
62.14-16 —117
98.13 —105
2 Baruch
50.2 —117
50.2-3 —118
50.4 —117
51.1-3 —118
4 Maccabees
18.23 —117
£V. Dead Sea Scrolls
Fragments from Cave 4

4Q385 frag 2 —118
4Q386 col 1 —118
The Community Rule (1QS) —65
The Temple Scroll (11QT)
   64.7-13 —104

VI. Rabbinic and other Jewish Literature
Babylonian Talmud
   b. Chagiga 4b —77
   b. Sanhedrin 43a —106
   b. Shabbat 104b —77
Mishnah
   Sanhedrin
     6.4 —105
     6.5-6 —105
     7.5 —130
     10.1 —12, 130
Pirke de R. Eliezer 24 —118

VII. Josephus
Jewish Antiquities
   13.127 —111
   18.17 —12
   18.18 —118
   19.64 —107
Jewish War
   2.154-158 —118
   4.317 —104
   5.449-51 —102
   6.309 —106

VIII. Nag Hammadi Literature
First Apocalypse of James
   39.15-20 —83
   40.20-29 —82
Gospel of Mary —27, 53, 85, 89, 90, 92
   9 —92
   10 —90, 91
   17-19 —92
   19 —92
Gospel of Philip —29, 53, 74, 76, 77, 89, 90
   58.30-59.5 —76
   59.6-10 —74
   63.22ff —76
   63.32-64.9 —75
   64.30-65.28 —75
   70.14-21 —75
Gospel of Thomas —82, 89, 92, 94
   12 —52, 80, 82
   13 —82
   21 —27
   114 —27, 92
Second Apocalypse of James
   56.14-15 —76

IX. Early Christian Literature
Apostolic Constitutions —21, 141
Eusebius History of the Church
   1.7.14 —161
   2.1.3 —80
   2.1.4 —80
   2.23 —19, 80
   3.11 —19, 21, 159
   3.22 —159
   3.32 —21
   3.32.6 —159
   4.5 —160
   4.22.4 —159
   5.12 —160
Panarion 66.21-22 —160

X. Other Early Christian Texts
Acts of Philip
   8.94 —90
   15.107 —91
   15.109 —91
   15.114-115 —91
   15.137 —91
   15.142 —91
   15.148 —91
Gospel of Peter
   2.3-5 —99
   6.21 —109
   6.23-24 —100
   6.24 —100, 182
Gospel of the Hebrews —82
Justin Martyr - Dialogue with Trypho
   97.1 —109
   107-108 —139, 141
Martyrdom of Polycarp
   17.2 —107

Origen Contra Celsum
   1.65 —78
   2.55 —78
   2.70 —78
Pistis Sophia
   I.36-37 —91
   II.72 —91
   IV.146 —91
Protoevangelium of James —82
Pseudo-Clementine Homilies and Recognitions —82

XI. Miscellaneous
Horace Epistle
   1.16.48 —102
Petronius Satyricon
   111-12 —101
Quintillian -Declamations
   274 —102

Author index

Note: References to C Pellegrino, S Jacobovici and J Tabor are not listed

Albright, W F —69, 70
Allison, Dale —62, 64, 97, 111, 112, 138, 168
Bagatti, B —133
Bammel, E —106
Barrett, C K —70, 108
Batey, R —57
Bauckham, R —11, 24, 30, 31, 33, 52, 71, 72, 79, 81, 88, 99, 122, 128, 129, 130, 131, 132, 133, 134, 135, 156, 159, 160, 162, 167, 169, 170, 178
Beasley-Murray, G —70, 108
Blinzler, J —106
Brown, R E —24, 70, 88, 99, 102, 104, 108, 109, 112
Bultmann, R —70, 108
Byrne, R —45
Cargill, R —144, 145
Carson, D A —70, 108
Caruso, S —154
Charlesworth, J H —36, 144, 145, 154, 179
Chow, S —138, 140, 141
Collins, J J —65
Cox, S —47, 48, 177
Crossan, J D —62, 97
Cross, F M —155
Culpepper, R A —88
Dahari, U —44
Davies, W D —64, 69, 138
Dodd, C H —68, 69
Ehrman, B —27
Evans, C —8, 10, 11, 12, 103, 105
Farrer, A M —136
Feldman, H —45
Feuerverger, A —32, 177
Finegan, J —142
Flesher, P —43

Funk, R —62, 64, 97
Gamble, H —130
Gärtner, B —92
Goodacre, M —92, 94, 134, 136, 144, 179
Goren, Y —44, 45
Gundry, R H —64, 71
Habermas, G —178
Hachlili, R —65, 132, 142
Haenchen, E —70, 108
Hagner, D —123
Harris, M J —120
Hengel, M —13, 102, 103, 110, 136
Hoover, R —62, 64
Horsley, R A —62
Humphreys, C —51, 63, 103
Ilani, S —45
Ilan, T —30, 33, 41, 156, 169
Ingermanson, R —176, 178
James, M R —27, 90
Jeremias, J —12, 92
Keynan, E —168, 170
Kloner, A. —17
Kronfeld, Y —45
Krumbein, W —45, 47, 177
Lemaire, A —42
Lindars, B —69, 70, 108
Lombatti, A —144, 145, 147, 150
Lüdemann, G —116
Lührmann, D —58
Mack, B —62
Magness, J —8, 9, 40, 105, 166, 179
Mann, C S —111
Marshall, I H —138
Martyn, J L —84
McCane, B —7, 9, 11, 13, 73, 105
McGrath, J —144
McNary-Zak, B —45
Meyers, E —148

Moule, C F D —69
O'Neill, J C —119
Painter, J —40, 79, 80, 81, 86, 129, 163
Pfann, S —155
Pixner, B —110, 123
Pleše, Z —27
Pryor, J W —57, 62, 63, 64, 71, 73, 74,
    77, 81, 87, 88, 97, 98, 103, 107,
    116, 121, 122, 159, 164
Quarles, C —30, 179
Quast, K —88
Rahmani, L Y —10, 11, 12, 13, 20, 22,
    23, 24, 25, 26, 45, 46, 127, 131,
    135, 147, 154, 155, 156, 157, 163,
    164, 165, 167, 170, 171, 173, 176,
    186
Reich, R —43
Robinson, J M —74
Rollston, C —59, 128, 133
Rosenfeld, A —45
Schaberg, J —27, 28, 29, 67, 68, 75, 76,
    78, 82, 83, 84, 85, 86, 87, 88, 89,
    90, 91, 92
Schäfer, P —78, 107
Schnackenburg, R —70, 103, 108
Shanks, H —12, 39, 40, 41, 44, 45, 48,
    49, 50, 154
Sherwin-White, A H —103
Shoemaker, S J —83
Smith, D M —99
Snyder, G —139, 140, 141
Spong, J S —69, 97, 116
Taylor, J —98
Walker, P —162
Wedderburn, A J M —116
Wilson, R McL —92
Witherington, B —36, 40, 108, 144, 156,
    161, 179
Wright, N T —117, 120
Zias, J —44, 49, 50, 65

Subject Index

A

Abraham —7, 117
Arimathea —96, 98, 99, 110, 111

B

Bar Kokhba —132
Bartimaeus —69, 93
Beloved Disciple —84, 88, 103
Bethany —52, 86
Bethlehem —12, 163
Beth Shearim —33

C

Caiaphas —11, 12, 167
Celsus —77
Clopas —71, 159, 160, 162
Cochaba —161
Constantine —139, 140, 141

E

Elijah —83, 84, 85
Elisha —83, 84, 85
Emmaus —122, 162
Epiphanius —21, 159, 160
Essenes —28, 64, 118
Eusebius —19, 21, 79, 80, 81, 159, 160

G

Galilee —8, 19, 29, 33, 40, 41, 52, 54, 62, 71, 77, 85, 93, 100, 110, 115, 123, 158, 161, 162

H

Hagab —131, 133, 134
Hebron —7
Hegesippus —81, 159, 160, 163
Herod Agrippa I —79
Herodion —12
Herod the Great —12, 40
Hippolytus —27, 28, 155
Horace —102

I

Irenaeus —27, 77, 141

J

James, brother of Jesus —1, 3, 19, 21, 22, 24, 32, 39, 40, 42, 43, 45, 50, 52, 53, 54, 71, 72, 79, 80, 81, 82, 83, 105, 106, 115, 122, 129, 158, 159, 160, 161, 162, 165, 174, 177, 178, 182, 185, 187
James, son of Zebedee —71
Jericho —12, 41, 142
Jewish Council —98, 105
Joanna —71, 72
John the Baptist —28, 61, 62, 63, 64, 92, 95, 182
Jonah —18, 20, 35, 36, 37, 136–152, 172, 183, 184, 186
Jordan —15, 27, 61, 91, 133
Joseph of Arimathea —1, 3, 19, 28, 36, 51, 53, 67, 71, 73, 93, 95–113, 115, 116, 148, 151, 169, 174, 181, 182, 184, 187
Joseph son of Caiaphas —11
Josephus —12, 97, 98, 102, 104, 106, 111, 118
Judah son of Jesus —16, 24, 157, 164, 165, 174, 175
Julius Africanus —161

K

Kerak —133

M

Machpelah —7

Martha of Bethany —93
Mary Magdalene —1, 3, 19, 24, 25–30,
    52, 53, 61, 63, 65, 67–94, 113,
    115, 135, 155, 156, 157, 164, 165,
    166, 172, 173, 174, 176, 179, 181,
    182, 184, 185, 186, 187
Mary mother of Jesus —71, 77
Mary of Bethany —27, 86, 90, 156
Mount of Olives —51, 142

N

Naaman —84
Nag Hammadi —74, 76, 80, 82, 89, 91
Nazareth —53, 63, 83, 98, 161, 162, 177
Nicanor —91
Nicodemus —71, 93, 95, 108

O

Origen —27, 77, 78, 141

P

Paul —28, 51, 52, 53, 54, 65, 79, 80, 81,
    86, 88, 89, 106, 110, 115, 116,
    117, 118, 119, 120, 121, 122, 123,
    129, 158, 159, 160, 161, 185
Peter —27, 29, 79, 80, 81, 82, 84, 85, 86,
    87, 88, 89, 90, 91, 92, 93, 115,
    121, 122, 182, 185
Petronius —101, 102
Pontius Pilate —95, 96, 103, 107

Q

Quintilian —102
Qumran —11, 28, 65, 104

S

Sarah —7, 31
Sejanus —103
Simon of Cyrene —93
Stephen —105, 106

T

Tertullian —77, 141
Thomas —69
Trajan —21

V

Valentinus —74

www.ingramcontent.com/pod-product-compliance
Lightning Source LLC
Chambersburg PA
CBHW051737230426
43670CB00012B/2064